Memoirs of a Brit on Death Row

(A true story of abduction, torture, years of solitary confinement in Ethiopia and vindication)

Andargachew Tsege

Contents

Dedication

To Major MesafintTigabu (Belgium), Shibabaw Bayu (Florida, USA), Tesfa Lakew (Colombus Ohio, USA), Yosef Haimanot (London, UK), Gezahegn G/Meskel "Nebero" (Johannesburg South Africa) and all those who have made the ultimate sacrifice for freedom in Ethiopia.

Acknowledgements

To write this book, I first had to survive death row and gain my freedom from imprisonment. Between 2014 and 2018, there were moments when I lost hope of survival and freedom. The unthinkable happened: I emerged alive and vindicated from an Ethiopian prison, rejoicing in a reunion with my family, friends, comrades, and those who tirelessly campaigned for my safety and freedom.

I express my deepest gratitude, especially to my children and close family members, for their unwavering support. My heartfelt thanks go out to the Ethiopians at home, whose struggle and sacrifices for freedom toppled the regime that abducted me, and to the Ethiopian diaspora worldwide, particularly in the UK, for the many rallies conducted for my release. I extend my appreciation to the members of the Ginbot 7 Movement for Freedom, Justice, and Democracy in the UK and all over the globe; notably the DC Task Force.

I am profoundly grateful to Reprieve, Redress, and Prisoners Abroad for their advocacy and support in those troubling years. Special thanks to my MP, the Hon. Jeremy Corbyn, representative of Islington North, for taking up my case and pushing the UK government to work for my unconditional release and Emily Thornberry, MP for Islington South, for all her efforts.

I also extend special thanks to the British public, especially those who sent me many books to the prison. An exceptional thanks to the very young students of Sidcup School in Somerset for remembering me one Christmas by sending me 80 of their handmade Christmas cards.

I also acknowledge the staff at the British mission in Ethiopia, including Ambassador Susana Moorhead, John, Kate, Catherine, and others who worked tirelessly on my behalf. I express my gratitude to the British media, including the BBC, ITV, Channel 5, Sky, as well as newspapers like *The Guardian* and *The Independent*, for dedicating time and effort to publicize my abduction and unjust imprisonment by Ethiopian authorities.

I want to express the immense sense of indebtedness I feel towards the Arsenal Football Club and the players of the time, including Theo Walcott and his teammates, for the moral support they provided to my young children. They invited them to visit the Arsenal stadium, which we love as a family and allowed them to watch some major matches for free.

Last, I thank Dr Moges G/Mariam for his enduring friendship and his generous support in publishing this book.

This book would not have been possible without the combined efforts of all mentioned. I acknowledge your efforts and sacrifices, and I thank you all immensely.

About the Author

Andargachew, a British citizen of Ethiopian descent, is a philosopher whose passion for the subject stems from his profound personal experiences.

Enduring the loss of loved ones, imprisonment, torture, exile, and the collapse of his familiar world, he was compelled to explore the essence of humanity and the meaning of life.

His philosophical journey, driven by an existential need to maintain mental health amid chaos, led him to politics, activism, and extensive writings in his native language.

For Andargachew, human freedom and the freedom of others are central to life.

Prologue

When my story began, I was a British citizen of Ethiopian descent, and I still am. I came to England in 1979 after fleeing the chaos and destruction of the 1974 Ethiopian Revolution.

I was the second child in a middle-class family with eight children. Growing up, I often heard my parents and their friends discuss Ethiopian history and politics. These conversations planted a seed in my mind, sparking a deep concern for the Ethiopian people and their struggles. This early obsession led me to join the Ethiopian student movements and later one of the revolutionary political organizations that sprung up with the revolution.

My involvement was driven by a profound empathy for my countrymen's suffering and a determination to fight against their pain. This passion led to frequent imprisonments and a life marked by sorrow and struggle. I survived while many comrades died, witnessing their deaths and feeling immense guilt. This haunting experience has left me with a persistent ache, constantly questioning the outcomes of their sacrifices.

I arrived in the UK from Sudan in June 1979, during Margaret Thatcher's rule, as part of a family reunion program to join my two sisters. When I landed at Heathrow Airport, I had no underpants because they had been infested with lice, and for fear that they might infest the aeroplane, I had to dump them in an airport toilet in Khartoum. The only possession I had was a plastic bag filled with nine packs of Rothmans cigarettes left from the pack that contained 10, which I bought using the ten dollars an American who used to work for UNHCR (United Nations High Commission for Refugees) and I met at the airport lounge gave me.

The customs officer's startled expression when I showed my tiny plastic bag as my only luggage is still vivid in my memory. My real burden was my emotional baggage: memories of a devastated country, massacred loved ones, and the horrors of prison and torture.

This emotional weight influenced my decisions. I abandoned my engineering studies to pursue philosophy in England. I chose a life on society's fringes, doing odd jobs and avoiding career, marriage, and property for too long. My obsession with Ethiopia's fate remained unshakable.

Years later, this quest led me from London to the wilderness of Harena in Eritrea to organise resistance against ongoing abuses in Ethiopia. This self-imposed mission resulted in my abduction and imprisonment in Addis Ababa under the threat of the death penalty.

Hence, this book, "Memoirs of a Brit on Death Row" (A true story of abduction, torture, and four years of solitary confinement).

Chapter I: When Fate Wants to Turn Nasty

Friday, May 27, 2014, 3:30 PM, Palmers Green, London.

The voice on the other end of the line crackled to life, a familiar tone cutting through the distance.

"Hello, how can I assist you?"

I recognised the voice immediately—it belonged to the Pakistani man managing the Eritrean Travel agency in Dubai.

"I'd like to reserve four return tickets from Dubai to Asmara. I'll settle the bill upon my arrival in Dubai in two weeks," I stated confidently, affirming my status as a regular client.

He requested detailed passenger information, travel dates, passport numbers, and other particulars via email for the reservation.

I asked for the agent's email address. He gave me one over the phone. I sent him a trail email to which he responded straight away.

"Thank you," I said, ending the call. Without delay, I forwarded our travel specifics and required documents to the ticket agent.

My journey to Eritrea from Dubai was scheduled ahead of the other three passengers. The three were members of the executive committee of the Ginbot 7. A political movement that emerged following the contentious national election of 2005, which was marred by allegations of vote rigging by the ruling party, that led to widespread protests across Ethiopia, which were violently suppressed.

The brutal crackdown included the tragic deaths of 197 innocent men, women, and children during a peaceful demonstration. Furthermore, tens of thousands of ordinary members of opposition parties, along with their leaders, were subjected to mass incarceration. Among those detained were over 50 elected parliamentarians, numerous journalists, human rights lawyers, and leaders of civic society.

The ill-fated election occurred on the unique Ethiopian calendar, specifically in the Month of Ginbot and the year 1997, equivalent to May 15, 2005, in the European calendar. This significant event marks the first and only democratic election in Ethiopian history. In tribute to this historic occasion and the sacrifices made by the people to prevent their votes from being stolen, my colleagues and I chose to name our political organization the Ginbot 7 Movement for Freedom, Justice, and Democracy.

The three members of the executive of Ginbot7 were planning to travel to Eritrea. One member travelled from the United States, while the other two hailed from Europe—Belgium and Norway, respectively. All three members would obtain return tickets to Dubai. My task was to secure their return tickets from Dubai to Asmara. Hence, I departed from London on June 19, 2014.

Upon arrival in Dubai, I proceeded directly to the Eritrean Airlines office to settle the ticket bill. For security reasons, most of our organization's transactions were in cash. While the agent finalized the ticket printing, I counted cash, his explanation of the ticket details providing a background soundtrack.

Amidst his dialogue, I discovered an error in the date of my scheduled flight from Dubai to Asmara.

The emailed dates of my travel plan had an error, resulting in my ticket displaying the wrong date. The other three tickets were prepared for collection, but mine was slated for a flight a month later. Acknowledging my mistake, I asked if the agent could rectify the reservation. Unfortunately, all seats for the intended date were occupied.

The ticket agent proposed a first-class upgrade for an additional US$400.

My prior journeys to Eritrea had been trouble-free. Flights often had open seats, and if filled, spots were available the next day.

Despite having ample cash on hand from the $4000 available to me, I hesitated to fork over the $400 for the upgrade. In our organisation, my role involved clandestine activities, offering me autonomy without accountability or audits. Solely reliant on my word to justify expenses, I refrained from utilising these entrusted funds for avoidable costs. It felt incongruent with their intended purpose. Contemplating this, I considered waiting, holding onto the $400, and trying my luck the following day.

The agent sensed my reluctance to part with the additional fee.

"Passengers often don't show up. Let's try tomorrow," he suggested.

With pending tasks in Dubai, I settled the bill only for my three colleagues.

"I'll return tomorrow," I bid the ticket agent farewell and departed.

The following day, I returned to the ticket office. The agent had not yet succeeded in finding me a seat. No economy class tickets were available. I hesitated, then decided to pay the additional cost for first class, only to discover it had been sold out. There were no seats available at all for the consecutive days that followed. The travel dates for the three colleagues were fast approaching. They were limited to a few days. Their schedule was intensely packed. There was a lot of urgent business that needed to be arranged before their arrival. I had to look for alternative flights.

The available choices were between Egypt Air and Yemen Airways. Opting for Egypt Air would entail a lengthy layover in Cairo, resulting in an arrival at Asmara around dawn. This would consume an entire day of travel. Moreover, my early morning arrival would undoubtedly inconvenience Belenay, my designated immigration officer, and his family.

Each time I flew to Asmara via Egypt Air, the necessity to rouse Belenay at 4:00 am for airport pickup weighed heavily on me. Belenay, an aged freedom fighter of Shabia – a popular name for The Eritrean People Liberation Movement- EPLF, bearing a limp from a bullet wound on his leg, resides in a modest home with his sizable family. My arrivals via Egypt Air routinely disrupted their sleep, leaving me increasingly uncomfortable with the inconvenience caused.

On the contrary, Yemen Airways offered a more direct route, ensuring I'd reach my destination by 8 pm on the same day, sparing Belenay any inconvenience. Logically, it was the right decision, yet a slight unease gnawed at me as I settled on Yemen Airways. While I had flown this route previously, I realized circumstances had shifted. The scrutiny from the Ethiopian government regarding my activities had escalated. Despite this lingering apprehension, I ultimately opted for Yemen Airways.

Chapter II: Bad omen, when June meets Monday

The idea of flying with Yemen Airlines made me uneasy. Travelling through Yemen wasn't sitting well with me. My instincts were on edge. I decided to reach out to Yemane Gebreab, the political advisor to Eritrea's President Isaias, explaining my situation due to the unavailability of direct flights.

Yemane responded swiftly: "Could you spell out your name as it appears in your passport?" I interpreted this as an attempt to secure a suitable seat through Eritrean Airlines. I'm not a fan of things being done for me through the influence of authority, so I didn't want Yemane's involvement to secure me a seat.

"I wanted to gauge your thoughts on the safety of travelling through Yemen. It's been on my mind. If you advise against it, I can cancel the purchased ticket," I conveyed. A thoughtful pause preceded Yemane's reply, "I don't foresee any issues."

"Perhaps arranging for an embassy staff member to see me off at the airport would be wise," I suggested. Shortly after our call ended, Yemane informed me that the Eritrean Ambassador in Sana'a would ensure my departure at the airport.

Arriving at Al Maktoum Dubai International Airport, the Yemen Airlines waiting area was filled with Habeshas—Ethiopian and Eritrean. The passengers appeared weathered. I was looking into the faces of poor traders who most likely lived as lodgers, ten to a single bedroom. They packed roasted barley flour from their homeland for food, avoiding spending what little they earned from roaming the markets under the blazing Dubai sun for goods worth just pennies.

Most couldn't afford to pay for excess baggage. Their collective anxiety appeared obvious from the knotted bags and suitcases lying at their feet, the turbulent rise and fall of their chests, and their hopeful, darting eyes desperately seeking to offload the extra weight on any sympathetic fellow passenger.

The sad sight though overwhelming, did not remove the unease I felt by choosing Yemen Airways. As I observed the diverse passengers, I couldn't help but ponder. How many were linked to Ethiopia's security network run by Woyane - another name for the Tigray People's Liberation Front (TPLF) that was practically ruling Ethiopia? Who could discern my identity? Might someone inform Woyane intelligence of my presence on Yemen Airlines? These thoughts lingered.

My reflections followed a logical pattern. Members of Ginbot 7 who reside in different countries provided me with information - including passport details and travel information - about the activities and movements of well-known Eritrean opposition figures.

I refrained from sharing the information with Shabia because I realised that, unlike Woyane, the Eritrean government paid little attention to the opposition in the diaspora. However, while waiting at the airport, , it dawned on me that Ginbot 7 members could also be under surveillance by the Woyane.

With these unsettling reflections, I boarded the ageing, unkempt Air Bus-350 Flight 516. Departing in the afternoon on Monday, June 23, 2014, I grappled with scattered thoughts and emotions.

I was acquainted with the superstitious saying among Ethiopians that 'it's bad luck when days of June fall on a Monday. Despite my familiarity with this belief, I hadn't connected it to my situation, nor had I entertained the idea. Reflecting on it now, had I considered this superstition, would I have cancelled my flight through Yemen just because the date of travel was on a Monday in June? It's a question that will forever linger unanswered. Regardless, the reality remains—I continued with my journey to Sana'a.

Chapter III: The Yemeni Judas

After a couple of hours in the air, the flight finally touched down at Sana'a International Airport. As we disembarked, shuttle buses awaited our arrival. Joining the other passengers, I stepped onto one of the buses. The journey was brief, ending in front of a large building where I and the other travelers alighted. That's when I began to notice telltale signs that validated my concerns.

Among the crowd, a man dressed in a distinct blue suit caught my eye. His bulging cheeks betrayed a stash of Khat, a narcotic green leaf. I watched as he manoeuvred his way towards me, greeting me as if we were old acquaintances. A casual touch on my shoulders and a kiss on the cheek marked his approach—a gesture that stirred up thoughts of Italian mafia rituals and the infamous betrayal of Judas with his kiss.

Amid this rather surreal encounter, I couldn't help but internally ridicule my fleeting comparison to the biblical figure. But the momentary smile that crossed my face quickly dissipated. The gesture, though seemingly harmless, set off alarm bells within me. A Yemeni man randomly kissing my cheek? That signalled trouble.

Feeling defenceless, I clung to a slim hope of receiving some assistance from the Eritrean Ambassador's diplomatic influence, whom I had assumed to be present at the airport.

We entered an open waiting area, bifurcated for passengers entering Sana'a and those departing for Ethiopia and Eritrea. First, passengers bound for Ethiopia were taken to the departure terminal. Another bus arrived, and the announcer informed those who were bound for Asmara to board. We were many and the first bus filled quickly. The rest had to wait for the arrival of another one. At this time, I decided to get to the front of the queue. My reasoning was being at the back would make it easier for those hatching something against me. I found myself mingling with those gathered at the entrance.

The bus arrived. The man in the blue suit was on the bus and got off quickly and made way for me to board the bus. Other passengers were not allowed to follow me. As the glass doors of the waiting hall sealed off the others from joining me, the bus pulled away, and I found myself alone.

It became apparent that stepping onto that bus was the end of any control I had over my fate. The man in the blue suit swiftly relieved me of my passport, mobile phone, and wallet, extracting credit cards and my driver's license. The bus veered right, coming to a halt at a dead end. I was instructed to disembark.

Accompanied by other men whom I suspected were security officials working alongside the Khat-chewing man—we entered a compound. The place was heavily guarded by soldiers wielding AK47 machine guns. At its centre stood a small rectangular house

(Zanigaba). Upon entering, we were met by a room lined wall to wall with what the natives call Arabian Majlise, a low-sitting sofa, a very old one. Seated on them were two men clad in Yemeni robes, each with a handgun on one side and a 'gilay'—a short sword-like blade—on the other.

Despite the ongoing 20th World Cup match on the flat-screen TV in front of them, the Khat-chewing men seemed disinterested in the game. Yet their fat figures resembling giant balls was something that didn't escape my notice. They scarcely acknowledged our presence as we entered, engrossed in their Khat leaves.

The man in the blue suit ordered two chairs to be fetched—one for himself and one for me—before meticulously rifling through my belongings. After jotting down an inventory of my possessions, he returned my cash but withheld my credit cards, driver's license, and passport.

Despite my inquiries, he offered no explanations. Suddenly, he left me with the two round figures and departed. As time passed, my apprehension dulled my reactions. The Khat-chewing men appeared to forget my presence, engrossed in their khat-induced daydreams.

While observing the room's features—the ceiling, floors, worn-out Arabian Majlis, and the TV—I noticed an overwhelming sense of unease. It struck me that all the airport staff in Sana'a seemed to be chewing Khat, their lips and tongues stained green from the narcotic leaf. Hours slipped by, the first match ended, and a second game began. The commentary was in Arabic but I could tell by the jerseys that Brazil was playing. I watched the game with interest.

Chapter IV: Tefadel and Tebeges/ Eat and Move

Dinner arrived promptly as the football game commenced, catching the attention of the two individuals who had been dozing off. Startled awake, each person probed their cheeks with an index finger, extracting the small balls of Khat nestled there. They retrieved small plastic bags from their chest pockets and carefully stored these Khat balls for later. Seated on the floor, they leaned over to scoop water from a nearby jug, wetting their hands before reaching for the plastic bag that contained their dinner. They meticulously arranged various containers holding boiled eggs, pita bread, salad, and cooked rice with meat, all placed on a cloth spread on the floor amidst the grime.

"Tefadel," they warmly extended in Arabic, inviting me to join them.

This gesture evoked memories of my time as a struggling refugee in Sudan during my early twenties, some forty years ago. Familiar with the polite phrase Tefadel, "let's eat", I respectfully declined their offer with a polite gesture.

Twenty-four hours had elapsed since my last meal, which was dinner the previous night at the hotel in Duba. For me, the idea of dipping fingers into a communal bowl and sharing a meal with men who used their hands to extract Khat from their cheeks was inconceivable. I found it astonishing that my choice not to eat didn't seem to trouble them despite my firm decision.

In Ethiopia, the insistence for others to join in a meal could be relentless to the point of becoming bothersome. Hosts wouldn't easily accept a refusal. The cultural norms here were significantly different. The men sitting before me indulged in their meal almost as if I was not there. The substantial mound of food vanished within minutes. Once their meal concluded, I was astonished to witness them retrieve the small plastic bags from their pockets to tuck the Khat ball back into their cheeks.

At that moment, I seized the opportunity to inquire about using the toilet. One of them promptly stood up to guide me to the facilities.

I realized the severity of my situation when I entered the bathroom. Through the crack in the door, I glimpsed people smoking cigarettes on the doorsteps, armed with folding Kalashnikovs. The number of armed individuals had significantly increased since the time I first arrived at the compound by bus. Evidently, the increase was directly related to my presence there.

The shock of seeing public officials chewing Khat in a filthy room at Sana'a International Airport heightened as I stepped into the toilet. Broken ceramics littered the floor along with an old large barrel of water, beside which sat a jug. The place emitted an overwhelming stench. The distressing absence of basic sanitation in Yemen surpassed any expectations I had harboured.

I had held an assumption that Yemen maintained better fundamental hygienic standards compared to Ethiopia. Even the airport toilets at Bole Addis Ababa appeared far cleaner in contrast. This realisation brought a twinge of guilt for my previous harsh criticisms of my people regarding basic standards. A conflicting thought accompanied this emotion, teasing a sardonic smile. It struck me that these individuals, whom I had admired for their better toilet standards, were the very ones behind orchestrating my abduction, intending to eliminate me.

Upon my return from the toilet, a third person, their Chief, joined us. His pristine white jellabiya conveyed an air of cleanliness and expense, indicating his elevated status.

"Are you Muslim?" he inquired.

I responded that I wasn't. I wondered what his reaction might have been had I answered affirmatively. He attempted to convey in broken English that many people, particularly prominent officials, held animosity towards me in Ethiopia. As his words morphed into a jumble of sounds, "people" became "beoble" and "Ethiopia" turned into "Ethiobia". However, this revelation was hardly surprising to me. I had spent considerable time pondering the identities of those behind my potential abduction and how they might have influenced the Yemeni connection.

I suspected that there must have been a financial incentive for my kidnapping. Corruption was a prevalent issue among Yemeni police and intelligence officers, notorious for exploiting refugees for financial gain and taking advantage of women sexually. I had come across this information in a book whose title escaped my memory, leaving a chilling impression that many of these individuals were akin to monsters. As much as I wanted to inquire from the person in front of me about the sum my adversaries had paid to have me kidnapped, I refrained from doing so.

The TPLF likely had multiple avenues for securing cooperation from Yemen. I had strong suspicions that Yemeni intelligence officers, the individuals I had witnessed in that unsanitary airport room, were strategically placed by former Yemeni President Ali Abdulla Saleh. Rumours of Saleh's relocation to Ethiopia after his expulsion from Yemen supported this notion. I assumed he would have willingly directed his old pals to carry out such a task, even without financial incentives.

Conversely, Sheikh Mohammed Alimuddin, the wealthiest individual in Ethiopia of Yemeni descent through his paternal lineage and known for his close ties with the head of Ethiopian intelligence, Getachew Assefa, might have faced minimal difficulty in seeking support from Yemen in such matters.

Indeed, TPLF intelligence likely faced hurdles in securing Yemeni assistance due to the awareness that their involvement in such actions, particularly in the case of a British citizen (myself), would violate international law. Therefore, financial incentives would have been the primary driving force for the Yemenis to engage in such risky activities. It became increasingly clear to me that the TPLF was the orchestrator of my abduction, leading me to question why the Yemenis would willingly take on such a perilous venture. In my assessment, it ultimately boiled down to monetary gain.

The departure of the high-ranking official left me isolated in that same squalid room at Sana'a International Airport, surrounded by Yemeni officers chewing on the remains of Khat. Midnight had long passed, and I found myself exhausted, frustrated, thirsty, and hungry. Fully aware that my destiny rested solely in the hands of my adversaries, I anxiously awaited the pivotal moment when the Yemenis would transfer me to the TPLF. Impatience for a resolution overwhelmed me.

Finally, two Ethiopians entered the room, accompanied by armed escorts wielding AK47 machine guns. Without much ado, these guys seized my suitcase and computer case, motioning for me to follow them. The two Yemenis remained seated on the Arabian Majlis, seemingly observing as the newcomers conversed in a language unfamiliar to them. I expected them to intervene, and I, too, remained seated, acting as though I hadn't heard the instruction to follow the Ethiopian men.

When one of the Ethiopians repeated his order, I responded defiantly, questioning their right to command me. At this moment, one of the armed escorts levelled his gaze at me with his gun. Reluctantly, I stood and followed the two Ethiopians. The armed man ensured from behind that I left the foul-smelling room.

Outside, a larger contingent of armed Yemenis stood alongside two more Ethiopians. Adjacent to them was a Russian-made UAZ jeep parked conspicuously. A TPLF officer, whose face seemed familiar to me, directed me to enter the vehicle.

Chapter V: An Unpleasant Flight

"I'm not getting in," I replied to the order commanding me to enter the parked jeep.

This marked my final opportunity to resist.

The three Ethiopians attempted to lift me into the jeep, while one of the four men, young and fair-skinned, seemed anxious, standing at a distance and pointing his handgun toward the sky. Despite their efforts, they couldn't move me. I clung firmly to the car door frame with both hands.

One of the soldiers struck me from behind with the butt of his Kalashnikov, but I didn't yield. I held onto the frame until a TPLF officer removed my left hand from the car's frame and twisted it off. A sharp snap accompanied excruciating pain in my twisted arm and wrist, making me wince. I surrendered.

I entered the jeep with my hands cuffed behind my back, my eyes and mouth sealed with silver masking tape. I must have resembled an Egyptian mummy. A sack was placed over my head.

The vehicle raced toward a small aeroplane waiting for me. Judging by the few steps I climbed before taking my seat in the cabin, I estimated the plane's size. A female flight attendant, likely from Ethiopian Airlines, led me to my seat. It was impossible to discern the flight's purpose or its intended passengers. The pilot, engaged in an English conversation with the stewardess, was clearly not Ethiopian.

After a tense wait, the pilot finally received clearance for take-off. The flight attendant, conversing urgently in Amharic, pressed the person she was addressing to proceed swiftly, hinting at a concern and tone that implied engagement in illicit activities. Such unlawful manoeuvres could easily transpire unnoticed in corrupt locations like Yemen, potentially without the approval of higher government officials.

The engine roared as the plane ascended. The customary Ethiopian Airlines "Bon Voyage" jingle remained absent, not an incongruity given the circumstances.

The flight dragged on in the cramped confines of the small aircraft. The TPLF officer seated beside me kept my veiled head down by pushing on it forcefully. It was agonizing to endure the journey with my hands bound behind my back, compounded by the added pressure of another person's hand forcing my head down. My shoulders and arm joints throbbed with strain, the steel restraints digging into my hands whenever I tried to alleviate the pain.

Amidst physical agony, thoughts of my children flooded my mind, momentarily easing the discomfort.

"Helu is the eldest teenager. She'll manage. Her friends will support her," I reassured myself.

But concern arose for her kind and gentle nature, imagining her tear-streaked face. The twins, aged seven, would likely feel bewildered. Their mother, struggling to control tears while explaining the situation, haunted my thoughts each time pain surged.

My laptop stored vital organisational information. The external drive contained crucial data for the Asmara meeting: records, receipts, and documents outlining our organization's global activities. I worried that revealing income-expenditure details and member names might compromise Ginbot 7. Yet, I couldn't dwell on sadness amid the persistent pain.

As the ordeal continued, images of my elderly father, siblings, and friends flashed through my mind. Memories of losing my younger brother during the '70s military dictatorship resurfaced, amplifying the weight of the present situation. I empathized with my father's potential added grief, imagining the anguish he would feel at my imminent demise. In that moment, I found solace in the thought that my mother had been spared from witnessing the tragic end of her beloved son, having passed away earlier.

Thoughts of comrades in Eritrean fields awaited supplies from Dubai. They trusted me when assembling from around the world for the establishment of the Military wing of the party in Eritrea. Names and faces of fellow Ginbot 7 members flashed before my taped eyes, fleeting in my clouded mind.

Momentarily, as pain gripped me, I felt breathless, and amidst the discomfort, I heard male voices whispering in Tigrigna on the plane. All four men from Sana'a bore Tigrayan features. Though I understood Tigrigna, I couldn't discern their conversation as they had lowered their voices. A part of me wished they intended to cast me overboard across the Red Sea—an option seemingly less daunting than enduring the agonizing discomfort.

Crashing 30,000 feet into the Red Sea or the Simien mountains in Ethiopia seemed a merciful compromise. Yet, no one tossed me overboard, dashing my futile hopes.

Chapter VI: Prisoner without a Cell

Our flight seemed interminable, much like my enduring pain. Eventually, we landed, following the laws of physics—what goes up must come down. My exact location was indiscernible, yet the voices that greeted the driver unmistakably spoke in Tigrigna. I pondered whether we were in Mekelle, the capital of the Tigray region, rather than Addis Ababa, the capital of Ethiopia.

The sack still veiled my head as I disembarked the plane, leaving me to ponder the events unfolding around me. The vehicle that awaited me at the airport felt imposing, perhaps a Land Cruiser—a vehicle often favoured by high-ranking Ethiopian officials.

The air carried the essence of dawn, cool and fresh, accompanied by gentle rain and the rhythmic swish of windshield wipers. Sensing a presence on either side, I couldn't shake the notion that the subtle nudge against my ribs might be a handgun.

We traversed miles before halting abruptly, the driver honking insistently. After a brief pause, a gate opened, initiating a hushed conversation with an unknown arrival. Although barely audible, it seemed my abductors were being informed that the intended secret detaining place was unavailable. The driver manoeuvred multiple times before retreating from the tight driveway and stopping anew.

Repeated horn blasts echoed as gates opened and shut, frustrating attempts to secure a clandestine jail. Despite three failed endeavours, the captors eventually found what they sought. I couldn't shake off the disheartening realization of a network of villas used for detaining hostages. A wave of sadness engulfed me as I contemplated the multitude of security agents engaged in the kidnapping of citizens and holding them prisoner in the city's villas.

The throbbing pain in my hand urged me to focus, discarding the luxury of sadness. I concentrated, willing, soothing relief to my aching limbs. Led out of the car, I remained blindfolded, mouth sealed, hands cuffed behind my back. My mind conjured a small courtyard outside the building we approached.

The jangling of keys, followed by a door swung open. I was guided inside. "Sit down," came the command. Confused by such a simple instruction, I hesitated. Before I could respond, hands patted me down, rifling through my pockets and seizing my wallet. They counted my money, withholding both my wallet and cash. Then, they removed the sack from my head, peeling off the tape, causing stinging pain yet granting me the relief of normal sight and breath.

I didn't recognize these two men. They differed from those at Sana'a Airport, but certainty eluded me. Nonetheless, they were unmistakably Tigrayans. Still cuffed, I was told to sit on a sponge mattress in the dimly lit room, blood and sweat stains catching my attention.

With my hands restrained behind my back, sitting proved challenging. I manoeuvred onto one knee, then another, shifting onto my heels. The men forcefully pushed me onto my side, reapplying the sack over my head. Darkness enveloped me as they extinguished the lights, leaving me in solitude.

Chapter VII: Torment and Desperate Decision

My suffering got worse than it was in the aeroplane. Lying down intensified the strain on my already stressed shoulders, struggling to support my body weight. Agony surged to the point where I feared losing consciousness. I attempted to sit up but found myself unable to figure out a position. So, I opted to lay still on my front.

After wriggling, I managed to press my face against the mattress. The stench overwhelmed me, and I rotated my cheeks to alleviate anxiety and avoid suffocation, but it proved futile. Desperate, I decided to stand.

I missed my elbows dearly, yearning to remove the handcuffs. Holding my breath, I wedged my head into the sponge mattress and manoeuvred my legs underneath. But lacking support for my head, I couldn't raise my face.

Applying greater pressure on my head, I manoeuvred my legs forward. In a series of caterpillar-like movements, I painstakingly crawled towards the nearby wall. Leaning my forehead against it, I utilized it as a brace to finally stand upright. Despite my efforts, expressing these hours of unwavering determination and physical strain fails to capture the excruciating pain accompanying every movement.

I vigorously shook my head until the sack finally slipped off. Yet, it made no difference to my vision; the room remained pitch black. My bare feet registered the coldness of the icy concrete floor, and I cursed the men who had removed my socks and shoes. I groped my way around the room, using my shoulder against the wall for guidance.

In the darkness, unable to use my hands, I used my forehead instead to explore the surroundings, sensing the metal plates that now occupied the space where windows once stood. Apart from the foul-smelling sponge mattress, the room seemed empty. As I shuffled along, relying on the wall for support, I felt an object jutting out from it. I contemplated whether I could reach it with my cuffed hands, realizing it was an impossible task.

Curiosity led me to touch the object with my forehead; it felt like a blocked water pipe. Just to confirm, I used my mouth and teeth to thoroughly examine it. It was, without a doubt, a sturdy metal pipe. I entertained the idea of befriending it in my predicament, contemplating whether I could utilize it to end my life by forcefully impacting my head against it. The pipe's awkward positioning demanded precision.

Trying to manoeuvre my head towards the pipe with my hands restrained behind my back was awkward. After pacing back and forth, feeling along the wall to gauge the pipe's position, I gathered all my courage and took the decisive step. I thrust my head towards the pipe.

Minutes or perhaps hours elapsed before I regained consciousness. Lying flat on my chest, I experienced a pulsating headache but detected no signs of blood around me.

"How can this be?" I mused.

"Can dead people have a headache?"

My hands, still cuffed, intensified the pain. I must have missed the pipe, hit my head against the wall, and blacked out. How would I manage to stand and return to where my abductors left me?

Standing seemed inconceivable without the sponge mattress to support my head. Crawling with my chest demanded cooperation that my legs couldn't offer. I attempted to roll like a barrel, each landing on my shoulder excruciatingly painful. It took an hour to cover a mere two meters until I finally reached the sponge mattress.

Worry mingled with pain; I was certain my forehead was swollen. I didn't want my kidnappers to know I'd made physical efforts.

I retrieved the sack that I shook off from my head with my teeth, keeping it nearby, hoping it would seem to have come off on its own. Time felt like standing still. Drained of energy, escape from the mattress's stench seemed impossible. My shoulders throbbed incessantly, the silence around me deafening. I felt I was left in the world of pain all alone.

I had heard about the concept of eternal suffering in hell, but my current situation felt worse than that. Despair and hopelessness appeared to be engaged in their usual uninterrupted conversation, a peculiar condition unique to humans.

Chapter VIII: Mekelle or Addis Ababa?

It was incredibly disorienting. When the plane landed, I believed it was dawn. Since then, a significant amount of time had elapsed, or at least it felt that way. I was startled to notice daylight seeping through the cracks in the walls and around the window seals. My cell didn't entirely block out natural light. The room didn't appear as dark as it did during the night, signalling the arrival of a new day.

I could discern voices speaking in Tigrigna, footsteps drawing closer to my location. The jangling of keys and the creaking of the door indicated someone's arrival. The lights flickered back on. Unable to lift my face from its downward position, I sensed the presence of more than one person in my cell. I couldn't catch a glimpse of their faces while lying on my chest. I presumed it might be the same two men from before.

One of them bellowed, "Why did you take the sack off your head?"

The second man didn't pause for my response.

"Need a piss?" he asked matter-of-factly.

The vile odour of the sponge mattress silenced me. I couldn't muster a reply.

Seemingly uninterested in my answer, one of them struggled to remove my handcuffs, managing only partially. It hung loosely from one wrist while my stiffened arms rendered me immobile, still lying on my front.

"Get yourself up and come out for a piss," I was instructed.

I remained motionless, offering no response. Someone present seemed to understand the situation, manoeuvring my numb, rigid arms to my sides. Gradually, sensation returned, allowing me to face them. However, I had to convey my inability to lift myself. I lacked the strength. They assisted me to sit on the mattress. Once more, I was asked if I needed to use the toilet. Although I didn't feel the urge, I feared they might reapply the handcuffs.

"Yes, I'd like to go," I replied.

They helped me rise to my feet. I attempted to move my arms, hoping for improved circulation. That's when I noticed the shocking indentations the handcuffs had left on my wrists.

The toilet was adjacent. We were inside a small villa. Ahead, a long corridor stretched with doors lining both sides—perhaps bedrooms. I pondered whether I was in a guest room. The other rooms, stark and unadorned, diverged greatly from the aspirations of their original owner. I couldn't help but wonder if each held abducted individuals.

Despite its modern seat, the toilet was deplorable, filthy and lacking a lock on the door. Reflecting on the conditions at Saana airport, I couldn't help but recant my previous views; we were no better than the Yemenis. With my abductors standing just outside, not too far away, I found myself neither willing to proceed nor in a hurry to return to my cell. Instead, I sat down, lingering in the bathroom for as long as possible.

After a few minutes, one of the guards called out to me. "Are you done?" he asked.

"Just finishing," I replied, feigning a toilet flush.

Guided back to the room, I was directed to sit on the mattress. The handcuffs promptly returned to my wrists, followed by the sack over my head. The guys extinguished the lights, secured the door, and departed.

Sitting was unbearable; my shoulders felt as though they were being wrenched from their sockets, with my arms forcibly pulled back. I toppled onto my side, then rolled onto my front.

The house seemed constructed of stone. My shirt, useless in the freezing cold, stirred thoughts of thermal underwear. A blanket might have offered some comfort. Eventually, the cold subsided, but the persistent pain in my shoulder and wrist joints continued to torment me.

I could hear the men conversing with a woman in Tigrigna, mentioning something about food. Hope surged within me at the prospect of freeing my hands. The door swung open, and the sack was lifted off my head. Subsequently, the handcuffs were removed, allowing me to move my arms this time. I shifted onto my side and sat upright.

A plate of macaroni was placed on the floor, but I had no appetite. I dreaded having the handcuffs reapplied. In that moment, I wished they would simply end my life.

"Have your breakfast," I was instructed.

"Okay," I replied.

As the men exited and closed the door behind them, relief washed over me. I had no intention of forcing myself to eat. I planned to bide my time until their return and then feign eating. I gazed at the macaroni, unmoved. Roughly twenty minutes later, the men returned to find me holding the fork but the food untouched.

"You haven't eaten," remarked one of the men, his demeanour less stern.

"My mouth and throat are so dry. I need some water. I can't swallow," I replied.

"We'll get you a cup of tea," responded the first man kindly, ignoring his stern colleague as he exited the room.

The other man followed him, audibly locking the door, which felt like a small triumph to me.

After a while, the first man returned with the tea. "Come on now, drink this and eat your breakfast," he urged before leaving and securing the door behind him. I calmly drank the tea. With no reason to resist further, I nibbled at the macaroni, forcing myself to eat it piece by piece. It was tough to swallow and repulsive to consume food under such degrading conditions.

Some twenty minutes might have elapsed before the security men returned.

"You haven't touched your food," one of the men observed.

"I've had enough. I'm diabetic and shouldn't be eating macaroni. The tea was also very sweet. That's why," I lied, hoping for sympathy with my diabetic story and, perhaps, the removal of the handcuffs. However, I had no such luck. The restraints remained, as did the sack. They gathered the empty cup and the leftover macaroni as I rolled onto my front. The door was locked behind them.

My pain was excruciating. I regretted missing the chance to end my life just the day before. Though motivated to try again, I lacked the physical strength. The idea of lifting myself into a standing position seemed nearly impossible.

How protracted is a solitary minute when every second is inundated with agony? How extensive are each of these hours when every minute is riddled with suffering? How much more interminable does a single day feel when inundated with hours of affliction? I sensed the encroaching darkness, even from behind the weathered sack shrouding my face. That one day spent on the stinking sponge mattress felt like an entire year had elapsed.

Now, enveloped in total darkness, it must be late in the evening. The jangling of keys startled me once more. I couldn't fathom any reason for my abductors to arrive at this hour except perhaps to torture or execute me. This grim reality wasn't new in Ethiopia. Memories resurfaced from the military dictatorship era, recalling executions that occurred after nightfall when the prison guards emerged in the dead of night. The legacy seemed to persist, now inherited by the TPLF that replaced the Army. Picturing death offered a semblance of solace, an end to this relentless agony.

The men entered, handling me brusquely, bundling me up, and placing me in a car. Unaware of our destination, the journey was brief. An iron gate creaked open, and we seemed to have entered a large compound. I winced as they pulled me by the arms, forcibly removing me from the car. Led up a flight of stairs and into another room, the echoes of multiple voices conversing in Tigrigna surrounded me. My shoulders throbbed with searing pain as I was dragged along by my handcuffs, the sack blinding my sight.

Once in the room, I felt cold hands unbuttoning my shirt, followed by the release of my trouser buttons. Left in my undergarments and the sack still over my head, the handcuffs were removed. New clothes were draped over me, the zipper of my jacket zipped up, and my trousers slipped on. Regrettably, the handcuffs soon returned. It transpired swiftly, within five minutes, before I found myself lying on my front on yet another sponge mattress.

The intense brightness of the room persisted as the lights blazed on. Although the door lacked a lock, a guard, seated on a chair leaning against the wall, remained vigilant, keeping a watchful eye on me through the open doorway. The sounds of people conversing in Tigrigna reverberated throughout as they traversed from one room to another. As the darkness enveloped, any lingering hope for a swift execution waned. It became apparent that I was likely in Mekelle.

Chapter IX: Heaven and Hell

I accepted the reality that my death wasn't imminent and shifted my focus toward restoring the blood circulation in my arms. My primary goal was to get the handcuff off as many times and as long as possible at all times. My strategy to do that was to take as long a time as I could to eat and use the toilet. That way, I could relieve myself of the pain on my shoulder.

In the morning, a routine settled in, becoming a fixture for the days ahead. The guard routinely asked if I needed to use the toilet. I obliged, knowing that the absence of handcuffs during this time provided a brief respite. Afterwards, the restraints returned promptly. Breakfast followed not long after, prompting another brief release from the handcuffs. This cycle repeated for lunch, dinner, and a visit to the toilet before the guards retired for the night. Despite enduring severe discomfort due to the handcuffs, I managed to consume a small amount of food each day. However, the fourth day marked a turning point.

On that particular day, when the man arrived to remove my handcuffs for lunch, he was taken aback by what he saw. The cuffs had embedded themselves so deeply into my flesh that they had to be dug out. The sight of my excessively swollen hands was frightening. The handcuffs dangled from one wrist, the clasp hardly visible, buried within the swelling. I could sense the distress it caused the guard; he was the one who had shown me sympathy earlier in the other cell. It was the first time my eyes met his kind gaze.

Lunch had been placed on the floor, but my hands were too stiff to reach out for the food. The gentleman shook his head in disbelief. "What is the meaning of this?" he muttered to himself, staring at my hands. He crossed the hallway into the adjacent room, stood by the door, and pulled out his mobile phone. It was evident he was describing the precarious state of my hands to his superior. Upon returning, he placed some utensils on the floor, removed the dangling handcuffs, and gently massaged my forearms and hands with soap and warm water. His act of human compassion brought tears to my eyes.

"Why?" asked the man with kind eyes, glancing up at me.

"I've always believed that a little kindness defeats a mountain of cruelty," I replied.

"You've just confirmed my belief," I continued.

"So why the tears?"

"Of joy, not of sadness," I replied.

It became clear that rubbing my hands would not alleviate the swelling.

"It won't be long before it goes back to normal; nothing to worry about," he reassured me.

"You have to eat," coaxed the man. Lunch consisted of bread and stew, but my fingers were numb, making it impossible to pick up anything. The man noticed this.

"Allow me to hold the bread up so you can bite into it," he offered. At that moment, my appetite craved sleep and pain relief rather than food.

"Do you mind if I could skip the meal and get some sleep instead?" I asked.

Finally, I slept, free from handcuffs and a sack over my head for the first time in a long while. It was a blissful feeling to lie down on my back rather than on my front.

As darkness fell, the door opened, and the bright light switched on. I saw the man who had tended to my hands sitting in the dimly lit room opposite mine. I marvelled at how swiftly I drifted back to sleep, unable to determine how many hours or days had passed in slumber.

Someone shook me, urging me to wake up. It felt like being pulled out of paradise. I struggled to open my eyes and realized it was daytime, evident from the natural light filtering in from the opposite room. Next to me sat a bun and some tea.

"Get up and eat your breakfast. Visitors are coming to talk to you," he said.

The swelling in my hands had significantly reduced, allowing me to move my fingers. Attempting to rise, I felt the tightness of the blue tracksuit they had dressed me in. Accompanied to the toilet by the man with kind eyes, I had my tea and the bun upon returning to my room. The handcuffs, which I thought had disappeared for good, were placed back on me after I finished eating. However, this time, they were cuffed to the front, providing relief to my arms and improving my blood circulation. It felt like a moment of solace, a glimpse of a new kind of providence.

"I am grateful," I whispered to this God.

Chapter X: Softening before Interrogation

The anticipated visitors failed to show up that day, leaving me to pass the time by dozing off intermittently, shifting from side to side and occasionally onto my back. Surprisingly, the shift of the handcuffs from behind to the front provided a newfound comfort, enabling me to catch up on much-needed sleep. It seemed the guards had opted to let me rest instead of rousing me for meals or other activities, perhaps recognizing that I wasn't the dreaded figure they were led to believe. Their empathy translated into a reprieve, granting me an unexpected respite.

As I drifted into slumber, a whole day slipped by unnoticed until an evening awakening by one of the guards disrupted my sleep. It was then that I was handed a pair of inexpensive slippers, valued at 30 Ethiopian birr, as informed by the guard who had purchased them. Until then, I had been forced to tread barefoot. Gesturing towards the slippers, one of the guards instructed, "Put these on, let's go."

Assuming that the long-awaited individuals who sought to converse with me had finally arrived, my expectations were quickly shattered as a sack was placed over my head once more, leaving me in a state of blindness as they guided me. The sensation of being outdoors was apparent, yet the veil of night obscured any understanding of why I was being escorted outside at such an hour.

The chilling fear of being executed and discarded in an unmarked grave flooded my mind once again.

"Mind yourself; there are steps here," a voice cautioned.

We descended the seven steps calmly. I counted each one as we walked for about 50 meters before another warning preceded the ascent of three steps. The surroundings hinted that we were inside a dwelling. Upon entering a room and the removal of the sack covering my head, I beheld an unkempt space with walls painted in a worn-out shade of blue.

Comparing it to the room I had occupied moments earlier—an orange-painted space with wooden floorboards—this room boasted a larger area with a concrete floor covered in grey linoleum. The signs of damage on the walls and concrete floor hinted at the room's history, housed within an ancient villa whose ceiling bore the scars of time. The window had been replaced by flat metal sheets, barricading any natural light from penetrating the room, rendering it hermetically sealed.

Thick layers of dust blanketed the surfaces, prompting a thought about whether a cleaner had ever set foot in this forsaken space. As was customary, an aged sponge mattress lay on the floor. "Sit down," came the command. With my hands cuffed at the front, it was a relatively easier task, although still challenging to lower myself without assistance. I leaned against the wall, slid down, and allowed myself to descend to a seated position on the floor while both guards observed, chuckled, and then departed the room.

Dinner soon arrived, and I followed when led through the labyrinthine house to wash my hands, the handcuffs dangling from my left wrist. The villa, sprawling with numerous rooms and a lengthy corridor adorned with doors on either side, assigned each room a number. Adjacent to my cell, the bathroom presented a picture of neglect with a sizable bathtub, a fixed shower, a water heater, a sink, a bidet, and a toilet.

Returning to my cell, I indulged in the injera – the traditional Ethiopian flatbread – and Shiro, a chickpea sauce for dinner. Accompanied by a plastic bottle of tap water, this meal surpassed the taste of all prior ones. After allowing me ample time to finish, the guards returned, cleared the dinner plate, and departed, securing the door upon exit.

Moments later, the door creaked open once more. One of the guards entered, carrying a lengthy, weighty chain along with a padlock. "I'm here to chain your legs since your handcuffs are now in front," he explained, his undertone carrying a hint of apology, seemingly emphasizing that he was merely following orders. Methodically, he secured the chain around my legs, clicked the padlock shut, wished me a good evening, and then departed. Under the circumstances, the guard wishing me goodnight looked cruel to me.

The addition of the chain to my legs proved more of an inconvenience than a source of pain. I had recently endured what true pain felt like; the physical discomfort in my shoulders and arms over the past few days had been relentless. The intelligence officers knew well that depriving me of sleep by restraining my hands behind my back was their method of torture, designed to exhaust and weaken me before interrogation.

Resigned to the discomfort, I drifted off to sleep. Typically, I am not one to lose sleep over worries; my mind has developed a coping mechanism to shield me from excessive anxiety by shutting down. The more pressing the issue causing distress, the deeper my slumber becomes. To evade mental anguish, I can immerse myself in sleep for twenty-four hours, even days, if needed.

Chapter XI: Interrogation

The following day beganearly with the opening of the door and the removal of both the handcuffs and the chain. The morning routine ensued, involving washing up and breakfast. After these rituals, the restraints were once again placed on my wrists and legs. Later, the door reopened, freeing my legs from the chain but leaving the handcuffs intact. I was escorted to another room and informed that someone wished to speak with me.

The solitary figure awaited in what seemed to be a relatively spacious area, resembling a former reception room adorned with aged photographs in one corner. Seated at a distant desk, a man with bulging eyes, a dark complexion, a receding hairline, and a sturdy build captured my attention. The desk was adorned solely with a vintage home phone apparatus, an antiquated relic of communication. Behind him, an open window offered a view of a courtyard entangled with a rampant berry climber scaling the stone wall.

A sense of familiarity stirred within me, prompting thoughts of where I might have met this man before. Yet, my memory failed to provide certainty. His gaze pierced through me as he gestured with a plastic water bottle towards the empty chair opposite him.

"Please, take a seat," he invited.

"How are you?" he inquired.

"Hanging in there, if I can still be counted among the living," I replied.

At his beckoning, a guard entered the room.

"Get him some water," the man ordered.

The guard reappeared, holding a one-litre worn plastic bottle filled with tap water retrieved from my cell. The expression on his boss's suggested displeasure.

"What is this? Have you been giving him tap water? Go fetch him some bottled spring water," he directed.

Silently, I speculated that this might be the classic ploy of 'good cop, bad cop.'

The room fell silent momentarily, and I sat upright, scanning for any hidden surveillance. The man scrutinized my every movement.

"What are you looking for?" he asked.

"Hidden cameras," I replied, with a suspicious look at the odd home phone apparatus in front of him.

He half-smiled. "So you don't remember me," he stated.

I concentrated, trying to recall. "Are you Aderaw?" I ventured a name I associated with this man for a particular reason.

He had interrogated me when I was detained in Zeway after the 2005 election. It was my first encounter with him. I had shared details of my imprisonment with friends in London, including the features of a man who had told me he was sent to talk to me by Prime Minister Meles Zenawi.

One of my friends identified him based on the description I provided.

"He's from Tigray, worked during the final years of the military dictatorship, and later joined the Woyane regime to reorganize national security," confirming that his name was indeed Aderaw.

As I confronted the man in front of me, I sensed his scepticism regarding my recollections. "Who is Aderaw?" he volleyed back.

His response confused me momentarily. Yet, I remained steadfast, convinced I had met him in Zeway. I studied his face intently.

Without hesitation, he confirmed he had indeed interrogated me, but the name was incorrect. "I'm surprised you don't remember me more vividly," he remarked.

"I can't see well without my glasses," I fibbed, hoping to coax him to ordering the guards into returning my reading glasses. And thus, the interrogation commenced.

Chapter XII: Mind Game

The interrogator employed amicable tactics throughout our interaction. He maintained courtesy from the onset, adopting an approach that encouraged conversational dialogue rather than the typical question-and-answer format. Instead of bombarding me with a barrage of questions, he delved into topics such as politics, Ginbot 7, the economy, and Shabia, all with a gentle touch.

It was evident that he had two primary objectives. First, to gather evidence, and second, to identify content that could bolster his government's propaganda. Aware of the potential scrutiny from hidden cameras and sound recorders, I carefully devised a safe strategy on the spot, mindful that every gesture and every word uttered could be captured.

First, I decided to provide evidence that I knew he already had in his possession. Then, I planned to acknowledge the information they would likely discover in my computer files. I had to be cautious with my words, ensuring that nothing I said could be misconstrued to incriminate the Ginbot 7 movement or align with their propaganda.

Once again, I returned to the issue of hidden cameras and audio recorders.

"It wouldn't be beneficial even if I were to make comments that you could use for your propaganda. Nobody believes your news reports due to your reputation for falsehoods. Even if you present evidence, it's unlikely anyone will believe it. That's why there's no point in using hidden cameras," I asserted.

He smiled in response and shifted the conversation to questions about Ginbot 7 and the popular force. "You already have all the data from my computer files. It tells you everything you need to know; why do you need to hear it from me?" I questioned.

"The Yemenis didn't give us the laptop," he replied.

"Of course, they did. My kidnappers were quick to claim my computer bag and suitcase. I've seen them load it onto the jeep that took us to the smaller aircraft. In any case, I can give you my computer password if you wish," I offered.

"Tell me," he commanded.

Knowing that Ethiopian security likely had access to my password, thanks to Chinese assistance, I shared it as a gesture of cooperation rather than institutional betrayal. My laptop had two passwords, and intentionally misspelling the second one might prompt him to return for the correct one.

My interrogator recorded both passwords in his notebook. As I observed him write, I recalled his earlier claim about the Yemenis failing to hand over my computer. While they might find a way past the password, my hopes dimmed at the prospect of him not returning for the correct second password.

A subsequent examination of my laptop unveiled potential avenues for purchasing armaments on the black market. The interrogator's questions aligned with this research, making me certain that he had posed those inquiries after accessing my computer. His colleagues were likely reviewing my notes at that very moment.

The same interrogator continued questioning me for a few more days. The sessions became confusing at times, as I struggled to discern whether his focus was on engaging in political discussions or extracting answers to fill a standard form loaded with endless questions. His final remark took me by surprise – it was a question.

"Did you notice that the Eritrean Ambassador was present during your detention?" he inquired.

"I knew he intended to come to the airport, but I'm not sure he ever did," I replied.

"He's a little on the older side. He was present," he disclosed. That final conversation essentially marked the conclusion of his investigation. However, it left me with a lingering suspicion regarding the Eritrean Ambassador.

Chapter XIII: David and Goliath

A few days later, the same investigator returned, this time accompanied by a much shorter man. He introduced the new man, not by name but by the task he would be performing. The newcomer would be taking the lead in future interrogations, and I could ask him if I needed anything. With these words, the initial investigator abruptly left.

Before the new interrogator could ask any questions, I inquired, "How may I address you?"

"You can call me Dawit," he replied.

I understood it wasn't his real name, yet he must have chosen "Dawit" (Amharic Version of David) for a reason. Given his short and skinny stature, I couldn't shake the feeling that he had picked the name mockingly, perhaps to allude to the biblical story of Dawit and Goliath. While I didn't see myself as a Goliath figure, I was intrigued by the choice.

Dawit differed from my first interrogator. The latter exuded professionalism and demonstrated self-respect and respect for others. The national security body trusted Dawit, and there was likely a significant reason for his introduction. He continued to see me regularly until my transfer from the extrajudicial solitary cell to the prison in Kaliti.

During his interrogations, Dawit would use slurs to pose provocative questions. The guards, well aware of the importance of capturing every moment, would meticulously arrange my seat to align with the optimal position of the hidden cameras. In anticipation of this routine, I would consistently and deliberately shift my chair before sitting down, prompting the guards to swiftly rush in and readjust my position to ensure thorough coverage for the hidden camera.

In one of these sessions, I asked Dawit the same question I raised to his boss. Why did they invest so much effort in building propaganda that nobody believed?

My question seemed to annoy him, and he retorted, "What do you mean?"

"You don't seem to notice that your propaganda only convinces you. Well-trained publicists may save you from the humiliation your media is bringing upon you. Public relations requires skill. It's not an art that your cadres can intuitively pick up and apply," I remarked.

Dawit appeared visibly restless, but observing the impact of my words seemed to content me, prompting me to continue.

"Look, nobody knew anything about Ginbot 7 until your media started talking about us. You created an image by planting a sensational story about military generals collaborating with Ginbot 7 to carry out a coup d'etat. Then, within less than 24 hours, you backtracked and reported that it was not a coup d'etat attempt but terrorist activity.

This change of mind gave us significant exposure in the international media. I'm sure you won't forget how I responded to the questions from Voice of America's Tizita Belayneh.

I recalled the details of that interview and pointed out to my interrogator how we have exploited each one of their public relation disaster to our advantage to the extent that we could fabricate anything and still be believed by the public. At the time, I simply told VOA that we had information about why the change in narrative was decided at the Prime Minister's office.

"We used to find all sorts of information about the state from your people. However, we had no information abouta meeting taking place at the PM's office on the case of the Generals. I had invented the information I shared with Tizita. But you helped me by making anyone who heard my side of the story believe that we had an informant on the inside reporting the content of meetings within the Prime Minister's office. You would have been better off just arresting the generals without much commentary. Instead, you ended up giving huge publicity to Ginbot 7 and the generals."

Dawit continued listening, restraining his anger and impatience with apparent difficulty. Repressing his annoyance, he asked, "What else?"

I was eager to express my thoughts on the slurs they directed at leaders of Ginbot 7, particularly the one portraying me and my comrades as the errand boys of Shabia.

"Do you think people believe what you say on your TV and radio programs? Older folks know who the real Shabia errand boys are." I said.

"The younger generation isn't tuning in to your media; they're listening to what is being said by their parents, grandparents, aunts, and uncles. What they hear is that you are shameless eye-pluckers. You sent the young people of Tigray to Eritrea and forced them to fight for Eritrea. The political and military language you use, the way your fighters dress, the way they walk, and the emblem on your flag all demonstrate your awe for Shabia. The whole country knows that. Everyone, including children, still remember how you once claimed to share the same lung with Shabia to breathe. If I were in your place with that kind of backstory, I wouldn't go around making public comments or private jokes about leaders of Ginbot 7 being Shabia errand boys," I asserted.

Both Dawit and the guards became visibly upset, particularly one guard who happened to be tall and bald. He was shaking and frothing at the mouth as he hurled insults at me, to which Dawit added, "Woyane has never been subservient to Shabia, but we have proof that you kiss Isaias' feet!"

"As far as I know, you had a sycophant master who believed it was better to speak to Isaias for an hour than to read a thousand books," I retorted, referencing PM Meles, a figure these individuals used to idolize, and it struck a raw nerve. One of the guards began raining threats and insults on me.

Realizing it was time to check myself, I decided to pause and assess the situation.

"Look, I can sweet talk you guys, but I thought you dared to take a bit of criticism. I had imagined talking would be useful; I didn't want to be pretentious, but I can stop here if you like," I stated. My words seemed to put them on the defensive; Dawit calmed down, holding his face and squeezing it in his hands.

"No need to lie, so what else have you got to say?" asked Dawit.

"Well, how about the time you gave Birtukan media visibility after her release from prison?" I questioned without hesitation. Silence fell over the room, and I took it as a sign to continue.

"You manipulated Birtukan to appear on television and express hope that foreigners would help secure her release. You knew that she echoed a public statement Meles had made about prisoners who believed foreigners could secure their release. You thought she would be humiliated, but the humiliation turned out to be yours. Shall I tell you what people say about you?" I asked.

Nobody objected, so I proceeded, assuming their silent approval.

"Is it appropriate for a head of state to demand that a woman who has suffered enough in jail echoes a public statement he made in return for her freedom? People out there are saying that your lack of ethics is scandalous," I asserted.

"Some people..." I began, but before I could continue, Dawit lost his temper. The rageful words he used against Birtukan were too foul to repeat here, further fueling my anger.

"Don't forget, Birtukan was a Supreme Court judge who, up until the moment she refused to give in to servitude, was a hero you dragged into jail," I spoke out.

I believe that took away Dawit's appetite for further interrogation.

"Get him out of here," he instructed the guard. It marked the last day of the official investigation, and the full-day interrogations had finally come to an end, most likely in Mekelle.

Chapter XIV: World Cup Finals

One morning, as I made my way to the washroom, I overheard the guards talkingabout the World Cup Finals. The guard on duty, the one with kind eyes, was the same individual who had previously eased the discomfort in my swollen hands with soap and water. Seizing the opportunity, I engaged him in conversation while he prepared to reapply the handcuffs and secure my legs.

Curious, I inquired, "Which teams have advanced to the final round?"

"Argentina and Germany," replied the kind-eyed man. Maintaining a light-hearted tone, I suggested, "So, we'll be watching the game together tonight."

He smiled but left without responding, locking the door behind him. Ever since the interrogations ceased, daily life had assumed a new routine.

The guards, appearing in pairs at their discretion, often at sunrise, would open my door. One would observe as the other removed my handcuffs and leg restraints. Over time, my consistent refusal of breakfast resulted in the guards discontinuing their early morning visits. In my altered routine, lunch became my first meal around 2:00 p.m. I would be escorted to the washroom only upon my request, signalled by banging on the door.

Set against the backdrop of the rainy season, the stone house where Woyane detained me lacked heating. A persistent, tickly cough had developed, and it was unclear whether the cause was the cold or the dusty environment. Asthma, a condition not experienced for many years, began to resurface as the cough intensified, making breathing a struggle.

On the evening of the World Cup finals, wrapped in chains and handcuffs, I lay on my sponge mattress. Given the absence of alternative activities, I was free to sleep throughout the day. As a light sleeper, I would awaken at the slightest noise. That evening, my ears became attuned to the sound of a running car, with the closing car door confirming my acute hearing

I sensed that this might be the day of my dreaded apprehensions—the day they would lead me out, end my life, and discard me into some obscure pit in the earth.

I could hear people taking. Amidst faint voices, it was challenging to decipher their words. Despite the uncertainty, a voice queried why the phone calls went unanswered. Perhaps the purpose of the car's arrival was to investigate the unresponsiveness.

Attempting to quell my rising anxiety, I considered the possibility that the car hadn't come for me at all. The person who emerged from the car didn't depart as one might after delivering a message. Instead, I detected footsteps approaching my room and the sound of a key turning in my door. No one had ever entered my cell before at such a late hour.

Revisiting the notion that the car had come for me, I found an unexpected calm settling within me. A peculiar quote by Gabriel Garcia Marquez surfaced in my mind: "Many years later, as he faced the firing squad, Colonel Aureliano Buendia was to remember that distant afternoon when his father took him to discover ice."

Recalling that I had memorized this quote from the opening sentence of "One Hundred Years of Solitude," a book I had read multiple times, I pondered what thoughts might occupy my mind in a scenario akin to the Colonel's. Imagining my final moments, I pictured my young twin children standing before me, their faces at the forefront of my mind as the door creaked open.

The man who entered wore a bright, cheerful expression, a stark contrast to the ominous look I had anticipated. To my relief, it was the kind-eyed man, and I felt assured that he had not come with harmful intentions.

"Get up. You have permission to watch the World Cup final," he announced.

I had forgotten the casual remark I had made earlier, jokingly and certainly unexpectedly. He assisted me in standing, and with chains in tow, I shuffled behind him down the entire length of the corridor, trailed by the horse-faced, bald guard.

We entered the lounge that was previously used as the interrogation room. A small TV sat on a plain table opposite an empty chair. Following instructions, I took a seat while the two guards settled into sagging yellow armchairs on either side. Carefully made single beds adorned each corner, presumably where my guards would sleep.

The game began shortly, but the aerial TV's signal was less than ideal. The guards took turns attempting to rectify the reception without much success. Despite the unclear image, we proceeded to watch the World Cup finals. Engulfed in the peculiar reality of my situation—legs chained, hands cuffed, and guards at a distance—I found it surreal.

By halftime, it was evident from the flickering screen that neither Argentina nor Germany had scored. I had assumed the guards might take a break, perhaps even offer a cup of tea or coffee as a gesture of effort in organizing the event. However, not a word passed through their lips, let alone a provision of hot beverages before the second half began. The Germans scored, but neither guard reacted, and my own indifference mirrored theirs. Perhaps I would have preferred Argentina to score.

As the game concluded, we observed the German team receiving the cup. Simultaneously and seemingly synchronized, the guards rose from their seats. I, too, stood up as they approached. With my chain jangling, I made my way back to my cell. As I entered, the door locked behind me.

The entire experience was bizarre and inexplicable, lingering in my thoughts as I reached for the edge of my sponge mattress and dropped onto it.

Chapter XV: Cough and Asthma siding with my abductors

A few days following the World Cup final, my cough worsened into a full-blown ordeal that persisted both day and night, making it increasingly challenging to breathe. A rusty, unsettling sound emanated from my chest, harmonizing with each laboured breath. Even the simple act of eating triggered a disruption in my respiration.

Concerned about my deteriorating health, the kind-eyed guard, who had previously permitted me to watch the World Cup, reported my condition to the principal interrogator. In response, the interrogator visited, his scrutiny apparent as he observed my distressed state.

"What do you need?" he inquired with a measured tone.

Expressing my urgent need for medication, specifically an inhaler, I emphasized the gravity of my respiratory struggles. Without hesitation, he assured me that he would procure the necessary treatment and hastily left the room.

Shortly after that, the interrogator, followed by a woman, arrived with the promised medicine. The lady appeared to be a nurse, roughly fifty years old, and her attire, despite her age, mirrored a youthful style—perhaps an attempt to present a more urban image. Clad in white, tight-fitting trousers, she resembled a Woyane fighter with a rural background but with the kind eyes that had become a rare source of comfort in my challenging circumstances.

From her handbag, she retrieved a stethoscope and a blood pressure monitor. While taking things out a leftover hair extensions fell to the ground unnoticed by her. Her eyes revealed a subtle hint of compassion as the guard removed the chains and handcuffs, but her focus quickly shifted to her professional duties.

"Open your jacket, please," she requested, noting my bare chest underneath.

Observing the absence of an undershirt, she inquired about it, directing the question to the principal interrogator and the guard. Their silence provided no answer. Undeterred, she proceeded to place the cold stethoscope on my chest, attentively listening to the sounds within.

With a calm yet firm tone, she instructed, "Inhale, exhale," as part of her thorough examination. The room, fraught with tension, became a makeshift clinic as she efficiently carried out her medical assessment amidst the peculiar circumstances of my detention.

Complying with the nurse's request, I opened my jacket, allowing her to attach a blood pressure cuff to my right arm. She diligently monitored my blood pressure and then delivered the relieving news, "It's good."

Following this assessment, the guard inquired about my familiarity with using the asthma inhaler. Confirming my knowledge, I was then asked to demonstrate by inhaling twice.

"The guards will keep it. Knock on the door whenever you need it," they instructed, seemingly indifferent to the practical challenges I faced with my hands cuffed and legs chained.

Attempting to convey my difficulty in reaching the door under such constraints, I met resistance. The guards, seemingly unwilling to let the nurse overhear further discussions, promptly asked her to leave. Remaining behind, they informed me that I could not retain possession of the inhaler.

The principal interrogator, noticing the hair extensions on the floor, questioned their presence. I explained that they had fallen out of the nurse's handbag.

"Women!" he muttered disapprovingly as he kicked the hair extension out of my room. The guard, resuming his role, reattached the handcuffs and chain before leaving, securing the door behind him. The brief reprieve offered by the nurse's visit gave way to the harsh reality of my confined existence once more.

Despite diligently using both the inhaler and antibacterial medication, my persistent cough showed no signs of improvement. The security guards attempted to address the situation by changing the sponge mattress and blanket, yet my condition remained unchanged.

Frustrated by my ongoing discomfort, I persisted in requesting permission to keep the inhaler within reach, but my appeals were consistently denied. It seemed the guards were concerned about potential misuse or harm.

"It's harmless," I tried to assure them. "I could use the inhaler as often as needed, and it would not pose any danger to me," I explained. However, their stance remained firm: "Knock on the door whenever you want it."

As my cough worsened, keeping both me and the guards awake, they eventually relented and started coming into my room to provide the inhaler upon my request.

A few days later, a new challenge emerged as I developed a rash on my legs. Despite the visible discomfort and bleeding resulting from scratching around my handcuffs, my pleas for medication went unanswered. It seemed they doubted the legitimacy of my ailment, suspecting an attempt to manipulate them into freeing my hands.

One evening, overwhelmed by the persistent cough, the sense of suffocation, and the constraints of the chain and handcuffs, I found the situation intolerable. In a moment of despair, I thought about my children, and waves of grief engulfed me. Pleading with God for relief yielded no answer.

Suddenly, a childhood memory surfaced—the Biblical story of Job, with the verse "He giveth, he taketh." Reminding myself that my suffering was not as severe as Job's brought a modicum of solace, helping me endure the hardships I faced.

Chapter XVI: A New Sports Attire

"What size of clothing do you wear?" the man inquired.

"I used to be a size 34, sometimes size 36 around the waist, but I've slimmed down since then," I responded.

Upon reconsideration, the man rephrased his question, "Would you be a small, medium, or large for a jogging suit?"

Puzzled, I questioned, "I have two already; why an additional one?"

He conveyed my response over the telephone to someone else, and the reply came, "We've been asked to buy him a set, so we have to. Which one?"

Slightly confused, I suggested, "Small is tight, large is loose, how about medium?"

They resolved the issue amongst themselves, leaving me with lingering questions. Why were they providing me with additional clothing? Could there be a hidden motive, perhaps a new ritual preceding an execution, akin to the Americans offering sumptuous meals to prisoners before their demise? While scepticism clouded my thoughts, a glimmer of hope emerged. However, the uncertainty continued to gnaw at me, leaving me restless and disturbing my sense of inner peace.

The jogging suit arrived in the afternoon, and the handcuffs and chain were removed so I could try it on. As I inspected the material, expecting to find "made in China" labels, to my surprise, it turned out to be an original Adidas tracksuit made in Turkey.

One of the guards observed my examination and inquired, "Do you like it?"

"Why would that concern you?" I retorted, knowing I was mocking him. He chose not to respond, realising the futility of engaging in banter.

I tried on the jogging suit, and to my surprise, it fit perfectly.

"We can return it if it doesn't fit. How is it?" inquired the man who had handed it to me.

"As you can see, it fits," I replied.

Regrettably, the satisfaction was short-lived. I was instructed to remove the new outfit and return to my old clothes. The handcuffs and chain were reapplied, and the man who had brought the jogging suit carefully packed it back into the plastic bag before departing. I couldn't help but wonder when the moment, my "Epiphany" reserved for that jogging suit, would finally arrive. It manifested the following day.

In the morning, the kind-eyed guard opened my door, holding a pair of scissors.

"You're going to have a trim," he declared, referring to my hair and beard.

Indifferent to the prospect of a haircut, my primary concern was the time it would take. Seeing it as another opportunity to liberate my body, I readily agreed. Accompanying the kind-eyed man was a young, familiar-looking lad with a fair complexion, reminiscent of the people in Sana'a, Yemen. It occurred to me that he might be the same individual who had wielded a handgun, perhaps as a symbolic gesture, aimed at the sky—perhaps a way of signalling a warning to a higher power not to intervene—when I resisted getting into the car.

After removing my handcuffs and chain, the guard led me into the bathroom, where I complied with the guard/barber's instructions. Following a trim, I took a leisurely shower, cherishing the rare moments of personal care. Upon completion, my new jogging suit was handed to me. Additionally, the guards returned the black leather shoes confiscated at Sana'a airport, and under their direction, I put them on.

Though the combination of leather shoes and a tracksuit didn't particularly appeal to me, I adorned them quietly, avoiding any confrontation. It was evident that I was now being prepared for something. My curiosity and impatience grew as I eagerly awaited to discover my destination.

For the first time, the guards did not rush to restrain me. Embracing this newfound liberty, I began to stride back and forth.

My hands, free from restraints, felt as though they had returned to their rightful place. As I contemplated the impending journey ahead, I couldn't help but approach it with a mix of anticipation and uncertainty, akin to a fortune teller predicting the future.

Chapter XVII: Rendezvous at a Guard room

As suspected, the door opened in the afternoon, and security guards threw a blanket over my head to obstruct my view. They must have misplaced the sack that I was used to. The covering, while perhaps a mild improvement from the sack, was a welcomed change. The sound of a running car engine reached my ears as soon as I stood up, and the security guards guided me to the vehicle. Following their instructions, I lay down on the back seat as the journey began.

We travelled a considerable distance, or it seemed, and I could sense gates opening and closing before the car eventually stopped. I rose from my lying position upon instruction, and as the blanket was removed from my head, I found myself in a compound surrounded by tall trees. A prominent white multi-storey building dominated the scene. Two security guards firmly holding to each of my arms led me towards a room near the gate, presumably reserved as a guards' room.

To my surprise, Dawit, my second interrogator, had been the one driving. It was unexpected to see him take on the role of a driver, given his seniority. This unusual responsibility might be linked to the secrecy surrounding my location.

Inside the room, which housed four chairs, one positioned behind a computer desk caught my attention. Puzzled by the presence of a computer in a room apparently designated for security personnel, I suspected there was more to the situation than met the eye.

Dawit settled into the chair in front of the computer, instructing me to sit on another chair away from the window. Two security guards who had escorted me stood outside, and the door was left ajar, providing a glimpse of the surroundings.

As Dawit and I sat in silence, I sensed that we were waiting for something, although the nature of that wait remained elusive. Eventually, Dawit broke the silence, and I braced myself for whatever revelations or inquiries lay ahead.

"Tamagne Beyene (a charming and famous artist-activist, a friend of mine) will snivel a while," Dawit declared.

His comment caught me off guard, and I quickly composed myself. "Why?" I asked.

"Because of your detention," Dawit replied.

As he spoke, I sensed a satisfaction in his demeanour at the thought of Tamagne's distress. He seemed to relish the notion that he had succeeded in making Tamagne cry. Swallowing my own emotions, I chose to remain silent. Dawit appeared to derive pleasure from adding salt to the wound, further mocking Tamagne's tears.

"Tamagne was lamenting on ESAT television that you deserved, more than he did, the silver lion awarded to him in London," he continued.

Dawit, unwittingly offering me valuable information, persisted in his spiteful narrative. Until that point, I had been anxious that my whereabouts were unknown to anyone. Tamagne's public expression of grief on ESAT hinted at his awareness of my abduction, suggesting that my friends might also be informed. Familiar with Tamagne and his inclination for tears, I pictured his distress, burdening my heart with profound sorrow.

As Dawit continued with his disdainful remarks, two individuals entered the room—one tall and dark-skinned, the other a balding, stocky white middle-aged man.

The white man, seemingly recognizing me, extended a hand in greeting. "Greg Dorey, British Ambassador," he introduced himself. Both he and his Woyane escort took the remaining seats.

Suddenly, clarity dawned regarding the recent fuss over the Adidas jogging suit and the haircut. It was all orchestrated by the Woyane to showcase their supposed care for me during the British Ambassador's visit. The young man accompanying the Ambassador, with his persistent interventions, seemed adept at managing language barriers. Dawit remained seated, silent and unmoving.

After inquiring about my well-being, the Ambassador delved into a rigorous interrogation. I observed his demeanour and gestures, noting the casual attire that marked a departure from typical diplomatic formality. One of his unbuttoned shirts strained over a bulging torso, and I couldn't help but imagine the hearty lunch he might have enjoyed before our meeting. Despite the urge to inquire about his lunch, I restrained myself, recognizing the inappropriateness of such a question.

"Do you know the exact location of your detention?" the Ambassador inquired.

"No. I'm not even sure if I am in Addis or Mekelle," I responded, maintaining a serious expression.

My confusion stemmed from the fact that everyone around me spoke Tigrigna, including the lady cook, the interrogators, and the guards. During my outings, my eyes were always sealed shut, and I never heard anyone speak in another language. Therefore, the assumption that I could be in Mekelle seemed reasonable.

"The Ambassador contradicted, "No, you are in Addis Ababa."

He continued to probe my knowledge of my location, asking about the date and the duration since my abduction, indirectly assessing my mental state. Utilizing a sharp object in my cell, I had marked lines on the wall to keep track of the days, making it easy for me to answer his questions. Confirming it had been a month, he then pulled out a piece of paper from his pocket, delving into a series of health-related inquiries.

The questions mirrored details recorded in a health report prepared by my GP, Doctor Aaron of St Johns Way North London. The Ambassador covered topics such as malaria, eyesight, asthma, diabetes, and other ailments I had experienced. Although not diabetic, my doctor was aware of my family history and had advised precautions. I appreciated that the Ambassador's inquiries justified my refusal to consume certain foods, a point noted by Dawit, who listened attentively.

I openly discussed my deteriorating health and the limited medical attention available. The Ambassador, seemingly concerned, pledged to follow up on my needs. The young man with him promised to find a solution for the eczema on my leg.

After the health discussion, the Ambassador conveyed personal messages. "Yemi and the children send you their love," he said, with an Amharic translation automatically coming to me. He also mentioned a request for a kiss. That was the translation.

Moving on, the Ambassador sought to understand the circumstances of my kidnapping, asking about my British passport and the specifics of the event. I answered each question, yet the British government's stance did not include a condemnation of the Woyane's illegal actions. I awaited a statement urging my immediate release, but the Ambassador did not make such a demand.

Ambassador Creg persisted in assuring me that the British government opposed the death penalty and would advocate for my court appearance. However, he omitted any mention of the British Government challenging the illegal abduction of one of its citizens at an international airport or fighting for my unconditional release. Sensing the hopelessness of being released through UK pressure alone, I resigned myself to the fate of prolonged imprisonment.

Although not surprised by Ambassador Greg's diplomatic approach, I responded in detail, stating,

"Ambassador Greg, I am well aware that what I am involved in is not child's play. I am struggling to bring an end to this government."

I continued by critiquing Western governments for their immoral actions in defence of national interests and highlighting Woyane's repressive measures against dissenting individuals. Expressing my disappointment with the British stance, I emphasized that prolonging my life under the threat of death was much worse than death itself. Their opposition to the death sentence was no favour.

The Ambassador and security guards abruptly halted my discourse, declaring it enough for the day. Woyane officials escorted the Ambassador out, expressing appreciation for their courteous conduct. Once again, a blanket covered my head, and I was instructed to repeat the same actions as when we arrived. I was then returned to my unidentified cell.

Chapter XVIII: Gifts and Travel

One afternoon, the cell door swung open, and the nurse entered, accompanied by the kind-eyed guard. He positioned himself by the door after granting her access. Had the accompanying guard been the tall one, he would likely have followed the nurse into my cell.

Expressing empathy, the nurse inquired about my well-being without awaiting my response. She promptly issued instructions to the guard, "Could you remove the handcuffs for a moment so I can check the prisoner's blood pressure?"

Efficiently, she retrieved her tools from her handbag, mirroring her actions during the previous checkup. Once done, she stowed away her equipment and revealed an item wrapped in a plastic bag.

"I brought you some undershirts," the nurse announced, unveiling white Indian-made T-shirts from the packaging. "These cotton T-shirts will keep you warm, and the prison authorities allocated a budget for their purchase," she clarified. Delving into her bag, she produced a blue coloured men's underwear, adding, "This, however, is a gift I bought for you. I suspected you might not have any if you don't possess undershirts." Her thoughtful and kind gestures touched me deeply.

The undershirt instantly warmed my skin upon wearing it. Recalling the prior kindness of the guard stationed by my door, I was moved by the nurse's compassionate act.

"Take your medication regularly and have courage," the nurse encouraged before departing.

However, the persistent cough and breathlessness endured.

One evening that same week, I heard the sound of a car entering the compound. Despite the late hour, I felt no anxiety. Ever since my encounter with the British Ambassador, my apprehension about being taken out and harmed in the dead of night had diminished. The door opened, and a guard removed my handcuffs and chains while I lay on the mattress without explanation. The tall and short guards helped me stand, draped a blanket over my head, and secured it around my neck to obstruct my vision. Guided like a blind man, I was ushered into a sizable car, its engine audibly humming.

"Lie down," the guards instructed.

Where," I asked sarcastically.

Someone was already seated next to where I would be. "On the seat," a male voice barked. Hands dragged my blanket-wrapped head down. I could feel something scraping against my head; I suspected it was a handgun. The car started moving left and right on rough dirt roads before hitting an asphalt road. The bumpy ride was soon over, and it was now smooth sailing. I had no idea where we were going, and I did not feel anxious.

We travelled for a long time as if heading to a far-off land. Finally, the car drove into a driveway and stopped. I rose from the seat and followed the guidance as I stepped out of the car with my head wrapped up in the blanket. A few minutes later, a door opened, I entered, and the blanket came off.

I found myself in a spacious room. In one corner, a new and expensive-looking mattress lay on the floor and nothing else. The security guard declared that my transfer here was due to the dust in my cell, which was now scheduled for renovation. I was to stay in this place until then.

"That is your bed; it's much better than your old mattress. We will give you an additional blanket," said the tall guard. They both left, locking the door behind them. I wasn't sorry to see them go. I was delighted that my legs were left free of the chain. I felt as though I'd never see the chain again and walked around the room.

A little later, I felt as though this wasn't the first time I'd been in here. I looked around carefully. The mattress lay next to a locked door, and I could see through the crack. It was dark on the other side, but the opening was wide enough to let some light from my room filter through. It was a bathroom. I didn't need to do much more sleuthing to find out where they had brought me; the bathroom tiles gave away my destination.

I stayed at one of the guest houses at the Ghion Hotel, a historic establishment constructed by Emperor Haile Selassie. In the earlier days, prior to the emergence of more contemporary hotels in Addis Ababa, the Ghion Hotel stood as the sole accommodation dedicated to hosting state Presidents and other esteemed foreign dignitaries at the highest levels.

On one occasion, I spent two nights, and the second time, just one night. The room I now occupied had French-glazed windows leading to a private garden. The authorities that turned this prestigious guesthouse into a makeshift prison had sprayed the windows with white paint, giving them the appearance of double doors.

Scraping the white paint off the windows was easy, but I didn't have any tools. I looked around, noticed a crack in the linoleum floor, and broke off a piece which I used to lightly scrape off some of the paint.

From behind, someone had covered the French windows with iron sheets. I could still see beyond between the opening of seams. I couldn't believe that part of the garden had transformed into a multi-story building construction site. The tower lights shone over the vast lawn.

The Ghion Hotel garden, once meticulously maintained, now appeared neglected and overgrown. The contrast between the faded grandeur of the hotel's history and its current state struck me as symbolic of larger shifts in the country.

As I observed the garden, memories from my previous stays at this guest house flooded back. The Emperor's era was long gone, replaced by a new political order. The Ghion Hotel, once a symbol of prestige and power, had transformed into a relic of a bygone era.

I was now sure of my whereabouts. My idle observation lasted no more than five minutes.

The guards returned. I leapt onto my mattress as they unlocked the door. They walked in with an extra blanket, a pillow, a bottle of spring water, and the dreaded chain for my legs. I fumed as they locked it in place. I had to say something biting.

"This chain seems to be a permanent accessory. Are you afraid I'll run away in this spacious room?" I remarked with a sarcastic tone.

As I continued to survey the room, the metallic jingle of the chain around my legs seemed to mock the grandeur of the Ghion Hotel. My captors, seemingly unfazed by my sardonic remark, maintained their stoic expressions.

I decided to play my trump card, injecting a note of gravity into my voice. "It's a pity you are using the Ghion Hotel as a prison," I declared, making sure my words carried weight. I could sense a subtle shift in the room; the nonchalant atmosphere was punctured by a sudden tension.

Their carefully laid precautions to conceal my whereabouts began to unravel. I watched as my captors exchanged wary glances, realizing that I held information that could cause serious trouble for their higher-up masters. Without a word, they left.

I walked back to the new mattress and sat down, contemplating my current situation. The dust in my previous cell, the transfer, and now this temporary residence hinted at a series of changes in progress. Yet, the details remained elusive.

Hours passed, and there was no sign of anyone returning. I wondered if this was a momentary respite or a prolonged stay. Unlike the all time deadly silence at my previous cell, here I could hear noises. The room's silence was occasionally broken by distant sounds from the outside world – perhaps a faint murmur of voices, the rustling of leaves, or the distant hum of traffic.

In the quiet solitude of the guest house, I couldn't shake the feeling that my stay was not merely about the renovation of a dusty cell. There were deeper currents at play, and the uncertainty of my circumstances loomed over me like a shadow. The events that led to my transfer, the guarded secrecy, and the historical backdrop of the Ghion Hotel all merged into a complex narrative, leaving me with more questions than answers.

Chapter XIX: At the Imperial Ghion Hotel

In 1992, I served as the Secretary of the Addis Ababa City Council during the period when it was referred to as Region 14. It was at that time that I initially experienced staying in the guest houses of the Ghion Hotel. The emerging Woyane regime successfully orchestrated an election that paved the way for establishing administrative regions across Ethiopia. Each region was assigned a president and a deputy, who oversaw and ruled the respective areas.

The leaders of the eight regional governments found themselves unfamiliar with officials from both the Federal government and Region 14, prompting the ruling party EPRDF (Ethiopian People's Revolutionary Front) to orchestrate an event in Addis Ababa aimed at fostering introductions. Each region was instructed to send a delegation comprised of its three highest-ranking officials – namely, the President, the Deputy President, and the Secretary of the Council of the Regional Parliament.

In a welcoming gesture, the national flag was prominently displayed on the city's main thoroughfares, symbolising the warm hospitality extended to the visiting delegations. Notably, these regional officials were to be accommodated at the prestigious Ghion Hotel, a venue traditionally reserved for African heads of state.

During that period, Teferra Walwa, the Chairman of Region 14, and his deputy, Ali Abdo, maintained private residences in Addis

Ababa. Despite this, they chose to participate in the event organised by the ruling party and opted to stay at the Ghion Hotel. Similarly, even though I had a residence in the city, I was instructed to join the Chairman and his deputy at the Ghion Hotel as invitations for officials from other regions, including the Secretary of the Regional Parliament. This marked my introduction to the guest houses at the Ghion Hotel.

The Ghion Hotel guesthouse maintained an exemplary standard of service. Consisting of several rooms akin to those in a small villa, each space was meticulously designed to evoke the ambience of an ideal private residence. A charming touch was added with the presence of welcoming beds of plants and flowers at the front door, creating a warm and inviting atmosphere.

The French windows located at the rear of the house opened up to the refreshing sight of a manicured lawn and other well-maintained gardens. Inside, guests were treated to a spacious, furnished double bedroom, a comfortable reception area, and a bathroom equipped with hot water sourced directly from the city's magnificent hot springs. This thoughtful combination of aesthetics and comfort made the guest house a truly leisure-oriented haven for those fortunate enough to stay there.

It is profoundly disheartening to witness the transformation of such a prestigious presidential resort into a prison for those allegedly kidnapped by the Woyane regime. The very location that once hosted esteemed African leaders like Nkrumah, Nyerere, and Nasser, deserving to be preserved as a historical site, now bears witness to degradation through criminality. This touching shift highlights the stark contrast between the noble history of the place and its current misuse, evoking a sense of sadness at the loss of its dignified past.

The Woyane had taken the troubling step of sealing off the door to the ensuite bathroom with a steel door, a stark indication of the grim conditions within the cell. Evidence of previous occupants was visible, discernible through Ethiopian names inscribed on the walls. A striking discovery was the presence of handwriting in East Asian languages, possibly Chinese or Japanese has raised intriguing questions—was this place used to imprison Chinese nationals, or was it once a dwelling for them?

I pondered over these surprising thoughts; the night unfolded with a cascade of unsettling reflections that persisted until dawn. The blend of Ethiopian and East Asian influences within the confines of the cell added an additional layer of complexity to an already distressing situation.

The purpose behind my confinement in this strange place remained elusive to me. The Woyane authorities seemed disorganized and unprepared for the shift. The following morning, as the guard opened the door and informed me of their instructions.

"We are instructed to obtain food from a nearby restaurant during our stay here for a few days," he explained. "What would you like for breakfast?"

"I don't want anything made in a restaurant," I insisted.

Concerned, the guard inquired, "What will become of you then?"

"Did you not bring any kollo (roasted barley mixed with roasted peanuts) from where we were?" I asked, suggesting a more simple and traditional meal option.

The security guards did bring kollo and water as I had suggested, yet they continuously reminded me that I couldn't sustain myself on kollo alone. Despite their concerns, I persisted with this simple and traditional diet.

Days passed, first three, then six, and eventually, we remained in the same location for a total of 15 days. My diet had not changed, consisting solely of kollo and water, and the toll on my body became evident as I appeared visibly wasted.

On the evening of the 15th day, the guards arrived to prepare me for my return trip. Reflecting on my ordeal, I couldn't help but draw parallels between my misfortune and that of the guest house, both having endured their own trials. Wrapped up in my blanket, my head shrouded in sad thoughts, I allowed the security guard to guide me to the car like a blind man. Unlike previous instances, this time, my head brushing against the seated person next to me did not result in the brutal impact of a gun. As we embarked on a journey, the distance we covered was vast, leaving me to contemplate the uncertain path that lay ahead.

Returning to my former cell after leaving the Ghion Hotel guest house, the security guards followed their customary procedure of chaining and locking before departing. As I surveyed my surroundings, I noticed the changes within the room - it had been transformed with new plaster, painted a shade of blue, and featured matching floor laminate. The familiar "Addis Foam" mattress rested in its usual corner. However, all electric outlets and switches had been removed and plastered over.

Despite these alterations, the room's illumination remained as bright as the sun and persisted throughout both day and night. A noticeable improvement was a hole high up on one of the walls close to the edge of the ceiling that allowed for some ventilation, providing a welcome change. Yet, the old prison routine continued unabated the following day, perpetuating the monotony and uncertainty of my confinement.

Chapter XX: A Threat to Force-feeding!

The series of interrogations, my encounter with the Ambassador, and the peculiar visit to the Ghion Hotel guest house had all concluded.

The rotation of my two security guards on 15-day shifts continued, accompanied by a succession of new faces who stayed overnight. The tall and short guards, whom I perceived as high-ranking security officials due to their apparent command over others, remained with me until the end. The newly appointed team members joined for only a few months before undergoing further rotations, maintaining the cycle of changing personnel during my period of confinement.

My eczema improved significantly after receiving treatment, but it had never completely cleared and was now beginning to flare up again. On a positive note, my cough and breathlessness had completely ceased. The handcuffs were removed a few weeks later, coinciding with my first interrogator seeking permission for a video recording.

"What's the point of the handcuffs and the leg chain?"

I asked him at that moment. He replied somewhat surprisingly, "It's for your own sake to prevent you from harming yourself."

He promised to instruct the guards to take them off, but I couldn't agree to his request for video recording me. He wanted someone to interview me about my well-being for dispatch on the Internet.

Of course, I asked myself why they would want to do that. Why was it essential for them to publicly demonstrate my well-being? I assumed there was a rumour going around that pointed to the contrary.

"I don't have a problem with the video recording, but I want journalists from the VOA and Deutsche Welle to be present for the interview. I don't want to be interviewed simply for the benefit of your propaganda," I told him. He didn't apply much pressure. He argued a little and then left, surprising me with a parting comment.

"It's a bit like 'Free Mandela' outside," he said. I wondered what exactly he meant.

His words, "Free Mandela," echoed in my ears as I returned to my cell escorted. My detention and public perception had never been raised until that moment, not even by Ambassador Gregg.

The security guards removed the handcuffs, but they adamantly refused to take off the chain on my legs. Despite reminding them of the interrogator's promise that the chain would also be removed, they insisted that it was not the instruction they had received. They assured me they would inquire on my behalf, then locked me up and left.

In the confines of my cell, I restricted myself to one meal a day. To avoid constantly calling out to the guards whenever nature called, I had requested plastic bottles for relieving myself, which they provided with the tops sliced off. These bottles became my makeshift solution for both day and night. I had developed an aversion to using the regular toilet due to the unsettling behaviour of one of the guards, particularly the tall one whom I branded as cruel. Whenever I ventured to the bathroom, he would leave the door ajar and position himself against it.

At a certain point, I couldn't help but ask him outright how he could tolerate the smell.

"I'm under orders," he replied.

"Why don't the others behave the way you do?" I wanted to inquire but caught myself, realizing I might inadvertently implicate the short one if he wasn't following the same orders. Fortunately, I seldom had any bowel movements in a week, which eventually became a problem, leading to the development of haemorrhoids.

When I informed the short man that I was unwell, he summoned the nurse, who kindly examined me, prescribed treatment, and helped alleviate my discomfort. She scolded me severely upon learning I was not eating, emphasising the importance of maintaining a proper diet for my well-being.

"You've developed haemorrhoids because you are not eating well and straining during toilet visits," she remarked. "You'll attract more ailments. Don't worry; you'll see your children," she said. She spoke freely because the guards had left during her physical examination.

"I'll be back to take blood and urine samples," she continued. "Your weight loss does not look healthy," she added.

Even though I imagined the guards might be eavesdropping, I suppressed the question I so badly wanted to ask, mindful of the sensitive nature of the situation.

The following day, the nurse returned with containers for blood and urine samples, along with a gadget to check my blood pressure. After collecting the samples, she left briefly and returned with empty containers, an air of urgency surrounding her. She explained that she needed me to draw more blood and fill another container because the initial lab results indicated an unbelievably low blood sugar level that required confirmation.

"He's at the stage of passing out in a coma; I need to have him rechecked," she said urgently and left with new samples. Unfortunately, the results were no better.

Suddenly, the short security guard, whom I hadn't seen for a while, along with others, barged into my cell, causing me alarm. The short and rude interrogator, Dawit, launched a barrage of accusations.

"We know what you are up to. You stopped eating to kill yourself. Your objective is to enter a state of coma. You will eat from this day on," he declared.

I explained that I had no such intention of killing myself, but he wouldn't listen. Frustrated, I remarked, "It's up to me; I'll eat if I want, I won't if I don't."

This provoked a strong reaction. "You don't have any rights; we will use restraint and forceful measures to feed you if necessary," he threatened.

Not wanting to escalate the situation, I made an effort to calm him down. "I didn't know that my blood sugar was so low. In any event, it would be useful if you could find the glucometer I had in my bag at the time of my detention. High blood sugar levels are equally dangerous. I reduced my food intake to be careful," I explained.

I had initially purchased the glucometer for a small Government Clinic in Eritrea that took care of the fighters of Ginbot 7 popular force. Surprisingly, he agreed. In a rush, a bun and a cup of tea were brought to me. From that point on, I started eating twice a day, closely monitored by my abductors.

Chapter XXI: The Glucometer Reveals a Secret

Before I was transferred to the main federal prison at Kalait, I had spent a year and a month in various illegal places serving as makeshift detention centres to keep abductees out of sight. Along my journey, I added up the number of people I encountered, which amounted to 23, all Tigrigna speakers. I was amazed that not a single person spoke a different language.

One day, as Dawit arrived to subject me to one of his surprise interrogations, I confronted him, asking, "Do you not have any other trusted, non-Tigrayan individuals working for the security?" His response left him speechless.

On another occasion, I cynically remarked, "You know, sometimes abductees crave interrogators and torturers from diverse ethnic backgrounds. Don't you have individuals from Oromo, Amhara, Gurage, and other ethnic groups?" His frightening response that day solidified my determination. If I survived, I vowed to pen a detailed memoir of my harrowing ordeal.

It was astonishing that out of more than 80 diverse ethnic groups in Ethiopia, the entire security apparatus ended up being dominated by Tigrayans, constituting less than 7 per cent of the entire population. From the individuals who kidnapped me in Yemen at Sana'a airport to those who held me captive for 13 months in a series of residences transformed into illegal prisons, and even the shift-working security guards, nurse, interrogators, and the unseen cook who communicated in Tigrigna, all hailed from the same tribe.

Nonetheless, I refused to view myself solely as a prisoner of all Tigrigna speakers. Such a sweeping generalisation would starkly contrast with the pleasant and cherished memories of my youthful days spent in Tigray, where I interacted with ordinary folks who reflected warmth and kindness. The goodness shown to me during my imprisonment by certain individuals with close ties to the TPLF convinced me that I cannot view all Woyane members in the same harsh light, let alone the people of Tigray.I recognized the importance of distinguishing between the actions of specific individual Tigrayans and the broader Tigrayan community.

Except for Dawit, I didn't know any of their names. I even have a suspicion that the name Dawit might be fictional. The guards and other staff never made the mistake of addressing each other by name. Instead, they referred to one another as "Ah-l-oo." Even when the cook called out to the guards, it was always "Ah-l-oo." "Lunch is ready," she would holler, and they would respond, "Is lunch ready? Ah-l-oo?" The phrase "Ah-l-oo" sounded like a kind of greeting, perhaps a colloquial or coded term. It was unclear whether it was a derivative of "hello" or had an entirely different meaning. There was no way of knowing for certain.

One afternoon, a security guard came to my cell and gave me a parcel in a large brown envelope. Noticing my confusion,

It's your glucometer," he said.

The guard hadn't noticed the name lightly written in pencil on the envelope. It felt wonderful to finally be in contact with the paper, and I turned the package over and over between my hands. The writing addressed the envelope "To Leteberhan." It wasn't hard to figure out that Leteberhan was the nurse. The name is definitely a female name.

Leteberhan paid me frequent visits, mainly equipped with alternative treatments for my haemorrhoids. She often kicked out the guards whenever she examined me, as they consistently made every effort to stay in the room.

I prepared myself for her visit one afternoon.

"I think I know you," I said.

"Where?" she asked.

"Weren't you a fighter?" I asked, referring to the guerrilla war.

"Yes," she replied.

"That's where I remember you from; you were very young back then," I said.

"Are you saying that I'm old now," she asked.

"Just saying that you've changed since," I replied.

"Inevitably," she remarked.

What I said next drew her attention.

"I also believe I know your name."

"I don't think so, but you can try telling me," she said.

"Not entirely sure, something related to Mariam, is it Weletemariam, Ehetemariam, or something like Letemariam, letebrehan?" I asked.

She was alarmed. She gathered her things immediately, "I'm done here," she said and left.

I felt sorry that my attempt at humour had alarmed the kind nurse. She did look shocked, possibly because she didn't want the guards to overhear our conversations. They must have all received a warning not to reveal their names. If any of them found out I knew her name, she would likely get into serious trouble.

Leteberhan had spent her money on my underwear. She made every effort to examine and treat me for various ailments, including my cough, asthma, eczema, haemorrhoids, diarrhoea, toothache, and more. I'll never forget her attentive, empathic behaviour towards me. Leteberhan will be remembered for much more than all that.

"Don't worry, you'll see your children," she had said many times, soothing my deepest anxieties.

For some unknown reason, Woyane female members of the security services are notoriously known for mistreating their prisoners. When acts of kindness contradict such cruelty, it's the kind actions that leave a lasting impact. Leteberhan's compassion alone could overshadow the wrongdoing of thousands of prison keepers. Individuals like her contribute to the hope of many in need. Without her kindness, we would be left in despair.

Chapter XXII: Groundhog Day

Many months had elapsed since I was confined to solitary isolation. It was a monotonous existence with no discernible activity or conversation. The door opened once a day, granting me a brief reprieve as I disposed of the accumulated waste in plastic bottles. Meals were delivered, utensils collected, and within minutes, the door would close, sealing me back in solitude. The relentless routine and uncanny resemblance to Bill Murray's predicament in the famous film Groundhog Day played in my mind. Unlike Murray, who was aware of the fictional nature of his predicament, I found myself on the verge of believing that I was trapped in an endless loop, reliving the same day over and over.

Two huge Florescent electric bulbs illuminated my surroundings persistently, both day and night. Occasional relief presented itself during power outages as if my silent plea for respite from the constant light had been answered. In those moments, I would sit contentedly in the darkness until the light inevitably returned.

The cell, devoid of any windows, featured only a high opening in the upper corner of the ceiling for ventilation. Unfortunately, it was beyond reach, denying me the chance to catch even a glimpse of the outside world. Slanted sun rays would filter through this opening, serving as the sole indicator distinguishing between day and night within my confined space.

That same opening, while providing ventilation, also ushered in a breeze. Accompanied by either a chilling current or pollutants that posed a threat to my asthma, the breeze followed the sun's rays into my cell.

With the breeze came insects, eager to engage in their biting antics. I would futilely thrash at them, ending their lives, only to be troubled by a sense of conflict with the Creator.

"Why create them and bring them to me? So I can extinguish their lives and then suffer from guilt?" I vented my frustration aloud.

In the midst of my discomfort, I couldn't help but draw a poignant comparison between the vulnerability of these insects and my own vulnerability. As I crushed them, an overwhelming sense of revulsion and self-reflection engulfed me. I felt like I had transformed into a ruthless mass murderer in the miniature world of insects. I couldn't escape questioning the terror my actions might have unleashed in their tiny existence. "How many lives have I snuffed out? Whose futures have I ruthlessly dismantled? "

I questioned earnestly, searching my soul for answers. Unlike Tamrat Layne, the former Prime Minister who found redemption and claimed to have encountered God in prison, I didn't share his fortune of receiving divine guidance.

I regarded the sun rays streaming in through the hole as cherished companions, treating them with a sense of warmth. As I lay on my back, I observed these rays gracefully traverse the walls and ceiling, faithfully mirroring the sun's journey. Occasionally, the presumptuous wind would amass clouds, stifling the sun. During such instances, I would silently rally against the wind, standing in solidarity with the beleaguered sun.

I remained cut off from the world, barred from receiving visitors or any messages. The British Ambassador, Mr. Gregg, never returned.

In solitude and in silenceI voiced my grievances to every government and security official within reach, decrying the injustice of my circumstances. Aware that life imprisonment and death sentences had been handed down in my absence, I hesitated to file an appeal, convinced it would be a futile endeavour. My lack of faith in the country's judicial system fueled my reluctance; the absence of justice had been a driving force behind my political resistance.

I harboured a grim hope for swift execution of the death sentence, a consequence of my service to the Woyane during their initial rise to power. I envisioned that my modest contributions to their consolidation of authority would be acknowledged, perhaps influencing the fulfilment of my final wish. However, that day of resolution seemed elusive as I languished away in my wretched cell.

With nothing to occupy my time but the company of my thoughts, I delved into reflections on what had aged me before my time. At the tender age of 25, I recognized a startling truth: more of the people I had known were deceased than alive.

The Italian writer Italo Calvino's words, "You reach a moment in life when, among the people you have known, the dead outnumber the living," resonated with me in my solitude within the prison walls. I longed to convey to him that such an experience need not accompany ageing, especially in Ethiopia.

During Ethiopia's tumultuous revolution of the 1970s, in my youth, there was a dark period when I knew more deceased individuals than those still alive. Living in a nation ravaged by war and famine, where hundreds of thousands, sometimes millions, fell victim, the stark reality emerged even before reaching adolescence. Calvino's words, I realized, held true, primarily for Europe and America, regions that had recently shielded themselves from the upheavals of bloody wars.

In my case, the years that witnessed the loss of numerous young brothers and sisters during the revolution had passed. In their place, a semblance of relative peace had emerged, allowing for healing and recovery. At my current age, I find comfort in knowing more living individuals than those who have departed. The chance I would soon join the departed looks real.

I overcame the pain of the Military dictatorship's red terror. Opting to defy the harsh regime that followed, I found joy in sharing life's journey with new, trusted friends. Ethiopians globally rallied against the regime, supporting our fight from a distance. Some answered my call for a freedom struggle, relocating to Eritrea, prepared to sacrifice for justice. I envision these comrades, at times huddled playing board games, braving the cold. In other moments, I see them, proud and singing, "For you, Ethiopia!"—words I crafted.

For the glory of the land, restoring Unity

Breaking the yoke, embracing Liberty

Ready to give my life.

I heard them singing. My friends might feel disheartened temporarily by my capture, but undoubtedly, they will bounce back. They'll chant "For you, Ethiopia" to dismantle the corrupt and cruel regime of Woyane. I trust they'll endure any sacrifice, and my imprisonment or death will only fortify their resolve.

I pondered extensively on the children I hadso late in life. I've long acknowledged that my political involvement would be all-consuming, leaving me little room for family life.

From my youth, I've dedicated myself to the betterment of the lives of the less fortunate who educated me without receiving an education themselves. Despite setbacks and sacrifices in the struggle, I couldn't abandon it. What pained me more was my kids being at such a sensitive age—they're not infants unaware of much, nor are they teenagers capable of coping with my imprisonment. The twins were only seven years old.

My thoughts drifted to the last summer day before my abduction at home. London had an unusually clear sky, and the warm day saw oak trees proudly adorned with leaves over the estate's common grounds.

The twins and I descended to the common playing area in short-sleeve t-shirts. My son ventured off to amuse himself. Resting on a wooden bench in the courtyard, his twin sister pulled out a chessboard, and we began to play. A Jamaican with a head full of dreadlocks popped out of an adjacent office building and called out, "Who's winning?"

My daughter Menabe's voice chimed, "I'm winning!" Her innocent face beamed as she glanced up at her newfound acquaintance. Dressed in a multi-coloured dress with geometric shapes, she looked adorable.

That summer scene revisits me whenever I think of my children. Lost in my thoughts, the days passed swiftly. Around that time, the guards permanently removed the chain on my legs.

Chapter XXIII: Abductors craving to convince the abducted

Shortly after my abduction, I underwent an extensive interrogation that spanned over a week, all under the surveillance of a concealed camera. The interrogations were far from conventional, marked by numerous dialogues. When they asserted, "We have developed the country," I countered with, "What has developed?" This sparked heated arguments.

I found it perplexing why they were so eager to convince me of their accomplishments. The Woyane firmly believed in the progress they claimed to have brought to Ethiopia. This issue of development didn't die even after the interrogations were over. My abductors seized every opportunity to articulate the economic progress their government had brought, and on the other hand, I kept on refuting their claim.

"You have achieved nothing; taking into consideration your tenure in power and the conducive political climate you had, the country has actually regressed through time," I would assert.

Then, one day, the door to my cell swung open, and Dawit walked in.

"You insist there's no economic progress. How about stepping out with us? We'll show you the kind of 'development' we've been implementing," he proposed.

Surprisingly, their reaction caught me off guard, and I embraced the suggestion wholeheartedly. Who wouldn't, after enduring such a prolonged period in that dismal cell? Only someone who has experienced solitary confinement can truly grasp the essence of the emotions I felt in that moment.

Having received my consent, "We will arrange something soon", said Dawit and left. When the guards locked the door, I saw the idea of going out and visiting places as a big joke.

The next day, the joke turned into reality. The guards came in and said are you ready to go with us to see places?

Clad in the same jogging suit I wore day and night, there was nothing else to change into, so I was ready in a minute, sporting the worn Birr 30 plimsolls.

However, my anticipation waned when they blindfolded me with my blanket, contrary to their promise that I would witness their developments. Negative thoughts began to infiltrate my mind. Oddly, the driver had turned on the radio, and the air was filled with occasional drifting music and mostly nonsensical commentary. It felt like we had been travelling for an extended period, and an eerie silence enveloped us. Then, a familiar voice emerged from the quietude.

"That's enough, time for him to rise," the voice instructed.

I obediently rose from the seat as the blanket was removed. The Nissan Patrol we were in had black glazed windows, obscuring visibility for anyone outside. Dawit, the driver, was behind the wheel, and my head had been resting on the short security guard's lap. The tall, stern-looking security guard occupied the front passenger seat. All three wore dark sunglasses, prompting me to humorously label them as "hill-billy wanna-be James Bond."

As I gazed outside, I realized I couldn't recognize our location. The people and cars bustling about signalled we were in Ethiopia. When I asked, "Where are we?" they nonchalantly replied, "Around Sar Bet."

Struggling to orient myself, I questioned if my extended confinement had led to disorientation. Though I had knowledge of the area Sar Bet none of the streets seemed familiar as we drove. After navigating through suburbs, we entered a semi-rural setting, eventually turning onto a dirt road that wound its way up to a summit.

The men disembarked from the car, surveying the landscape. Following their instructions, I stepped out and beheld a panoramic view that captured the city's expanse. They pointed toward a cluster of high-rise buildings, identifying them as condominiums in a location called Hannah Mariam. They went on to claim they had constructed similar condominiums and roads throughout the city.

To be honest, I was genuinely impressed. Although I had heard people discussing the city's transformation, I had no idea that the hometown where I grew up would undergo such a remarkable change.

Standing on top of a hill, feeling the sun's rays directly on my skin, was a welcomed sensation. The breeze collaborated with the sun, gently caressing my face. A flood of memories rushed in, reminiscent of a similar experience one summer morning in London.

In the backdrop of that morning, the ambience of my emotions was set to Joan Armatrading's "Love and Affection." The café adjacent to the small park where I found solace was playing her lyrics, "Now I can feel the sun in my eyes, the rain on my eyes... why can't I feel love? This memory resonated deeply within me, suddenly taking on a richer meaning, shaking my being to the core.

It was a thoughtful gesture on the part of my captors to bring me out into the sunshine, but a nagging suspicion lingered that they were playing some sort of game. Despite the pleasant moment, I still couldn't fathom the possibility of ever being truly free from them. As quickly as the sunlight lifted my spirits, a dark space of gloom enveloped me once again.

We lingered on the hill, Dawit occupied with plucking leaves from the eucalyptus tree stumps. It occurred to me that he intended to use them as a remedy for his cold. Eventually, we returned to the car, but a noticeable shift unfolded as we embarked on an unfamiliar route back. Wrapped in a blanket, I found myself lying on my back, and the passage of time felt elongated, as if we had covered a considerable distance.

The transition from the expansive hilltop to my confined cell was abrupt. The unsettling sound of the key turning in the lock reverberated in my mind like a cannon blast. It struck me with a sudden awareness that the security guards wielded the freedom to traverse wherever they pleased while I languished in the confines of this forsaken place.

A surge of resentment welled up within me, fueled by a profound sense of envy for the freedom they enjoyed. The stark contrast between their liberty and my captivity ignited a flame of hatred that burned quietly within the confines of my imprisoned existence.

Chapter XXIV: The bizarre outing and its effects

I was taken out on several occasions to witness firsthand the scale of construction unfolding in the city. My abductors, however, were keen on keeping me hidden, orchestrating these visits from a distance and in secluded areas. The sights that met my eyes were predominantly condominiums and road construction projects.

Despite the external exposure, each return from these visits plunged me into a deep sense of depression. The stark contrast between the emotions evoked during the outings and the subsequent return to my cell became the catalyst for these bouts of despair.

During these periods of depression, my thoughts delved into the origins of the first prison and the audacity of the individual or community responsible for confining others behind locked doors, assuming a power akin to that of God. I pondered on who might have been the first person to endure the confines of a prison cell. The very concept of imprisonment now seemed overwhelmingly malevolent, intensifying the emotional weight of my reflections.

During one of the site visits, the focus shifted from high-rise condominiums to road works. We traversed miles, the familiar routine unfolding. As the security guards uncovered my face, I realized we were on the Chinese-built motorway from Addis to

Nazareth. The Nissan Patrol glided so effortlessly that it felt like we were sliding on butter rather than driving on the road.

It marked my first encounter with that particular motorway. My captors took the opportunity to explain its significance and our location. A new driver guided us that day. Seated between Dawit and another security personnel on the rear passenger side, I shared the space with a third guard in the front passenger seat. Throughout the journey to Nazareth town and back, they provided a live commentary about the motorway.

Rain poured heavily around Nazareth, but as we approached Addis Ababa, the weather cleared, and we drove into the welcoming embrace of sunshine. The contrasting scenes and the smooth ride on the motorway provided a surreal backdrop to the unfolding events, punctuating the peculiar nature of my experiences during these excursions.

"Let's stop and take a souvenir photograph over here," Dawit suggested.

"Come on, you too, get off the car," he instructed, and I stepped out, expressing my exasperation at Dawit's straightforward approach with a roll of my eyes.

They took turns wrapping their arms around my shoulder, posing for photographs with me using their cell phones. Subsequently, they took pictures of each other without including me. Finally, they requested a solo photo of me, and I complied. Throughout this unusual episode, I couldn't shake off the sense of unease, wondering about their true motives and holding my breath. Were there details they were concealing? Why did they desire a souvenir featuring me when, to my knowledge, I had not been released yet? The mystery of their actions hung in the air, leaving me with lingering questions and a heightened sense of apprehension.

I harboured no suspicion that one of those photographs would find its way onto the Internet. Little did I know that they were executing one of their conniving mini-projects.

The security guards orchestrated a remarkable charade aimed at pacifying the Ethiopian diaspora. Their message was clear: "You are protesting for his release; he is visiting the motorway in peace." The carefully crafted narrative sought to present a benign image of my activities, a stark contrast to the reality of my captivity. The manipulation of perception through these staged photographs added another layer of complexity to the enigmatic world I found myself entangled in.

I came across this truth months after the visits stopped, and I was transferred to Kaliti Federal Prison.

During one of his permitted visits, the British Ambassador, Creg, casually remarked, "We saw you on the Internet."

"Really, me?" I responded in surprise.

"Yes, standing at a major motorway," he answered.

In that moment, I grasped the reality—they had taken me out to carry out the video recording project that I had openly refused. The realization dawned on me that the Woyane had orchestrated my temporary release from the cell to capture footage in the open for propaganda purposes.

The entire charade had nothing to do with convincing me of the economic progress they purported to have brought about. Instead, it was a carefully calculated move to manipulate public perception and advance their own agenda.

Despite my attempts to convey to my abductors that the Woyane were notorious for their dishonesty, my words fell on deaf ears. During interrogations, I had warned them, "People won't believe you if you speak the truth." However, they chose to ignore my advice and proceeded to post the deceitfully acquired pictures on the internet.

When Creg informed me about the pictures, I couldn't help but anticipate that the Ethiopian diaspora would likely dismiss the images as a fabricated Photoshop creation.

Chapter XXV: A Christmas Gift of Mischief

Every passing day brought forth a new dawn until we arrived at the Christmas season. From the birth of my children to the present moment, I hadn't missed a single Christmas or the subsequent birthdays. The approach of Christmas intensified my sorrow, and I speculated that my family, particularly the children, would experience a mix of hope and uncertainty as their birthdays approached. The anticipation stirred my anxiety, leaving me to ponder their emotions.

On a Sunday afternoon, I found myself in a contemplative state when the door opened, inviting me to speak with a visitor. Breaking from the routine, I traversed the corridor's full length, stepping into the reception area without the customary blanket covering my face for the first time.

The worn yellow sofa accommodated the astute interrogator, the first one I encountered. He rose to shake my hand, pulling me into a half-embrace as if we were old friends, a sentiment not reciprocated on my end. I recalled his claim from some time back, asserting our supposed friendship from ten years ago during the time he came to Zeway prison to talk to me.

Taking a seat on the armchair beside him, the interrogator launched into the routine questions, inquiring about my health, food, and any grievances against the security guards.

With the exception of one guard who was new but notably pleasant, they were all unfamiliar faces. Surprisingly, I wasn't the one forming bonds with my captors in a manner resembling Stockholm syndrome. Instead, it seemed the reverse was happening.

Over time, all the security guards, barring one, appeared to have developed a certain camaraderie with me. Those who once regarded me as the embodiment of evil now spoke in my defence when given the chance. There was a noticeable improvement in their attitude towards me, and individually, each guard found discreet ways to extend favourable treatment. The dynamics within the captor-captive relationship were evolving, revealing nuances that defied conventional expectations.

I initiated the conversation after exchanging greetings with the interrogator.

"What brings you here today?" I inquired.

"Oh, I've meant to come and see you for a while, just never found a moment to fit in," he responded.

Without much fuss, he got talking about the purpose of his visit.

"The Independent newspaper is quite a large one in the UK, is it not?" he asked.

"That's right," I replied.

"So why does it publish lies? You would be amazed to see what they have written about you," he revealed, lamenting, "Pity I didn't think to bring the paper with me," he added.

The mention of the article sparked my curiosity, and I couldn't help but wish I had the chance to scrutinize the contents for myself.

"What did they say?" I inquired.

"What did they not say is more like it," he responded. "That you are in torture with a plastic bottle carrying a litre of water hanging from your private parts, that kind of thing," he continued.

"These types of lies terrorize people; I feel sorry for your wife and children; they will have read that paper. How do you think they feel?" he asked me.

"If that was published, they would have certainly read about it," I replied.

"It's not fair. We have to calm them down," he stated.

"How?" I asked.

"It might be a good idea for you to speak to them on the phone," he suggested.

"Where am I going to get a phone from?" I asked, feeling a sense of frustration and helplessness.

"You can use my mobile phone," he offered.

"That would be great if you let me," I responded, feeling a surge of relief.

As he pulled his mobile phone out of his pocket, I sensed a stroke of luck shining down on me.

"Tell me the number," he urged.

I intended to call Yemi on her mobile phone, but to my dismay, I couldn't recall the number.

"Sorry, I can't remember the number," I admitted.

He looked surprised. "You don't remember any family phone number?" he asked.

I, too, was taken aback by my lapse in memory. Frustration and regret welled up, realizing that despite my intact memory in other aspects, I couldn't recall a single telephone number. Then, a fleeting idea crossed my mind—I remembered the landline. It was worth a try, even if nobody bothered to answer it.

"We never answer the landline. We normally look at it when it rings, but I do remember that number," I explained.

He dialled the number, and after a moment, he handed me his mobile phone. The call rang as expected. With each passing ring, my hope waned. It seemed like nobody was at home or everyone had chosen to ignore the landline, as was the usual practice. Just as I was ready to give up, a young lady unfamiliar to me answered.

"Hello," she greeted.

I immediately knew I didn't recognize her.

"Who is this? Is there no one at home?" I asked.

She identified herself as my older daughter Helu's friend and then went to fetch Helawit. I exchanged brief greetings with Helu and asked her to get her mom on the phone.

I could hear her cry out to her Mum, "Come quick, it's Papa." Only God knows how Yemi (Yemiserach) felt when she listened to what the child had to say.

I wasn't sure how long the interrogator would allow me to stay on the phone, so I spoke to Yemi with a sense of urgency. She was confused and was also speaking fast with caution.

"We are all fine. The children are well. They are playing outside," she replied.

"Do you want to speak to them," she asked. I turned to the interrogator and asked if I could speak to them. He appeared relaxed as he gave me the go-ahead.

The children were called inside. My son spoke to me with enthusiasm. He told me he was fine.

"Where are you, Pappa? When are you coming? Will you come for Christmas?" his innocent voice asked. I couldn't reply. My ears felt as though they were splitting.

Yemi could tell this wasn't easy for me. "That's enough, Yilak; give your sister a chance," she said and passed the phone to Menabe.

"Peace be with you, my Menabe," I said. There was no reply. "Are you well?" I asked. Still no reply. "Have you forgotten how to speak," I continued. There was silence. Yemi took the phone and said, "Never mind, it's ok to leave her alone now," she said.

"What?" I asked.

"She is crying," said Yemi. I felt a bitter sadness piercing my heart.

Bizuayehu, my elder sister, happened to be there as well, and I got a chance to speak to her. Finally, I had to address the reason that brought the telephone to me.

"Yemi, the Independent has issued an article about how I'm being tortured. Have you read it?" I asked. "It's not true; there's been no torture at all; no need to believe that article," I reassured.

"I haven't seen such an article," replied Yemi, "I'll look for it," she promised.

"Don't give the children hopes that we cannot fulfil. It will only hurt them; tell them the truth," I pleaded.

"I hear you," she replied.

Feeling a sudden urgency that further opportunities might be denied if news got out about my call, I turned to the interrogator, knowing Yemi was within earshot.

"Should I ask them not to tell anyone I called?" I inquired.

"There's no problem; they can tell whoever they want," he replied.

Alarm bells started ringing in my head. Something felt off about this.

I abruptly said goodbye to Yemi, cutting out all formality. It marked my first and last telephone call to her while I was in solitary confinement.

Before the interrogator left, I managed to request permission to read and obtain writing supplies.

"We'll see," he said.

*(**Author's note**: After my release, I discovered that the Independent had never published an article about me. The Woyane had orchestrated the entire scenario in response to the pressure exerted by the diaspora. The primary objective was to compel me to make a phone call, reassuring my family of my well-being, and to disseminate that information widely. Additionally, they sought video recordings of me for the same purpose – to counteract a campaign tarnishing their image. I grasped this motive as soon as my interrogator permitted my family to claim they had spoken to me.*

Although the British Ambassador urged me to contact my family and the Woyane were willing, I declined. My rationale was that my children were too young; my sudden call would disrupt their innocent playfulness, and I wished to spare them from further distress. This justified my decision not to make the call, proving advantageous as it thwarted their propaganda efforts and spared my children from additional anguish.)

Chapter XXVI: Pen and Paper replaced with Laptop

I communicated my interest in doing some political writing to my captors, deliberately using it as bait to capture their interest. I anticipated that expressing an interest in politics would prompt them to relent, eager to know the details of my political views. My speculation proved correct, and one morning, I was provided with paper and a pen.

One of my profound regrets during my abduction was that it disrupted my plans to write a book about Ethiopia's political situation, with a specific focus on opposition group politics, particularly Ginbot 7. In fact, I had expressed my interest in writing to the G7 leadership and had reached an agreement with them to take a six- to eight-month sabbatical.I was captured in Sana just before my plan to take leave from organisational work and dedicate some time to writing was put into effect. This unfortunate timing prevented me from pursuing an endeavour that held great significance for me and my understanding of Ethiopia's political landscape.

Despite this setback, I believed the impact of my abduction on G7 would be minimal.

However, my abductors held a different perspective. During interrogations, they repeatedly questioned the future of G7 without my involvement, seemingly unconvinced that the movement could endure without my contributions. Their persistent inquiries focused on the potential consequences for G7 in my absence.

I consistently provided a detailed explanation asserting that my imprisonment would not significantly impact Ginbot 7. I told my abductors not to underestimate Ginbot 7's international network, as it operates independently and is not reliant on my singular involvement. I also informed them, that although I held the position of Secretary, it had been quite some time since I actively assumed that role.

"y efforts had shifted towards to establishing a guerrilla army in Eritrea, a project thathad progressed sufficiently to operate without my constant presence. The G7 popular force now has its own bylaws, commander, political commissar, and chiefs holding other departmental posts. All training manuals, both military and political, have been prepared. Directives and instructions needed to guide other departments are complete and have been published. If G7 faces problems in the future, it won't be because I am not working for it but rather because others are failing to do their jobs properly." I insisted; but the interogators were not willing to listen."More likely, my imprisonment will inspire members to work hard, and many new members may join the movement. The organization stands on a robust foundation, and my current absence does not alter its trajectory. It might have made a difference if you had kidnapped or killed me a few years ago, but not now." I persistently stated these facts.

Aware of the voice recording in these investigative sessions, I deliberately emphasized certain points for the benefit of the movement. I also disclosed to my captors that they had kidnapped me at a time when I was preparing to resume my writing pursuits.

Once I received pen and paper, I took some time to ponder whether to document my pre-abduction ideas and assess opposition politics. I found myself in deep contemplation, considering the timing and how such writing might contribute to TPLF's propaganda against the opposition. It became a serious dilemma.

A thorough, critical examination of the opposition was necessary, but doing so would essentially provide Woyane with a tool to attack its detractors. On the other hand, remaining silent about the shortcomings of the opposition was also a precarious option.

After careful consideration, I decided to write in a manner that portrayed the ruling party in a much worse light than the opposition in my writing. The intention was to ensure that Woyane would not be able to use my writing to its advantage, aiming to maintain a balance that highlighted the issues within the ruling party without inadvertently strengthening its narrative against the opposition.

My clever interrogator visited a week after I received the stationery. I had written a few pages, and he asked me to read them to him. Despite my struggles, I managed to read to him.

The context was set around the 2005 elections and how the opposition outsmarted the ruling party. "Those who suffered hard of hearing by the noise at the Battle of Segalle live to their end by repeatedly saying 'Segelle and Segelle,'" he remarked sarcastically, suggesting that the opposition remained stuck at the point of the 2005 elections.

"I'd like to provide some historical background," I replied, "The 2005 election chaos is linked to our problems today. It was a turning point in our political history." I was trying to explain what had happened and to depict what could happen.

"What are you aiming for from that starting point?" asked the interrogator.

"When I was overseas, I hoped to focus on opposition politics and the Ginbot 7 movement. That has to change now. I need to write more holistically—something that you cannot use for your propaganda but will be useful for Ginbot 7 and you. Above all, for the nation and the people," I explained.

"How are you going to read your scribbles?" he asked, pointing at my messy handwriting.

"It's been a long time since I wrote on paper, you see," I said modestly, "I normally use a laptop. Do you think you could find me an old laptop? Or even better, how about returning my laptop?" I asked.

"I told you your laptop is still in Yemen," he started, rising from his seat. "I'll find out if you can get permission," he concluded and left.

A few days later, a small laptop was at my disposal, serving me well in prison. Its sole purpose was aimed at accessing my inner thoughts, and I wasn't prone to ever forget that.

Chapter XXVII: Love of the Laptop

The first problematic encounter with the laptop was the absence of AC sockets and light switches in the cell. They had all been removed and plastered over with cement.

The rationale was made to look like it was for my own safety, ostensibly to prevent me from using the current to harm myself or end my life. Although I had never asked, they never bothered to explain. This logic certainly applied to the handcuffs and leg chains.

I managed to get the attention of my captors, and they used an external connection to run a wire through the crack under the door, solving the power supply issue. Initially, however, my captors charged the laptop for me so frequently that they eventually got fed up and decided the effort wasn't worth the trouble.

I tested the Internet connection as soon as I obtained the laptop. Unfortunately, there was no software, and I had no Wi-Fi.

Surprisingly, they kept the free games that came with the purchase of the computer. I was delighted to discover Titan Chess, a 3D interactive game that allowed one player to play against the computer.

The laptop and I engaged in an unwitnessed competition that tested the strength of my patience and nerves. The computer won many times before I started catching up and had my laugh. I talked, scolded, cursed, and expressed both love and hatred to the laptop as if I had gone mad and was mistaking it for a natural person.

Certainly, the primary purpose of the laptop with the username Gogo was writing. I began deliberately with politics, focusing on the TPLF offering harsh criticism. My intention was to describe the nature of the TPLF in a discrediting manner, making my piece devoid of any use to them.

I proceeded to write in detail about the overall political situation in Ethiopia and the place of Ginbot 7 in that context. In case the piece reached my comrades in Ginbot 7, I addressed specific issues to the leadership. I expressed the great pleasure I found in knowing them in person and the joy it gave me working with them. "You are indeed a bunch of great guys," I declared, emphasising the camaraderie and dedication within the organisation.

I extensively addressed my concerns about the changing world and our collective inability to adapt, both as a nation and as individuals. The entire world has been confronted with rapid and complex transformations since 2005. I emphasized the need to resist emotional attachment to old ways of thinking and doing. Instead, I advocated for calmly observing and accommodating the accelerated changes unfolding around us.

I highlighted that we are not alone in feeling the challenges of this changing landscape. Many policymakers in Western governments and institutions, armed with information and staffed by sharp and experienced experts, are grappling with similar challenges.

The old world is crumbling before our very eyes, and the models and paradigms that dominated generations are fast being replaced by new ones, which themselves are subject to rapid evolution. It is a dynamic process where adaptability becomes paramount for survival and progress.

I argued that courage in the new world is not measured by rigidly adhering to ideas and methodologies but by the ability to embrace change. I feel a sense of dismay and foreboding as I realize that people are not adequately prepared to face the rapid pace of change, filled with both opportunities and challenges. Political intuition and decisiveness must play a crucial role in fostering flexibility and effectively managing these changes. Simply persisting with what has been initiated is insufficient.

I wrote about how I felt at the time, expressing my full awareness of the commitments I made when I chose to be part of the struggle we were conducting. I acknowledged my readiness to endure the necessary sacrifices.

My primary concern centred around the young children I brought up late in life. Even the pain induced by thinking about my kids was somewhat assuaged by realising how many children in Ethiopia grow up without parents and lack the social and material support that kids in similar conditions receive in the UK.

I reiterated my wish and hope for the future: that Woyane would relieve me from the agony by executing the death sentence their kangaroo court had passed against me. Recalling the incident when the government had sent a mercenary assassin to kill me in Eritrea and the publicised phone recording where a government official instructed the assassin to blow my brain out.

I argued that carrying out the death sentence would be congruent with the government's intentions and interests. I contemplated the prospect of death by stating that death will eventually catch up with all of us; however, extending my lifeline under the current conditions is nothing but a disgrace. I emphasized that even when I was a free man, finding meaning in a meaningless existence seemed unlikely.

I emphasized that enough sacrifices have been made in the past, and it is time to draw the correct lessons from them. Clinging to closed-mindedness and remaining prisoners to our emotions are unhelpful for Ginbot 7. A bright future is intricately linked to our capacity to adapt to change and glean insights from both our own history and the histories of other

Chapter XXVIII: A Mother's Motley Womb

The world slipped away from my consciousness after the laptop was handed to me. I failed to register the subtle movements of my captors as they quietly opened and closed the door, replacing my breakfast with lunch, only to return later and discover it untouched.

Months passed with my interrogators in apparent absence. My interactions were confined to the guards who had been keeping a watchful eye on me from the beginning – the kind, short one and the persistently mean, tall one. Remarkably, they remained unchanged; the short guard maintained his benevolence, while the tall one remained surly. Even during my moments of privacy in the toilet, the tall one lingered by the opened door.

The guard roster underwent a revolving door of faces every month or two, ranging from relatively kind to somewhat cruel. None of them uttered a single word in Amharic when communicating with each other. Some guards clandestinely extended small favours, actions that could lead to severe consequences if ever exposed.

The compassionate, short guard expressed genuine concern about my eczema. One morning, he was taken aback when he discovered that I had my hands ensnared in the cord from my jogging trousers.

"Why?" he inquired.

"To prevent me from scratching my legs," I explained, emphasizing the severity that had led to bleeding.

Given that the prescribed treatment had proven ineffective, he took matters into his own hands. Waiting for a moment of solitude, he opened my door and guided me to the second bathroom that is used by the guards without blindfolding me. A burst of sunlight flooded in through the window, revealing only a stone wall beyond.

"Your legs itch because you don't get any sun. Take a seat on the edge of the bathtub, bare your legs, and let the sunshine soak in," he advised.

Standing beside me, he kept a vigilant ear for the sounds of other guards. At the slightest indication of someone approaching, he would swiftly return me to my cell and secure the door, ensuring our covert excursion remained undetected.

I remember that one day, the short, kind guard clandestinely handed me a book—the first I had laid eyes on since my abduction.

"Don't let the other guards see you reading this. If you ever get caught, tell them you found the book on the toilet cabinet and helped yourself," he cautioned.

The book was titled "*Rosa*," its front cover adorned with a full-length picture of a beautiful woman, a slit in her skirt revealing her legs and thighs. Presumably, that was Rosa. The contents delved into the lives of women in the city's sex trade, clearly marked by explicit content. This was before I had received the laptop, and I lost count of how many times I read it. The book held an inexplicable allure, and it seemed as though no other book had ever been read as many times as I had read that one. It must be a record-breaking phenomenon, a testament to the unique circumstances that had made it my solitary companion in captivity.

Another memory lingers, prompting me to wonder if I'll ever encounter the short, kind guard again. A quarrel erupted between the lady cook who prepared my meals and the guards. Their heated exchange in Tigrigna echoed through the space.

"I'm not here to cook for you. From now on, you shall all cook your own meals," the lady cook vehemently declared.

After that incident, the guards shifted their meal preparations into the house. The enticing aroma of sizzling onions, frying meat, and simmering soup now permeated straight into my cell.

One day, the kind, short guard brought me a plate of lunch.

"Don't you miss being seated at a table for your meals?" he asked. "Come on up. You'll eat somewhere else today," he said, leading me across the corridor, past the guards' toilets on the left, through a reception room, and into a spacious kitchen. All the windows were tightly shut, and the lights illuminated the room. The remnants of a once dignified space were evident, with a small table and a few chairs.

"Do sit here and eat. I'm going to make my own lunch," the guard said, settling into the chair beside me. He began peeling onions right there, perching a stewing pan on top of a small electric stove on the floor to fry up the onions. As I started eating, he took out a mobile phone from his pocket and leaned it against the wall, displaying a music video. It was during this casual meal preparation that he began sharing details about himself for the first time.

He revealed that his mother's family, on his grandmother's side, hailed from Gondar and had relocated to Tigray through marriage. I couldn't help but wonder if his kindness towards me was influenced by this tenuous racial connection to the Amhara. I listened in silence, absorbing this unexpected glimpse into his personal history.

However, there was another guard who exhibited compassion. This guard worked shifts during public holidays when the others took the day off.

This person had a dark complexion and a distinctly sharp nose. Whenever he was on duty, and the days were holidays he would bring me a large plate of homemade assortment.

Fearing the potential health risks, I consistently declined his offerings. It wasn't so much my own well-being that concerned me but the realization that if I fell ill from the food he provided, it could have severe consequences for him as well. I would explain to him that his superiors had explicitly warned me not to consume anything that wasn't prepared by the lady on the ground. This became my cautious refrain, emphasizing the orders given by those in authority to dissuade him from offering me his homemade meals.

"My wife made it; please try some," he would coax, expressing a kindness that went beyond the prescribed restrictions. Politely, I sampled a bit of some of the bread and flatbread, explaining my dietary limitations. The young guard's considerate actions were not without a reason. It was because we shared passionately loved football.

The young guard, passionate about football, often delivered my meals while seemingly engrossed in radio broadcasts through his earplugs.

One afternoon, my curiosity got the better of me, prompting me to inquire about what he was listening to."What are you listening to?" I inquired.

"Football, English Premier League," he replied.

"Ah, I used to be an Arsenal fan," I shared with him.

Little did I know that the guard, too, was an ardent Arsenal fan. From that point on, we forged a friendship. Whenever he was alone and an Arsenal game was broadcast, he'd stand by my doorway, generously letting me listen through one of his earplugs.

We both tuned in to the games on Bisrat FM radio, captivated by the brilliant commentators who made our hearts race with anticipation. We shared moments of joyous applause when Arsenal emerged victorious and exchanged disappointed expressions when they faced defeat before parting ways. When circumstances prevented him from sharing the game with me, he would find any excuse to open the cell door just to inform me of Arsenal's triumph.

"Did I hear you were knocking?" he would loudly ask if his boss was around. Playing along, I'd reply, "Yes, I can feel my bowels; I'd like to go to the toilet." He would then lead me to the toilet, sharing the results of Premier League matches along the way. Occasionally, he'd promise to update me on the game and then mysteriously disappear. After a few such disappearances, I began to realize that he only avoided me when Arsenal lost a game.

The characteristics of this particular guard served as a poignant reminder that human beings do not possess a fixed nature defined by a singular trait or identity. While he held loyalty to his Tigre ethnic identity, it was clear that that aspect did not solely define him. His allegiance extended to our shared passion for football, demonstrating that individuals can embody a multitude of interests and connections beyond ethnic affiliations.

In a hypothetical situation where I might face trouble with Manchester United fans, he would stand by my side, ready to confront them, even if our adversaries belonged to his ethnic group. This stance challenges the narrow perspective of those who promote ethnic politics, emphasizing that a person's identity goes beyond ethnicity. In reality, humans share numerous common interests that unite them across ethnic origins. Humanity, indeed, transcends all limiting ethnic qualities.

As I reflect on these interactions, I often find myself wondering what has become of the short, kind guard and the loyal Arsenal fan. I am hopeful that he remembers, as I do, our brief encounter as Arsenal fans in a strange circumstance, and perhaps he smiles at the shared moments when he went out of his way to please another Gooner.

Chapter XXIX: Bread Rolls and Evidence

"I insisted that I was diabetic, initially met with scepticism from my captors. However, when the British Ambassador inquired about my diabetic condition based on the report from my GP in London, they had no choice but to believe me.

The doctor, in truth, had never explicitly diagnosed me with diabetes. He had only cautioned me to be watchful, considering both my parents were diabetics. Nevertheless, this seemingly small detail became a convenient tool for manipulation in my precarious situation.

I provided my captors with an extensive list of foods I claimed I couldn't eat, emphasizing white bread among them. The traditional Ethiopian bread, Injera, made from the grain Teff, was known to pose no concerns for diabetics, and I made it my staple diet. However, preparing Injera for just one person proved to be a headache for the cook.

It must have been at the cook's behest that one morning, a guard approached me, asking, "Would you mind having Barley bread? Diabetic patients can have it." Seizing the opportunity to break the monotony of Injera for every meal, I replied without showing much enthusiasm, "No problem at all."

From that day, I received a daily delivery of beautifully baked Barley bread in a plastic bag. Surprisingly, I found the taste to be delightful. While I was aware that barley wasn't fundamentally different from wheat, the change didn't bother me. I started collecting the plastic bags, realizing that I could use them to fashion a rope.

Amidst all the turmoil, I began to sense that the Woyane were no longer contemplating my demise. With this shift in perception, I decided to prioritize my health. Establishing a routine for daily physical exercises within the confines of the small cell became my focus.

To gauge the size of the room, I used the length of my jogging trousers, determining it to be exactly 3x3 meters. Through mental calculations, I deduced that the diagonal of the room should measure 4.25 meters. Confirming this with the length of the jogging trousers, I found my estimation to be correct. This small mental exercise brought me immense satisfaction, affirming that my mind was functioning well.

Motivated, I initiated my exercise routine at a modest level, gradually intensifying it. I incorporated five different types of sit-ups and push-ups, eventually reaching a count in the hundreds.

Every action I took in that confined space was a strategy to overcome the challenges of solitary confinement. I utilized the room measurements to track the distance covered as I briskly paced back and forth. My daily goal was to cover a total distance of 2 kilometres, requiring me to traverse the room 500 times.

The plastic bags used for the daily bread deliveries became the key to creating a makeshift rope. Soon enough, I had a sufficiently long rope to start skipping. One morning, as the tall and stern guard delivered my bread, he caught sight of me skipping. It was evident he was displeased, and an air of suspicion hung in the atmosphere.

"Where did you get this rope?" inquired the tall, mean guard.

"I made it from the delivery bags," I replied.

"Ropes are not allowed," he declared, promptly snatching the rope from my hands. From that day onward, this guard took it upon himself to collect the delivery bags whenever he was on duty.

On a particular morning, the same guard handed me the bread, and as I reached for the roll, I discovered a piece of paper in the bag. It turned out to be a sales receipt.

The receipt from Lafto Bakery in Nefas Silk sub-city bore the name of a Tigrayan lady, though it wasn't clear whether she was the owner or an agent managing the bakery. The three bread rolls were priced at three Ethiopian Birr each, totalling nine. I took this as a hint that I might be held close to that locality. Rolling up the receipt, I discreetly tucked it into the waistline opening of my jogging trousers after removing the tightening cord.

Upon learning from one of the guards that the lady cook managed my food budget, I suspected she had requested the receipt from the tall, mean guard. Soon after, he returned to my cell, instructing me to hand over the plastic bags. When I questioned the need for it, mentioning there was still a roll inside, he insisted I remove the fresh bun he had just delivered.

"Put it in your kollo container and hand the plastic bag over," he directed, and I complied. Observing him with sidelong glances, I was certain he was searching for the receipt.

The tall, mean guard refrained from asking me directly if I had seen a receipt. Silently, he left, not wanting me to realize that he was looking for something in the bag. I surmised that the knowledge of my location would discomfort him. If his superiors discovered that he had unintentionally left the receipt in the bag, it could lead to disciplinary action. His actions contradicted the purpose of transporting me with my face covered to keep me unaware of my whereabouts.

Chapter XXX: Book writing

It was in mid-January 2015, that I was provided with a laptop. Within a remarkably short span of 11 days, I completed my extensive 188-page political piece of writing. Shortly after that, the guy who gave me the laptop visited me in my cell to inquire about the progress of my work. I told him that it was finished. Fearing that he might reclaim the laptop, I hesitantly asked if I could continue using it for other writing purposes. Surprisingly, he responded without hesitation, saying, "Write whatever you want." It became evident that his sole interest lay in retrieving my political article, as he promptly transferred it onto a flash disk and left.

For the following three months, I immersed myself in writing and editing tens of articles on various subjects. I ventured into creating novels and dramas, attempting to explore different genres. One of my experiments led me to improvise a tragic drama inspired by the rise and fall of brothers Mengistu and German Neway. Their lives were tragically cut short due to a failed attempt to dethrone Emperor Haile Selassie in the early '60s, presented in the style of English playwright William Shakespeare. I even had a title for it, "Sons of Neway," but unfortunately, the endeavour did not resonate as I had hoped.

Every time I revisited my work, I felt discouraged by the perceived lack of quality. Dissatisfied, I deleted my drafts and started anew. My exposure to the works of renowned authors worldwide had elevated my standards, making it challenging to find satisfaction in my own writing.

Eventually, I made the decision to pen a narrative about my involvement in the EPRP (Ethiopian People's Revolutionary Party) and the events of the 1974 revolution. This revolution marked the end of Emperor Haile Selassie's reign and the 3000 years of monarchy rule in Ethiopia. I conceptualized a title for this endeavour as well, "Curbing Narrative Extremism and Revealing Truth."

One concern that weighed heavily on me was the possibility of this book surviving my imprisonment. Although facing the prospect of a firing squad has greatly diminished, I was also prepared for the likelihood of spending the rest of my life in prison unless a significant turn of events occurred. Consequently, I devised a strategy to ensure the survival of my book by keeping its content agreeable to my captors.

In line with this approach, I resolved to narrate the story only up to the era of the new rule's beginning and then halt. I understood that if I extended the narrative to the era of Woyane, I would have to write everything honestly, leading to a direct confrontation with my captors and risking the suppression of the book. Therefore, the book would cover the historical period from 1974 to 1978. Since 1978 marked the year of my first contact with Woyane, I had to refrain from going beyond it, fearing that my candid writing might provoke irritation from my captors.

I commenced writing "Curbing Narrative Extremism and Revealing Truth" on April 12, 2015, and successfully completed the book on July 9, 2015, as indicated by the start and final dates on the soft copy. Upon a quick calculation of these dates, I realized that it took me a mere two months and 27 days to complete 647 pages of a book on B5 pages. This starkly highlights the solitary nature of my life during this period, with my only companionship being the laptop.

When I initially embarked on creating the manuscript for this book, I made a request to my chief interrogator to provide me with reference books. Surprisingly, he agreed and asked me to provide a list. I submitted a list of 35 books, and to my astonishment, he delivered 31 of them. Having already read all of them during my time overseas, getting these reference materials proved invaluable to the writing process.

During the months I was engrossed in writing, I had another encounter with the British Ambassador. This time, the blanket covering my face was only used for a short distance, and I could sit upright in the car, enjoying the view of the city. Dawit, the driver, navigated the streets, and I could discern precisely where we were headed – towards one of the state guesthouses opposite the Jubilee Palace en route to the Filweha hot springs. I had stayed in one of these guesthouses upon my return from London when the EPRDF first assumed power in 1991.

Upon arrival, I waited in one of the guesthouse rooms with an escort. The meeting room was well-organized, capable of accommodating up to 20 people. The chief interrogator escorted the Ambassador into the room, and their conversation unfolded in English. The interrogator's fluency made me wonder if he had ever been a rebel fighter, as many rebels typically didn't have formal education.

The Ambassador greeted me with the customary shoulder-to-shoulder embrace, a gesture reciprocated by the interrogator. Sitting in the room, I couldn't help but compare it to the guardhouse where I initially met the Ambassador. This time, it felt as though the TPLF (Tigray People's Liberation Front) was meeting the Queen's representative in accordance with diplomatic protocol.

The Ambassador retrieved a piece of paper from his pocket, mirroring his previous meetings, and began his questioning. Health matters took precedence, and I provided a detailed account of all my problems. In return, he updated me on information about my family, England, and more. He mentioned that my constituency MP, Jeremy Corbyn, had expressed a desire to visit me but was denied an entry visa by the Ethiopian government. Casually, he also mentioned that Jeremy had become the leader of the opposition Labour Party.

The last information intrigued me. I knew Jeremy Corbyn personally and had consistently voted for him. I was confident that, in his constitutional role, he would inquire about my case with the government. His new position as the leader of the opposition would further facilitate raising my case publicly and privately with government officials.

Throughout our conversation, Ambassador Greg was careful not to offend the TPLF. It remained unclear whether his caution was a matter of personal choice or imposed by the British government.

The Ambassador was greeted with my ironic respect as I expressed, "I am well aware of Western government foreign policies and practices. Forget about me—a naturalized British citizen and a black man. I understand that you would not lift a finger to assist even an indigenous white English person if you believe such assistance conflicts with what you so-called the national interest. That is why I don't anticipate anything from you," I added. In response, he stated that the situation was more complex than I perceived. His departing message only solidified my scepticism about Western governments.

"He suggested that things might be easier if I apologized to the Ethiopian government," It remained unclear whether the TPLF had informed him about a potential resolution to my case through an apology or if he was merely relaying a decision made by his superiors in London.

Unable to overlook what I perceived as an insolent remark by the ambassador in the presence of my interrogators, I felt compelled to respond. I conveyed to Ambassador Craig that it was the criminal TPLF regime that owed both me and the people of Ethiopia an apology, not the other way around. Additionally, I pleaded with him to retrieve a copy of my writings that his associate had taken on a flash and pass it on to my family in England.

In response, Ambassador Greg mentioned that he had heard about my receipt of a laptop but chose not to bring it up, assuming I might be unwilling to discuss it. I explained the circumstances surrounding the laptop and clarified that whatever I had already written had been collected while I continued to work on additional pieces. He assured me that he would make an effort to retrieve the completed works, then swiftly emptied the remaining coffee from his cup and departed with his escort. This marked the final encounter with Ambassador Greg during my detention at an undisclosed location.

Chapter XXXI: Tears and Therapy

I was still confined to solitary when the first anniversary of my captivity arrived. I couldn't help but recall the traditional superstition that something ominous would happen when Monday meets the month of June. A curious thought crossed my mind – does the superstition apply to all Mondays in June, or is it specifically about the first of June falling on a Monday? Upon reflection, it didn't align with my situation, as I was abducted on a Monday in the middle of June.

The time also marked my second winter in prison. The old villa, its walls crafted from basalt stone, transformed into a freezer, enveloping me in an icy chill. Despite an extra blanket, I found no respite from the relentless shivers that gripped me.

Having finished my Amharic book, "Curbing Narrative Extremism and Revealing Truth," which delved into the history of EPRP in Addis Ababa—an organization I actively participated in until my departure from the city in January 1978—I halted my writing.

The conflict of interest was the primary reason for my decision. It became challenging to authentically depict the historical period, which also encompassed the history of TPLF, the organization of my captors. Being under their custody posed a dilemma, as my fear of displeasing them and compromising my ability to reveal the whole truth became a significant concern.

Choosing a different path, I resolved to produce multiple volumes under the title "Curbing Narrative Extremism and Revealing Truth." I had successfully completed Volume One, and with the remaining volumes, my task was to meticulously outline sections for each, saving the comprehensive plans on my laptop. That aspect of the job was also finalized.

Having nothing to write about, I was engaged in a constant battle with mosquitoes, passing both day and night playing chess on my laptop. The only indication of the time was the glimpse of dawn or the onset of dusk through the hole in the wall.

Persistently, rain poured down, creating a soothing symphony on the tin roof. Memories of my childhood flooded back. Having lived in London for an extended period in houses with concrete ceilings, I had nearly forgotten the unique sensation that the sound of rain on a tin roof brings. I listened intently, overcome with heightened emotions. Sleep eluded me, yet it felt comforting to curl up under the blankets and relish the nostalgic melody of the rain, much like I did in my childhood.

As the union between the tin roof and the rain persisted, memories of my mother's voice echoed in my mind. I recalled her calling out for her little boy, who once perceived the rain on the tin roof as celestial music. In my mind, I thought I heard the familiar call of "Ababu, Ababu," my childhood pet name, beckoning me from the rooms beyond my cell.

I pondered the disappearance of my childhood, along with my teenage and adolescent years, and in moments like these, my grief became profoundly intense. My sole solace was in revisiting the words I penned in "Curbing Narrative Extremism and Revealing Truth."

Writing that book and revisiting its pages proved to be a therapeutic journey for me. I found solace in the thought that if the writing endured and saw publication, it could serve as an explanation to my children about the reasons behind losing their father.

Emotions overwhelmed me as I penned the heartbreaking account of three of my father's younger brothers, all under the age of seven, being torn away from their mother's embrace and ruthlessly slaughtered like cattle at her feet. I could vividly picture the pain etched on my grandmother's face as she recounted this tragic tale, which unfolded during the second Italian invasion of Ethiopia just before World War II.

Expressing the suffering my father endured, surviving the brutal loss of his younger brothers and witnessing the death of his father on that fateful day left me grappling with the difficulty of putting such profound pain onto paper. A torrent of tears accompanied each word.

The anguish continued as I wrote about my father's dramatic reunion with his mother after two decades of separation, accepting the reality that he was truly an orphan. This poignant meeting occurred in Bekoji, in the Arsi province, where his mother sold homebrew to villagers. The tears flowed freely as I captured the emotional intensity of that reunion on the written page.

The military regime mercilessly took the life of my younger brother, Amha, at the tender age of 17 in 1977. He was buried in one of the countless mass graves whose locations remained unknown. The anguish that consumed my mother and the grief that weighed heavy on my father, who had seen Amha as a replacement for the brothers he lost four decades earlier, was indescribable.

A wave of bitterness and sorrow washed over me as I recalled how callous and indifferent we had been to our parents' grief. In those tragic years of the revolution, we passed through the ordeal without shedding a single tear, pseudo-rationalizing the entire affair as a necessary sacrifice for freedom.

We convinced ourselves that those who perished were not truly gone, as the fight for freedom, justice, and democracy would persist beyond their passing. It was a coping mechanism that now seemed like a callous evasion of the pain.

As if it were payback time for withholding my tears back then, I began sobbing uncontrollably until I was emotionally drained. The weight of the suppressed sorrow and the realization of the profound loss finally caught up with me, and the floodgates of grief opened wide.

The fate that befell my childhood friends—Zewdu, Japi, Markos, and Cherenet—mirrored Amha's tragic end. Like my brother, theirs, too, had no tombstones to visit, and I wept as I penned their stories. Their faces haunted the solitude of my cell, a constant reminder of the loss.

In the depths of my memories, I recalled Ephrem, Abdul, Lemenew, Dawit, Sheriff, Isaias, Asku, Belay, and many others who met a tragic end at a very young age. The question echoed within me as I asked God, "Why did you spare me to endure this fate? Why didn't you take me like them? Do you believe they lost by departing so early?" Tears streamed down my face as I confronted these profound and sorrowful questions.

In the absence of a wake, nobody entered my room. There was no need to worry about appearances, and the distinction between day and night lost its significance. No crier aided me, no women clung to the fringed embroidery of their shawls, and no elders donned dark wool overcoats to accompany, console, and restrain my uncontrollable tears. The solitude allowed me to experience the full weight of my grief.

The July rains seemed to pull at the melancholy settled deep within my stomach, yet this time, no tears were left for me to shed. The sombre atmosphere lingered as the dark clouds insisted on releasing rain throughout August. Then came September, and I witnessed the sun bursting its shine through the small aperture high up on the cell wall. September marked the beginning of the Ethiopian New Year.

Chapter XXXII: A Rendition of Some Sort

In September, the chief interrogator arrived with the sunshine, resembling a rural relative who had finally found a crossing over a flooding river. It happened to be a Sunday.

"Have you come to inquire about a prisoner's health?" I inquired.

My gaze fell upon the apples he carried.

"Yes," he replied, handing the security guy standing next to him a plastic bag filled with apples that he had brought for me.

The primary purpose of the chief interrogator's visit was to inform me of my impending move to a new destination. I refrained from asking him where exactly, and he did not disclose the information.

"I'll come and see you wherever you go," he declared before concluding his visit.

The warning proved valuable the following day when my cell door was opened at an unusual time. Dawit was the first to enter, followed by the tall and short security guards who had kept a watchful eye on me from day one.

"We are going to collect your belongings," they announced.

I had accumulated a substantial amount of bottled water, a small bag of kollo, and my pillow rolled up within one of my blankets. The guards meticulously stuffed my blood sugar monitor, jogging suit, and the underwear Leteberhan had purchased for me into a plastic bag. Every item underwent a thorough inspection before being carefully packed.

The tall, stern guard was particularly meticulous in his examination. He scrutinized every inch of my few collars and the seams of my trousers. Like a hawk, he managed to unearth the receipt I had carefully tucked into the waistline of my jogging trousers. Almost magically, my clothes from the day of the abduction reappeared, accompanied by my shoes, belt, and watch.

My long-time companion, the sponge mattress that had served as my bed, seat, dining table, and desk, was the only item left behind. I couldn't help but wonder if the mattress felt a sense of abandonment, and suddenly, a pang of grief washed over me for it.

All thirty-one reference books were meticulously counted and packed into a plastic bag, staying behind with the laptop. The thought of parting from my writings, crafted with tears and sweat, felt akin to separating from my own children. I clung to my laptop like a child holding onto his mother's dress, but alas, I had to let go.

As usual, my face shrouded in the second blanket, my escorts guided me into the waiting car, positioning my head on the rear passenger seat. After some time, someone removed the veil, allowing me to sit upright.

Wee commenced our journey in broad daylight with Dawit at the wheel, but now darkness enveloped us completely. I couldn't discern our location. Soon, the car veered off the main street and into the supermarket parking lot, parking beside a Toyota Hilux.

Dawit stepped out, conversing with the —a tall, stocky man with dishevelled hair and a gentle demeanour that had come out of the pick up. Others were inside the Hilux, including a soldier in uniform tightly clutching a Kalashnikov. Another uniformed soldier, also armed, aimed carefully with his finger on the trigger from behind the car.

Dawit instructed my escorts to transfer my belongings to the Hilux. I was told to disembark. All three of my captors embraced me, patting me on the shoulder bidding me farewell. Even the tall, mean one hugged me tightly as he said, "Goodbye." Seated in the rear passenger seat of the Hilux with a soldier beside me, we set off. A large gate opened in less than ten minutes, and we entered a huge courtyard. My whereabouts remained unknown.

The spacious courtyard extended into a driveway to the left. As the car stopped an older man that came to open the car door handed me a towel and instructed me to wrap it around my head, which I did. Beneath our feet, the soil was wet and red. The rains had not completely ceased in September, leaving the mud undried. Puddles dotted the pavement.

The man who gave me the towel unlatched a metal door, leading us into a small compound. Passing through another metal door that was unlocked by the old man and across a narrow corridor, another wooden door was unlocked, and we entered a room.

The room I entered was small, with a very low ceiling had, two beds and a man was lying on one of them. The man sat up, appearing startled, as though our arrival had disrupted his sleep. The bed near the door was designated for me. The guards unceremoniously dumped my belongings on the floor before departing, leaving the wooden door ajar while locking the metal behind them.

Approaching the man who seemed somewhat confused on his bed, I extended my hand and introduced myself.

"Andargachew Tsege," I stated, and we shook hands.

"Assefa Kusse," came his reply.

"Where is this place?" I inquired.

"Kaliti," was his brief response.

Chapter XXXIII: Overnight at the Federal Prison; Kaliti

After our introduction, there was a conspicuous absence of communication between Assefa Kusse and me.

The time had already passed 8:00, and the weight of the ensuing silence began to harass me. Restlessly, my eyes darted around the room, scanning every object within its confines.

The narrow gap between the two beds allowed only enough space for a single person to pass through. The unusually low hanging ceiling prompted me to rise and reach up to it. With a half-stretched arm, I managed to touch it.

The wall behind Assefa was cluttered with hanging cloth and utensils suspended from nails embedded in it. A similar assortment of belongings clattered beneath his bed. In his state of immobility and isolation, seated on the bed, Assefa's gaze was fixed solely on me. Though not an intense stare, I could discern a fascination in his eyes, as if I had transformed into an object of captivation for him.

I was excited and filled with anticipation for my first conversation to be with someone other than a member of Woyane. The prospect of engaging in various activities for the first time heightened my enthusiasm - from using the toilet without seeking permission to sleeping on a bed and utilizing it as a chair for reading, eating, and doing whatever I pleased.

However, my excitement turned into contemplation when I recalled the peculiar remark made by the chief interrogator during our last encounter. "Berhanu Nega is in Eritrea," he had declared.

Berhanu Nega, a professor of economics at Bucknell University in the US, served as the leader of Ginbot 7, my organization. Considering that September is a busy time for university inductions and admissions, with the beginning of the new term, I questioned the validity of this information.

I considered the possibility of Berhanu taking a sabbatical leave to support Ginbot 7's popular force in Eritrea. While I acknowledged the potential falsity of the statement, I also left room for the chance that it held some truth. Regardless, I concluded that this open prison would be the ideal place to gather more information about the outside world, putting an end to my inquiry about Berhanu and Eritrea.

Despite these contemplations, I remained in high spirits. Almost on the verge of singing aloud, I reflected on the traditional saying, "Humans are the best medicine for human pain." Even though I wasn't actively conversing with Assefa, I felt grateful for his presence. The solitude I had endured for so long was finally breaking, and the anticipation of human connection brought me a sense of joy.

I spread the curtain looking bedsheet over the sponge mattress, covered it over with my blanket and sat up on the bed.

"How long have you been here?" I asked Assefa.

"It's my third day," he said.

Why were you confined alone?"

"For possessing a cell phone".

Assefa had not been out of the room by day or by night since his arrival.

"Do you think we'll stay locked up in here?" I asked.

"The guards may decide to leave the door open in the daytime now that you are here," he said. Assefa addressed me formally with the honourable 'thou'.

"Do let's drop the formality unless you want to distance yourself from me?" I pleaded.

"Ok," Assefa agreed.

Our conversation persisted into the late hours of the night before we eventually retired to sleep. However, the light switch proved to be beyond the reach of either of us from our respective beds. As I moved to turn off the light, Assefa cautioned me.

"Don't," he said, "it is against prison regulations," he added. That shattered my hope of sleeping in a dark room, and the bright fluorescent lamp continued illuminating the small cell.

Chapter XXXIV: Dawn at the Federal Prison

I slept like a log. In the morning, a repeating thumping noise woke me up. Assefa was engrossed in exercising within the cramped prison corridor leading to the toilet.

I couldn't discern the exact time; perhaps it was just before seven o'clock. The brief joy of having my watch with me was short-lived, as I had to surrender it to the prison attendant upon my arrival at Kaliti. "You can't have it," he barked, and I silently watched as another officer walked away with my watch adorning his wrist. However, I noticed that Assefa had a watch on his wrist.

Attempting to console myself, I told myself that I didn't really need a watch. I reassured myself with the fact that I still had a digital clock on my blood-sugar meter.

The front door opened while Assefa was engaged in his morning exercises. A middle-aged man dressed in civilian clothes pushed through the second door and announced breakfast. Assefa paused his exercises to hand the man a plastic bag and a flask.

"Do you not have a bag for your bread roll?" the middle-aged man asked me politely.

"I have some barley bread," I replied.

Lacking a container for tea, we quickly agreed that I was better off without the tea that came with sugar put into it. The man handed the plastic bag with a bread roll back to Assefa and the tea in the flask, locked the door and left. Assefa informed me the man I had just seen was Major Berhane, an ethnic Tigrayan.

Major Berhane paid us another visit at lunchtime, presenting us with poorly fermented black injera covered in runny Shiro (spiced chickpea flour sauce).

Noticing the sauce lacked hot spice, I took out a bottle of Mitmita (extra hot chilli powder), I had saved from the other prison and asked Assefa if he would like to add some to his meal.

"Nobody in this prison is allowed Mitmita. Where did you find it? How did you get permission to bring it in?" Assefa asked, clearly surprised. I explained that Leteberhan had persuaded the prison attendant to let me have some when I had stopped eating in the other prison.

"I'm sure the guards here missed it when they searched you. I would keep that out of sight if I were you," Assefa advised as we evenly sprinkled the powder onto our Shiro. Heeding his suggestion, I didn't hesitate to conceal the Mitmita. Anyway, despite its disgusting look, the food didn't taste that bad, and I ate most of it with a sprinkle of Mitmita.

The same injera arrived that evening for dinner, and I opted for Kollo instead. Unfortunately, we soon ran out of Mitmita. Feeling daring, I decided to take a risk and approached Major Berhane, informing him that I had run out of mitmita.

"Where did the mitmita come from?" Major Berhane inquired, just as Assefa had predicted. I shared the story and insisted, "I need it." "That's not allowed here," he declared, promptly confiscating the container.

In the subsequent days, our confinement continued within the cell. One morning, after finishing breakfast, I was interrupted while gazing at a wall bordering our cell through the metal bars of the small window located in the corridor facing the compact courtyard.

A man entered through the front gate, announcing that I had a visitor. My mind immediately went to the possibility of a real visitor, thinking of my sister, the sole resident of Addis Ababa. I was taken out of the cell and led into an adjacent room whose entrance was on the other side of our compound.

Dawit sat comfortably behind the desk in a plush leather chair, a familiar sight in every kebele (neighbourhood) office, accompanied by a TV set. Without delay, he got straight to the purpose of his visit.

"Your cell is too small and will be merged with this office. You'll both transfer to a different cell for a few days," Dawit announced.

It was surprising that Dawit took the time to inform me of this change personally.

We gathered our blankets and other belongings and moved to a room 20 meters away. The new space was expansive enough to accommodate over twenty prisoners. In one corner, a lone prisoner lay on a bed under a mosquito net, who recognized me immediately and offered a respectful greeting.

I extended my hand, introducing myself, "Andargachew Tsege."

"I know, Dawit Dibabaye," he replied, shaking my hand.

Chapter XXXV: Who is the Spy?

The large jail room was in a deplorable state of filth. Taking the initiative, I began to clean up, and my fellow inmates joined in.

I assumed responsibility for maintaining the bathroom and shower room, a duty I would carry throughout the years. Since the cell only had running water at night, I also filled a barrel with buckets of water to ensure an adequate supply during the day.

I undertook these tasks for two reasons: to demonstrate to my fellow inmates the dignity of manual labour and to occupy my time, as there were no other constructive engagements available to me.

Our daily routine remained unchanged, marked by the front door opening for the delivery of breakfast, lunch, and dinner. The inside door was left unlocked, granting us access to the tiny courtyard surrounded by corrugated iron that seemed to reach the sky. Our vision was confined by the walls, and the only glimpse of the outside world was the expanse of sky defined by the perimeter.

It became a daily pleasure to spend an hour in relative freedom gazing upon the Ethiopian sky. Surrendering to the warmth of the bright sun, I closed my eyes and allowed the hues of the fiery red sun to permeate my being.

With closed eyes, I could hear Joan Armatrading's beautiful voice resonating in my ears repeatedly, singing, "Now, if I can feel the sun in my eyes and the rain on my face, why can't I feel the love?"

It may seem trivial, but even in a prison deprived of love, feeling the sunshine, the wind, and the rain caressing your face, hair, and eyes fills the heart with melancholic yet fond sensations.

Confined within a space chartered by our jailers in a universe of limitless expanse, it's not just the physical space but also our time that lies at the mercy of the guards. These restrictions elevate small, simple experiences, such as the touch of sunshine or the gentle fall of raindrops on one's face, into sweet moments.

To sit in a corner of the courtyard, immersed in silent contemplation, became a cherished privilege. For those beyond the prison walls, living in freedom, such feelings may be foreign. Having once been a free man, I understand what I am expressing. It wouldn't have occurred to me to thank God for delivering me from the daily stress by using the elements as soothing agents.

Stepping outdoors became a great novelty for me, and I found myself moving in and out constantly. This allowed my fellow inmates to communicate with me privately. If one went outside while I stayed indoors, the one inside would share many unfavourable details about the other prisoner, and vice versa. However, all these revelations boiled down to one consistent issue: "Don't trust him; he's a government spy."

Accepting any of their words at face value was challenging, as none could provide concrete proof. After listening to both sides, I carefully crafted my response. I made it clear that it wouldn't bother me in the least if the government planted dozens of spies in our cell. I had already disclosed everything to my interrogators, and if I happened to recall something unsaid, I would raise my voice beyond the prison walls and let the whole world know. Nothing would unsettle me.

Following that declaration, my fellow inmates never brought up the story of a planted spy among us again.

I sensed an underlying issue between my inmates, with their mutual discomfort evident in the unspoken communication of their eyes. Instances unfolded that exposed their mutual dislike.

Dawit, having little money, had the right to call the guards and ask them to buy him coffee from the prisoners' cafe. Strangely, he used Assefa's flask since he had none. When the coffee arrived, he reluctantly shared it with Assefa, compelled by the fact that the flask belonged to Assefa. Assefa accepted the coffee and added sugar, yet he didn't offer any to Dawit, who had none. I found myself intervening each time to demand that one of them share what the other lacked.

However, I personally harboured no concerns about either of them; they both seemed like decent individuals.

Inspired by Assefa's example, I decided to start exercising in the morning. The only hindrance was my flip-flops, making my movement challenging. Observing my predicament, Dawit eagerly offered me his training shoes, even though they were slightly worn out and rather tight. He seemed embarrassed by their condition. In accepting the shoes, I invoked a traditional saying, "If a man shares what he has, he cannot be accused of meanness." Dawit understood that the state of the trainers didn't matter; it was what he had, and he had offered it sincerely. I accepted his gift with utmost gratitude.

I and Assefa had moved with our mosquito nets from the other room, and Dawit was the one who hung mine up for me, a gesture that seemed to annoy Assefa. It was challenging to discern whether Dawit's acts of kindness were genuine or motivated by a mysterious tension shared between the two.

A new aspect of our cell was the presence of neighbours, and we could now hear voices and the sound of a TV coming from the adjacent room. One day, I beat my fist against the wall three times, and our neighbours responded. After this initial contact, I asked them, "Who are you?"

"Andualem Arage, Melaku Fenta, and Mesfin..."

I introduced myself and the names of Assefa and Dawit. Andualem, one of our neighbours, informed me that my family and the general public had finally learned about my presence in Kality Prison. Visiting family and relatives had heard about it from the international media. "Your sister told the foreign media that she was not allowed when she asked if she could visit you," Andualem revealed. All the information was gathered from his visiting wife.

This news was a great relief for me. My family needed to know my whereabouts. Andualem and I became friends, communicating through knocks on the wall to request to increase the TV volume during the news. They obliged. That's how I heard US President Barack Obama, during his visit to Ethiopia, declare, "The TPLF government is a popular government." It was disconcerting to hear the same person who had said, "Africa needs big institutions, not big people," complimenting the oppressive TPLF-led government.

While not surprised by Obama's speech, considering the historical trajectory of US foreign policy, I found it astonishing that he wasn't ashamed to label TPLF as "popular." Despite the discomfort caused by Obama's words, our stay in that stable/cell went well, and we returned to our old cell a week later.

Chapter XXXVI: A Day of Pleasure

The original cell was supposed to have been merged with the adjacent office, but it now accommodated a third bed. I was informed that Dawit Dibaba, the individual who stayed with us in the other cell, was to join our quarters. It became apparent that the narrative about Assefa and me requiring more space was misinformation.

Observing the cramped conditions with the addition of these two individuals, who mutually loathed each other, in a relatively small cell was ominous. I began to suspect that the entire arrangement might be a tactic aimed at me—either to inconvenience me through their conflicts or to introduce potential informants, hindering my ability to confidently formulate any plans I could hatch if I were to be only with one person or on my own.

Uniting two conflicting individuals in the same cell served as a strategy to prevent inmates from plotting ideas and sharing secrets. It stifled conspiracy, creating an atmosphere where one lived in fear of the other. This measure, developed by security experts, seemed to be effective in achieving its intended purpose.

From the first day we returned to the expanded cell, I decided to bring order to our collective life. I proposed establishing a routine and allocating responsibilities to each of us. To make it easier for everyone, I took on the least desirable task—I volunteered to clean the toilet and the shower room, just as I had in the other cell.

We reached an agreement on a cleaning schedule and committed to adhering to the agreed timetable. Additionally, we discussed how to use the tiny courtyard for morning exercise. Assefa was allowed to go out first and do his exercise, while Dawit and I would follow after Assefa finished. We granted Assefa the freedom to exercise on his own, considering the type of exercise he did required more space than our routines.

In contrast to the traditional way of collectively eating from large plates, prison life didn't foster the culture of sharing plates and communal meals. Each of us received our food individually and ate on our own. Assefa enjoyed a certain privilege – he received fresh tomatoes from his family, who visited him occasionally. Whenever he had some, he treated us to tomato and onion salad alongside our Shiro.

Unlike Assefa, Dawit and I did not have visitors. Dawit's relations and friends showed no interest in visiting him, and mine were not allowed to do so. As a result, only Assefa had access to money and food items that were otherwise unavailable within our cell.

I soon discovered that I had little in common with my fellow inmates. Both were younger, at least 20 years from me and serving life sentences for murder. It disappointed me that I found myself among them, having committed no crime other than advocating for human rights and freedoms. In my mind, I saw Assefa as Gestas and

Dawit as Dismas, the murderers crucified to the left and right of Jesus Christ. Despite not being a religious person, I found solace in the realization that I wasn't the first innocent being to be in the company of murderers. "What wonder that I, the sinful son of man, should find myself amongst killers when even the innocent son of God was crucified amongst assassins without cause." Such thoughts comforted me.

Assefa and Dawit exhibited no remorse for their heinous crimes. Instead, they took pride in recalling the gruesome details of their actions. As I listened to their callous recounting, I couldn't help but wonder how someone could be so devoid of empathy. Was their demeanour a calculated display orchestrated by my captors to instil fear within me? Was it a form of psychological torture designed to deprive me of peace and sleep?

My fellow inmates hailed from modest backgrounds with limited educational opportunities. They showed no interest in bettering themselves through the various programs offered within the prison. Before being transferred to our cell, they had access, like all prisoners, to educational services provided by the authorities. Their backgrounds and attitudes contrasted sharply with mine, leaving me feeling isolated and disadvantaged in this environment.

Assefa seemed to possess more belongings than Dawit, including money, sugar, a Bible, clothes, shoes, paper, a pen, onion, garlic, and various other items. However, despite his material possessions, he appeared to be somewhat mentally disturbed. He showed paranoid tendencies.

He initially lent me his Bible but later found a reason to take it back and stow it away in his suitcase. At the time, he knew that I had begun reading the Bible again for the second time because I had nothing else to read. I couldn't shake off the suspicion that Assefa might have been acting under instructions from the authorities.

My doubts deepened when he refused to lend me two cloves of garlic to alleviate a cold I was suffering from. I had hoped that a sense of camaraderie would develop among us, but any such hope had all but vanished.

Dawit, on the other hand, lacked family visits and had little to offer in terms of material sharing. Despite this, his actions, such as offering me his old pair of training shoes, hinted at a generous nature. However, another aspect of his character overshadowed this generosity. He was easily offended, resentful, and quick to resort to aggression and intimidation tactics.

My fellow inmates were far from easy-going individuals. However, Andualem, a political prisoner that I know well and whom we managed to converse with while we were in another cell, seemed to have better fortune. He was incarcerated with men of similar age, life experiences, and general knowledge.

From the conversations with Assefa and Dawit, I learned that Kaliti prison segregated inmates into cells with individuals of identical backgrounds. For instance, officials from the deposed military regime were confined together in one area, while officers and civilians accused of conspiring with the Ginbot 7 movement in an attempted coup d'état were imprisoned together elsewhere.

Given this pattern of imprisonment in Kaliti, I became convinced that the TPLF (Tigray People's Liberation Front) continued to isolate me deliberately, assigning me to a group of inmates with whom I shared no common ground. It seemed like a form of punishment aimed at demoralizing me and breaking my spirit.

However, amidst my struggles to envision my future in such circumstances, something remarkable and unexpected occurred.

It was over a month since my transfer to Kaliti when, one late afternoon, the unusual sound of a car pulling up in front of our cell courtyard caught our attention. Until that moment, no vehicle had ever approached the small dead-end road leading to the gate of our courtyard. All three of us were outside our cell, puzzled by the unexpected arrival. When Major Berhane opened the gate and motioned for me to follow him, I complied without any understanding of what was happening.

The car, a Toyota pickup, awaited me. I was instructed to sit in the back seat, accompanied by two armed prison guards—one in the front seat and one outside the back of the car—who were assigned to escort me wherever I was being taken. Berhane joined me in the backseat, and our journey barely covered a hundred yards before we stopped in front of a large villa, where I was directed to disembark.

Following Berhane and the two guards, I ascended a few steps and entered a dimly lit corridor, turning left as instructed. Beyond the door leading into the corridor was a lavishly furnished room, serving as an office, with an imposing desk and an empty swivelling chair positioned before me. Despite the poor lighting, I could discern a spacious area with leather sofas opposite the desk. Seated directly across from me was a gentleman, and though obscured from my view, an elderly man and a middle-aged woman were also present.

To my astonishment, the elderly gentleman seated before me was my father, and the middle-aged woman was Tadelech, the young wife he had married after his separation from my mother.

My father rose from his seat and embraced me warmly, followed by Tadelech, as we exchanged greetings and expressions of concern for each other's well-being. It was evident that my father was taken aback by my physical condition, having lost a significant amount of weight during my time in solitary confinement. Witnessing his reaction, I couldn't help but feel a pang of sadness, realising the impact my ordeal had on him.

Memories of my mother flooded my thoughts, and I couldn't help but grieve for her, thankful that she had been spared the anguish of witnessing my imprisonment and the looming threat of the death penalty.

The person who was seated on the sofa next to my father got up and moved to the administrator's chair. He was a tall, slender man whom I learned was a security officer, presumably overseeing our conversation.

My parents, visibly apologetic, explained that they hadn't been given any warning and were unprepared for the visit, having hastily jumped into a car to reach me. My father was talking in plurals when he told me about those who gave them instructions.

It was evident that multiple individuals had been involved in orchestrating this urgent visit, including the figure behind the administrator's desk, identified by the nameplate 'Abraham'. He was clad in a flashy suit that exuded a certain ostentatiousness, reminiscent of the New York pimps that I used to watch in old Hollywood movies.

Throughout our brief reunion, my parents remained mostly silent, offering only brief responses. When I inquired about my children, they assured me they were fine but swiftly changed the subject whenever I broached topics related to the outside world. It dawned on me that my captors had likely warned them against divulging any sensitive information.

As our time together dwindled, the man in the administrator's seat announced that our visitation period had ended. Before parting ways, my parents promised to come better prepared for future visits, offering to bring clothing and asking what else I might need. I requested two pairs of trainers in specific sizes, expressing gratitude before bidding them farewell.

Exiting the building first, I returned to the waiting car that promptly transported me back to my prison confines, a mere 50 meters away from where our encounter had taken place.

Chapter XXXVII: Family and Diplomatic Effort

A week later, my parents appeared again, informing me that they were the only ones permitted to visit me on Saturdays. They arrived laden with an extravagant supply of food and clothing despite it being unnecessary.

Our conversation remained limited, with my parents responding to me in simple and brief comments. I despaired at the futility of extracting any substantial information from them. During this second visit, I was escorted from my cell to our meeting venue by the Chief Administrator of Kaliti Prison. As we walked to his office, he shed his driver's cloak and assumed the administrator's seat upon our arrival.

I had learned from Assefa and Dawit that the former chief of the prison, Abraham, had been dismissed, yet his nameplate still adorned his desk. The description they provided of the new chief, Commander Gebreyesus, matched the man now seated in the administrator's seat. Additionally, I couldn't shake the feeling that this person was the same gentleman who had previously collected me from Dawit, the interrogator at the supermarket parking lot.

"Take a look at what we've brought for you today, and make a list for our next visit," my father urged.

Though the allocated half-hour may seem brief to some, it felt too long for both my father and me. Our conversations, constrained by a warning he had received, lacked any discussion of politics or life beyond the prison walls. Instead, I resorted to asking safe questions every week.

"Are the children safe? How is Yemi? Are my siblings okay?" I inquired.

My parents responded in a few words with, "All is well."

Our exchanges rarely lasted more than a minute, often with me carrying the conversation alone. I would inquire about my father's health, jest about his choice of attire, his new walking stick, his clean-shaven appearance, his hair, and his age. There were instances when we parted ways before our allotted time was up simply because we had exhausted all topics of conversation.

Major Berhane and his associates meticulously inspected the food brought by my family in the corridor of the administration office. My parents were compelled to taste everything, regardless of their religious fasts. They agreed to take turns, with my father assuming the role of taster on fasting days despite his own modest eating habits. I refrained from questioning why he didn't opt to fast like others his age.

After several visits, senior members of the security forces and the prison administration ceased attending our meetings. The chief administrator never returned, and Major Berhane assumed full control. However, little else changed; the venue and visiting schedule remained unchanged, and my parents continued their visits.

Our communication remained unchanged, although Berhane now seated himself beside my parents on the couch, rather than in the administrator's seat, engaging in casual conversation as if he were a family member. This lack of privacy deprived us of any chance for personal discussions.

Nevertheless, Berhane maintained a respectful demeanour towards my parents, even offering to carry their items into the office upon their arrival at the gates of Kaliti. I had no complaints about his treatment of me. I later learned from a that keeps watch on us from aprison tower that Brehane was assigned to oversee me due to his Tigrayan heritage and loyalty to the TPLF. He always kept the key to my cell with him, even when he returned home in the evening—a fact I confirmed later on.

On one Wednesday coinciding with one of my parents' visits, the British Ambassador, Greg, was granted permission to visit me. The day before his arrival, the tall, thin man in the glittering suit, escorted by Berhane, approached us.

Dawit and Assefa suspected the new guy of being from the intelligence services, as he had no apparent connection to the prison. While I remained inside the cell, he entered and began asking questions about my accommodations, my family, and whether they had provided what I needed. It wasn't until the following day, during the Ambassador's visit, that I realised he had been assessing my responses to gauge what I might disclose.

As usual, I was escorted by armed men and taken by car to the administrator's office, where I immediately noticed the intelligence officer who had visited our cell the day before occupying the chief administrator's seat. Ambassador Greg had taken my parents' usual place and seemed pleased to see me. We exchanged greetings with the customary bump of the shoulders, and I couldn't help but notice the books spread out on the coffee table opposite him.

"We are now allowed to bring in some books. These two have been with us for a long time since they arrived from England," Ambassador Greg informed me.

Among the books was "God in Every Stone" by Kamila Shamsie, a book I had pre-ordered after hearing her interview on the BBC. The second book, "Memoirs of a Geisha," delved into the rich history of traditional Japanese courtesans and their relationships with affluent Japanese men. I was overjoyed to receive the books, as I hadn't read any in a long time. Before additional books were provided for me to read, I devoured each of them a minimum of five times.

As Ambassador Greg began asking questions, it became apparent that the execution of Foreign Office guidelines was underway.

He informed me that British government officials had been discussing my case with the Ethiopian government and had already requested my appearance in court. Despite my previous reluctance to face the TPLF's kangaroo court, I had a change of heart since being transferred to Kaliti. While I knew justice would not be served there, I had calculated the complications and embarrassment my appearance would cause the regime. Transporting me to and from the court would be a logistical challenge, given their panic, even during routine visits in Kaliti. Furthermore, they wouldn't be able to control what I would say in court.

When Greg broached the topic, I informed him of my decision to appear in court. He turned to the TPLF official in the room for comment, but the man remained silent. I was surprised that an official escorting the British Ambassador lacked the necessary language skills, adding to the surreal nature of the situation.

The intelligence officer, speaking in broken English, uttered, "Terrorist, judge decide, no judge," while looking at me. I dismissed his remarks, informing Ambassador Greg that the man was an ineffectual intelligence agent who didn't comprehend the legal proceedings. I suggested that it would be best to address his superiors and clarified that under the law, a person convicted in absentia has the right to appear in court. The official appeared to understand my explanation, albeit reluctantly.

The officer abruptly declared to Craig, "You have to go," pointing at his watch and repeating, "Time finished, time finished." Despite Greg's plea for just one more minute to conclude his visit, the exasperated security man insisted, "Your half-hour is up. Not a single minute more." Reluctantly, Greg departed, forgetting his leather hat on the table, his disappointment palpable.

Returning to my cell, I now possessed three hundred Ethiopian Birr (£10 at the time) received against signature facilitated by Greg. This sum, sent to me by Prisoners Abroad, a charity in the United Kingdom, elevated my status within the cell. Now, alongside Assefa, I, too, held currency and a certain authority.

Weekly family visits and monthly visits by the British Ambassador continued for a while, although the intelligence agency managed the Ambassador's visits. Ambassador Craig couldn't simply turn up at the prison and demand to see me; his visits were subject to the agency's discretion. There were occasions when he didn't show up for three months, as determined by the agency's assessment of the necessity for his visit. Despite the disruption in the scheduled visits, it made little difference to me. While the embassy provided more information than my family, neither source supplied the specific information I sought.

Chapter XXXVIII: Ratcheting up Tensions

In the cramped confines of our cell, tensions simmered, hinting at an impending explosion. The catalyst came when Assefa declared that the food brought by his family had spoiled and needed disposal. A seemingly innocuous comment I made inadvertently offended both of my cellmates, with Dawit's reaction seemingly stemming from a deep-seated sense of inferiority.

The conflict ignited from my comment: "The food appears to be untouched and well-handled. It shouldn't spoil so quickly." Despite my assessment that the food was still edible after a quick inspection, Assefa remained adamant that it had gone bad. After a brief examination, I concluded otherwise.

Expressing my frustration, I urged Assefa not to waste the effort his family had made in bringing him food. "Your family went through the trouble of sending this to you. It would be a shame to throw it away. I'll gladly eat it." Assefa's response was abrupt, asserting his right to do as he pleased with his food. I retorted, highlighting the myriad of challenges faced by our community and the need to avoid unnecessary waste.

Unbeknownst to me, my remarks struck a chord with Dawit, who interpreted them as a personal attack. He sulked as if I had branded him a pauper. In a fit of anger, Dawit flung open his suitcase, hurling its contents – clothes and a pair of shoes – in my direction. These were items I had requested my family to bring for him in exchange for the favour of lending me his worn-out trainers. Assefa fell silent, sensing the escalating tension.

Seeking to defuse the situation, I quickly apologised to Dawit and helped him gather the items he had thrown, urging him to stow them away.

Communicating freely with my fellow inmates proved challenging. Having witnessed the endless disposal of food in Europe, where wastage held little consequence, I couldn't help but feel disheartened. Now, here I was in prison, embroiled in a conflict while attempting to persuade Assefa not to discard meals that many in Ethiopia desperately needed.

In the UK, the staggering amount of food discarded past its sell-by date by major supermarkets was appalling. Even more shocking was the quantity of food purchased but left uneaten. I was appalled to learn that the annual cost of food waste disposal in England exceeded the yearly budget of the entire Ethiopian government. These memories flooded my mind as I argued with Assefa, consumed by anger.

The vast disparity between the UK economies and Ethiopia's profound impoverishment was glaring. Abject poverty was a harsh reality in Ethiopia, starkly contrasting with the wasteful practices I had witnessed in Europe. It felt absurd that I had returned from England, where food wastage is common, to get into an argument with my cellmate, who should have been more reserved in throwing away good food. I was astounded that my fellow inmate stood his ground against me on this matter.

Following the food crisis, my relationship with Assefa and Dawit headed for deterioration despite my efforts. Assefa started complaining that the food prepared by my family was making him sick. Up until then, despite everything, we shared the food brought by our visiting family members. However, if Assefa wasn't interested in eating food from my family, I couldn't share his either, even if I didn't mind. Dawit had no problem; nobody brought him anything, and he was happy to eat whatever was brought to us.

After a while, Dawit sided with me and continued sharing food with me, severing whatever link he had with Assefa. It became clear that it was only a matter of time before the tension in our prison escalated to a dangerous proportion.

I had Assefa bring in a chessboard he kept in his previous cell, expecting a board game to give us a good pastime. However, it turned out that Assefa couldn't play; he was not a chess player at all. Dawit was a bit better. Nevertheless, I encouraged Assefa to try, and soon, he caught up with Dawit and began challenging him.

Initially, Assefa was the underdog, and naturally, I wanted him to win against Dawit. However, my actions upset Dawit. "I will not play with Assefa," he announced. Assefa reciprocated by saying he had no desire to play with Dawit as well. I told them both that I cannot always play against each one of them and suggested that testing their competence against each other would be more appropriate than playing against me, given the predictable outcome.

When I was transferred to Kaliti, the prison attendants allowed me to keep the electric shaver taken away with my hand luggage at the time of my abduction in Sana'a. They used it to trim my hair when I was in solitary confinement. In Kaliti, I used the shaver to keep Assefa and Dawit's hair in control. I stopped when our disagreements escalated. I knew if they requested, they could be taken out for a hair trim by the prison barber.

In the same way, they were taken out to the prison clinic and the hospital when they got ill. That was my excuse. I told them to use their outing to gather information about the outside world. And then we stopped exercising together and eating within proximity of one another.

I began to recall how much I craved to come out of solitary confinement and share cells with inmates. Before long I found myself isolated amongst the two inmates that shared my cell. In some ways, the situation I found myself in was worse.

To spend twenty-four hours in the same cell with two human beings, not exchanging a word for days, was very painful. I kept myself to myself. I had no issues with the other two. But once my moderating influence was removed from our group, the nagging and the bitching between Asefa and Dawit rose up.

Chapter XIX: Bust up Gestas and Dismas

Even after my transfer to an official prison, the authorities were adamant about controlling the flow of information both about me and to me. This not only affected my access to information but also curtailed the rights that my fellow inmates used to enjoy in another part of the prison.

Assefa frequently lectured me, emphasising the importance of adhering to the prison's rules and regulations whenever I encouraged him and Dawit to assert their rights. He reassured me that I could confidently speak up, hinting at the support I might receive from the British government due to my citizenship. "You can exercise your rights, but remember, they hold the power to act as they see fit with us; we're left without assistance," Assefa lamented.

One early morning, I was taken aback to see Assefa scaling the lone tree in our yard. Lying on my bed, I watched him through the slightly ajar door, unnoticed by Assefa, who was alone for his scheduled exercise in the yard. Dawit lay in his bed beside me, and I turned to him, asking, "What do you suppose Assefa is up to?"

When Dawit approached the door to observe, he witnessed Assefa dangling a twig with a sheet of paper attached to it towards a crack in the joint of the neighbouring women's prison tin wall. Seizing the opportunity to retaliate against Assefa, Dawit hurriedly shouted to the security guards stationed on the tower, "Assefa is violating the rules! Alert the prison administrators. I refuse to be implicated in his misconduct."

The guard at the tower disregarded Dawit's outcry. One possible reason for this could have been that both Assefa and the security guard shared an Oromo ethnic background. Additionally, Dawit's act of informing on another inmate might have been viewed unfavourably by the security guard, as it was unusual for one prisoner to "snitch" on another.

However, other security guards nearby overheard Dawit's outcry and intervened, eventually reporting the issue to the administration.

Major Berhane arrived, and Dawit provided his account of what he had witnessed. Assefa denied the allegations, prompting Dawit to ask for my testimony. I found myself in a difficult position.

I hadn't anticipated the situation escalating to this extent, and I regretted drawing Dawit's attention to Assefa's actions. I struggled with the moral dilemma of either lying or testifying against another prisoner. However, my body language betrayed my reluctance.

Major Berhane inferred Dawit's honesty from my demeanour. As a result, Berhane reprimanded Assefa and departed, leaving us all embroiled in unnecessary turmoil. Berhane's reaction to Assefa's actions surprised me, further fueling my suspicion that the prison authorities might have deliberately planted my fellow inmates.

Dawit was incensed by the perceived leniency towards Assefa. To him, this leniency served as confirmation of his suspicions that Assefa was collaborating with the state. Dawit seized upon this incident as further evidence to support his earlier assertions that Assefa was a spy.

I kept mostly to myself, engaging in solitary activities like reading and exercising. One morning, just before dawn, I was stirred from sleep by a disturbance. The front door remained closed, yet Assefa had already begun exercising in the corridor.

"Why not wait until the door opens? Some of us are still trying to sleep, and you're kicking up dust from the corridor," I called out. But my words fell on deaf ears. It seemed like conceding to my suggestion would be admitting defeat for my fellow inmates, who were always quick to challenge any suggestion I made for our collective benefit.

"It's my right," both Assefa and Dawit snapped back, their expressions dripping with condescension. Ignoring my protest, Assefa continued his exercises, raising dust as he went.

As he carried on, Assefa opened the window of our cell from the outside, directly above where he and Dawit slept. Dawit, visibly irritated, got up, walked out to the corridor and silently closed the window. This seemed to aggravate Assefa. While I couldn't see everything clearly from where I was, I overheard Dawit speaking, his voice tinged with anger and emotion.

"You attacked me from behind like a coward," Dawit accused.

It's uncertain whether Assefa had indeed struck Dawit after the window was closed or if he had attacked him from behind, as the former claimed. Nonetheless, a heated altercation ensued.

I rushed out of bed and attempted to intervene. Assefa had Dawit in a stranglehold, while Dawit had a tight grip on Assefa's groin area. Their twisted and erratic actions made it difficult for me to separate them. Desperate, I reached up to the barred windows and screamed for the security guards in the tower.

"They're killing each other!" I cried out in desperation.

The guards swiftly scaled the outer fence and entered our yard but were unable to access our cell without a key. They shouted from outside, urging Assefa and Dawit to cease their fight, but their efforts proved futile.

Struggling against their violence, I managed to momentarily separate them apart. Dawit then retrieved a wooden broom from the toilet and attempted to strike Assefa with it. I intervened once more, but Dawit's swing missed Assefa and hit the wall, causing the broomstick to snap in half. Seizing the broken piece, Assefa retaliated, and they began viciously attacking each other with the broken sticks.

It was clear that Dawit was at a disadvantage, and I feared for his life. With great effort, I managed to wrestle the broken broomsticks away from them. They loosened their grip to free their hands, holding the sticks and engaging in a physical struggle, which allowed me to discard the weapons. However, when I returned, Assefa had his hand firmly wrapped around Dawit's neck, choking him.

Struggling to separate them once more, I succeeded in freeing Dawit, who retreated to the toilet in search of another weapon. I locked him in from the outside and positioned myself in front of the door, preventing Assefa from pursuing him, while I waited for Major Berhane to unlock the front door.

Eventually, Major Berhane arrived with the key, allowing Dawit to emerge from the toilet, still determined to continue the fight. Now, with the help of the other wards it was easy for Berhane to control Dawit and Assefa.

It became apparent that the two couldn't coexist in the same cell. Consequently, Berhane made the decision to remove Dawit and his belongings from our cell. Despite my repeated attempts to explain that Assefa had instigated the altercation, my words fell on deaf ears. Dawit was subjected to punishment, being transferred to a dilapidated cell within the same compound, devoid of basic amenities like a toilet or running water.

Life didn't become any easier after Dawit's removal. It was deemed too risky for Assefa and Dawit to have any interaction, so whenever Dawit ventured out of his cell, I found myself locked in with Assefa. Dawit's makeshift toilet consisted of a plastic container emptied into our shared toilet each morning.

However, Dawit also needed access to wash his dishes, use the bathroom, and take a shower, prompting the guards to station themselves outside our cell to prevent any contact between him and Assefa.

Turning my focus back to solitary pursuits, I delved into Sudoku and chess books for entertainment. It was during this period that I began to devote long hours to light sporting activities.

I couldn't shake off the disappointment and sense of injustice regarding Dawit's punishment. While he was allowed occasional outings, the majority of his time was spent confined to his cell. I couldn't comprehend why the authorities chose to subject him to such torment when they could have easily transferred him to another prison zone. Assefa and Dawit seemed to have a better grasp of the situation right from the start.

"We won't leave this place until you're released," Assefa and Dawit declared solemnly. "Because if we do, we might end up discussing you, and that's something the authorities won't risk." They made it clear that the only scenarios in which they would be allowed to leave were if I were released, if I died, or if they perished themselves.

In contrast to the conditions they endured at our shared prison yard, other prison zones offered amenities like cable TV, shops, cafes, and recreational activities such as table tennis, handball, soccer, and baseball. Dawit and Assefa shared these details with me, highlighting the stark contrast in their experiences.

Kaliti Prison accommodated a diverse array of inmates who formed bonds and enjoyed certain privileges such as haircuts, medical treatment, and visits from loved ones. However, Assefa and Dawit were stripped of these rights due to the sharing of a cell with me, exacerbating Dawit's already challenging situation.

Despite the tension between them, I managed to communicate with Dawit through the barred window, offering him solace by teaching him Sudoku, sharing some of my sodoku books, and occasionally sharing meals prepared by my family. However, I knew that Assefa didn't approve of the attention I gave Dawit.

Chapter XL: Ethnic Extremism Kaliti Prison

Ethnic-based dynamics permeated various aspects of prison life, a stark reality that became evident during my confinement in an undisclosed facility under the TPLF dictatorship, characterized by Ethnic Tigrayan rule. This pattern persisted even after my transfer to an official federal prison.

TPLF supporters and other Zeregna/Ethno fascists vehemently deny the existence of Zeregnanet in our country, arguing that Ethiopia lacks the typical notion of racism based on skin colour. Instead, they pivot the debate to the Amharic word "zer," which they prefer to translate to "race." They insist on defining "zer" through the English lens of racism, a perplexing approach that disregards distinct contextual differences.

In Ethiopian culture, inquiries about one's "Zer" are rooted in curiosity about familial lineage, geographic origin, and ethnic identity rather than skin colour. Despite this, certain ethnic intellectuals deliberately attempt to equate "Zer" with race, perpetuating a misrepresentation that aligns more with English definitions.

I define a Zeregna (Ethno-Fascist) person as one who excessively identifies with a clan, tribe, ancestry, or Ethnic group for personal gain or to inflict harm on others. Ethnic politics in Ethiopia revolves around classifying and organising people based on their ethnic background, overshadowing traditional definitions of politics centred on citizen-government affairs.

The term "nation" is often associated with cultural, linguistic, and geographical attributes, distinct from the divisive connotations of ethnicity. However, in Ethiopia, ethnicity is elevated to the status of nationhood and has become the predominant political organising principle, sidelining the traditional notion of citizenship and government affairs.

Ethiopia's political landscape remains deeply entrenched in ethnic divisions, perpetuating social and political segregation. This pattern is exacerbated by the TPLF's rural origins, where ethnicity has more relevance than citizenship, which shaped their perception of politics and governance, influencing the country's political trajectory.

In my solitary confinement, Zeregnaet manifested in various forms, influencing the composition of my custodial staff and their treatment of me. The TPLF's top security officials, all Tigrinya speakers, meticulously controlled my interactions, limiting access to individuals who shared their ethnic backgrounds.

Zeregnanet (blind attachment to ethnic affiliations) also facilitated privilege and power within the prison system, as evidenced by the lavish lifestyles of the security guards tasked with overseeing me. They flaunted their wealth and enjoyed extravagant perks, underscoring the inherent disparities perpetuated by ethnic-based discrimination.

The unique dynamics of Zeregnanet in Kaliti prison further underscored the ethnic divide, with Tigrinya speakers dominating key positions of authority. Trust was exclusively reserved for individuals of the same ethnic background, leading to a heightened sense of segregation and suspicion.

In Kaliti, only two people were allowed to hold the keys to my cell. These individuals also provided a food delivery service for Dawit and Assefa's breakfast, lunch, and dinners.

According to prison rules, Dawit and Assefa should have collected their meals from the designated providers, but that meant risking information leaks to the canteen staff. Two police officers were explicitly assigned to oversee my family visits for three consecutive years in Kality prison—both from Tigray.

The people high up in authority did not trust anyone, not even the prison administration. Therefore, they never left spare keys to our compound or our prison cell at the administration office or anywhere else. The assigned Tigrayan officers, Brehane and Berihou, carried them home and to bed.

Staff from other ethnic backgrounds were not considered trustworthy. If a fire broke out in the night, Dawit, Assefa, and I would be at risk before the key holders were awakened from their beds in their private residences and arrived on time to open the door for rescuers.

In conclusion, I want to emphasise that while the majority of those assigned to guard me during solitary confinement and later in Kaliti were Tigrayans, it's essential to acknowledge that not all of them were inherently evil. Human nature does not dictate such absolutes. Throughout my experiences, I encountered individuals who were both kind and compassionate, as well as those who were cruel and wicked. However, the fundamental issue of a state bedevilled with ethnic apartheid remains unchanged.

How can a government composed predominantly of one ethnic group in a country with over 85 diverse ethnicities be anything other than a Zeregna government? Engaging in linguistic acrobatics to redefine the political system does not alter its fundamental nature—an inherently flawed and unjust political system.

Chapter XLI: Chaotic Dreams and Nightmares

Before my experience in prison, I rarely had dreams or nightmares. I didn't ponder much on the distinction between the two; having them a few times a year was my norm. However, in the early days of my abduction, sleep was a luxury I couldn't afford. The discomfort caused by the handcuffs on my hands and shoulders had a single destination — driving one to madness. When the handcuffs were finally removed, and I could start to drift off to sleep, not a single night passed without either a dream or a nightmare.

I came to understand that the occurrence of dreams and nightmares necessitated a minimum condition to be fulfilled: the privilege of sleep without pain. For four consecutive years, my nights were plagued by nightmares, each one continuing until I woke up in the morning. Even if they were momentarily interrupted when I had to get up in the middle of the night for the toilet, they resumed as soon as I returned to bed, akin to a movie resuming after a commercial break.

The variety of my dreams and nightmares was astounding, each one vivid in its own right. I experienced terrifying dreams where extinct dinosaurs relentlessly chased me throughout the night, a surreal scenario unlike any other.

In another instance, I found myself as the sole witness to the sun's energy fading, its last feeble rays extinguishing, plunging the entire planet into a frightening darkness. The only place illuminated was the mouth of the volcanic crater at Dallol, the hottest place on earth located in Eastern Ethiopia.

In my dream, I envisioned people from all races desperately seeking to escape the darkness and cold, migrating towards the Equator where there was still light and warmth. Many perished in their quest for transportation, as only the affluent could afford the limited number of ships to cross the seas and oceans leading to Africa.

The influx of refugees from Europe and Asia into Africa reversed the typical narrative of migration, with Africans now lamenting the inundation of white and yellow flesh.

Africa lacked the resources to erect barriers to stem the flow of refugees, and they arrived en masse, succumbing to starvation and lack of sunlight alongside Africans. Eventually, Ethiopia and its numerous volcanoes became the sole source of warmth, with even those extinguished one by one until only the Dallol volcano remained.

As others gathered around the volcano, they perished one by one, leaving me alone, sitting on the mouth of the volcano, which had diminished to the size of a stool. I basked in its warmth, reminiscent of my great-grandmother covering a red-hot piece of porcelain with her large skirt in winter in my childhood memories.

Contemplating my solitary existence, I questioned my species. Without another like me, could I truly be called human? The revelation that my existence alone gave meaning to the darkness around me was profound. Upon my demise, darkness would cease to exist, highlighting the significance of human presence in giving meaning to darkness itself.

Now I understand the true meaning of "if humans turn their back to it, the world doesn't exist." Without humans, there will be no one to make sense of the world. The idea of the darkness disappearing with my disappearance brought me unbearable pain, compelling me to awaken to the bright sunshine filtering through the cracks and holes in the ceiling of our cell in Addis Ababa.

In one of my dreams, I found myself transported back thousands of years to the time of the ancient Egyptians constructing pyramids. As one of the Jews slaves, I laboured under the weight of flagstones, enduring relentless floggings and harsh orders to hasten my pace. Struggling under the immense burden, the boulder slipped from my back and tumbled down the pyramid's slope, sending me tumbling after it upon receiving an angry kick from the overseer.

In the distance, a mountain loomed, and atop its summit stood Sisyphus from Greek mythology, condemned by the gods to an eternity of rolling an immense boulder uphill, only for it to roll back down on its own weight each time he reached the top. Yet, in my dream, Sisyphus looked down at me with a sense of empathy, whistling the tune of an old EPRP song, "Victory is Ours." He spoke to me, predicting that one day, I would rise against the overseer and seize him by the neck.

My dreams then shifted to centuries-old wars between Ethiopia and the Arabs and Europeans, where I rode atop a golden horse named Worku, given that name for being gold-coloured. I marched at non-stop high speed like the wind amongst hundreds of thousands of horsemen from Nazret (Adama, a place 90 km away from Addis) to Adwa (Battle of Adwa 1896, where Ethiopia defeated Italy) to fight the Italian invaders.

In another surreal sequence, I married a white woman, hoping for the birth of zebra-coloured twins to challenge racial prejudices. However, when the babies came, the community's response was far from acceptance; they cruelly disposed of our multicoloured beautiful children, throwing them on a trash site on the outskirts of town.

Soldiers with machine guns forbade us from picking them up, and my wife and I were forced to watch while stray dogs had a meal of our beautiful Zebra twins. I saw the horrifying scream of my wife, turning the blue sky into dark and bringing it down. I was so scared of being crashed and woke up as I was trying to escape the tumbling down sky.

Further turmoil unfolded in my dreams as Obama, the US president, and Isaias, the Eritrean president, engaged in a heated argument that led to a fistfight on Mount Keren in Eritrea. Obama slipped the precipice of a huge gorge and went down. The US retaliated by raining cruise missiles on the area. I saw the small town of Keren melt as if its buildings were made of butter. Despite the chaos, Isaias emerged unscathed, ascending Mount Keren armed with a folding Kalashnikov rifle.

Amidst these tumultuous dreams, I also experienced poignant moments, spending nights with my ancestors and loved ones, only to witness the tragic demise of the children I left behind, their lives cut short in a harrowing accident. Each night, my nightmares delved into a myriad of unsettling scenarios, leaving me bewildered by the depths of the human brain's capacity to conjure such vivid and tumultuous imagery.

Chapter XLII: A Dream with a Remission: Before the Break

I sat huddled in a corner, marking the passage of thirty long years since my arrest. Time had etched its cruel marks upon me; I was nearing the century mark, my once robust frame now frail and contorted with age. I resembled more a gnarled creature than a human being; my form twisted like that of a giant worm. Upon my head sprouted only seven sparse and wiry hairs, a pitiful testament to the years gone by. My nails, once trim and tidy, had grown into grotesque lengths akin to the cork-pulling twisted metal of a wine bottle opener.

The efforts to secure my release had long since ground to a halt, fading into obscurity like a forgotten dream. Ages had passed since I last received any word about my children. I could only imagine that they, too, had aged and perhaps even had children and grandchildren of their own by now. Or perhaps fate had dealt them a harsher hand, and they were no more. Alone in my thoughts, I delved into every conceivable topic, pondering and philosophizing over the vast expanse of existence. Yet, in the vast tapestry of life, it seemed the world had all but forgotten my existence, leaving me to wither away in the solitude of my confinement.

Lost in contemplation on the cyclical nature of existence, akin to the concept of Groundhog Day, I was startled from my thoughts as the door to my cell creaked open. In strode the short, gentle security guard, a familiar face after our three decades of shared confinement.

The once sturdy stone walls of the prison had metamorphosed into a crude structure of corrugated iron, a stark testament to the passage of time. Anger radiated from the security guys's demeanour as he forcefully kicked the tin wall in frustration, a poignant display of his disillusionment with our shared reality. From my corner, I observed him silently, recognising in him not just a prison guard but a fellow inmate bound by the chains of time and circumstance. "What does it mean? If they had to do it, why didn't they do it earlier?" he muttered. I didn't get it.

"How shall I clothe you? I can't take you wrapped up in a bedsheet," he remarked, his voice tinged with a mix of concern and practicality. I remained silent, observing his movements with a sense of detachment. From a box resting on the ground, he retrieved the Adidas tracksuit his boss had him purchased for me in anticipation of the British Ambassador's visit three decades prior.

"That's better," the short, kind security guard remarked with a hint of satisfaction as he gently helped me into the tracksuit, a simple yet significant gesture of care amidst the bleakness of our circumstances.

He draped the jacket around my hunched form, the fabric hanging loosely like feathers on a misshapen bird. The pants, when pulled up, only accentuated the awkwardness of my gait.

"What to do," muttered the short, kind security guard, adjusting the garments around me with care, though his intentions remained a mystery to me. For three decades, I had not ventured beyond the confines of my room, my existence confined to the space within those walls. Yet, here he was, dressing me as if preparing me for something unknown.

"I'll be back," he assured me as he locked the door behind him and disappeared briefly, his voice mingling with the murmurs of unseen others outside. Through the thin barrier, I caught snatches of his conversation.

"We've been instructed to guard him, not to hand him over. We will never separate. He will remain in our control even if he leaves," he declared firmly, his resolve unwavering.

Moments later, the door creaked open once more, revealing the guard holding a pair of old slippers; their once vibrant colours faded over time. He dusted them off and gestured for me to put them on, their size a comical mismatch for my aged feet. With his support, I complied, sliding my feet into the worn shoes.

With a gentle hand to steady me, the guard guided me out into the unknown, marking the beginning of a journey shrouded in uncertainty yet tinged with a glimmer of hope.

For the first time in three decades, I lifted my eyes to behold the vast expanse of the sky, the sun casting its golden rays upon my age-worn face. The touch of the wind, crisp and invigorating, sent shivers down my spine as I stepped into the courtyard, greeted by the sight of a magnificent chariot adorned with shimmering elegance.

Four majestic horses stood regally before me, their sleek coats glistening as if bathed in butter, their noble presence commanding respect. With a grace that belied their strength, they swatted away pesky mosquitoes with their tails, a display of their unyielding pride.

The charioteer, dressed in a formal black suit and pristine white shirt, sported a black bicorne hat atop his head, his hands clad in elegant white gloves as he held the reins with precision and control. Surrounding the chariot were four men clad in uniforms reminiscent of a bygone era, their attire a symphony of white tights, red morning coats, and braided collars peeking through the openings in their coats.

Their black bicorne hats, reminiscent of those worn by French Emperor Napoleon, added an air of regal authority to their presence, while their hands, too, were enveloped in gloves as white as milk. Together, they formed a tableau of splendour and grandeur, a vision from a time long past yet vividly alive before me.

As the charioteer swung open the door, my security guard and I stepped inside, greeted by the opulent interior of the chariot. Two of the four uniformed men took their positions in the front seats while the remaining two balanced themselves with practised ease on the handrails to the left and right.

With a gentle lurch, the chariot began its journey, gliding effortlessly through streets that seemed both unfamiliar and yet strangely reminiscent of home. Wide avenues stretched before us, flanked by verdant parks, while the absence of cars lent an air of tranquillity to the bustling cityscape. The buildings, adorned with intricate architectural details, stood as testaments to the passage of time and the evolution of our nation over the past three decades.

Though the streets were sparsely populated, those we passed appeared impeccably groomed and attired, a reflection of the newfound prosperity and order that had swept through our country. I marvelled at the transformation that had taken place during my years of isolation, awestruck by the vibrant tapestry of life unfolding before me.

The chariot moved with a smoothness that belied its equine power, the rhythmic sound of hooves echoing faintly beneath us as we traversed the city streets. Soon, we arrived at a grand square, its cobblestone courtyard flanked by three-story buildings adorned with ornate facades.

Passing through one of the bow-shaped open tunnels that marked the entrance to the courtyard, we entered a bustling hub of activity, the air alive with the hum of conversation and the clatter of hooves against stone. Here, amidst the bustling energy of the city, I felt a sense of anticipation stirring within me, eager to discover what lay ahead in this new chapter of my life.

At this point, still in a sleepy state, I woke up to get to the bathroom.

Chapter XLIII: A Dream with a Remission: After the Break

In a sleepy state, I returned to bed.

The square teemed with activity, bustling with the energy of countless visitors patronising the array of hotels, restaurants, and cafes that lined its perimeter. Tables and chairs spilt out onto the cobblestone pavement, inviting patrons to linger over meals and drinks amidst the lively atmosphere.

On the western edge of the square, a wooden platform commanded the attention of a curious crowd; their eyes fixated on the approaching chariot as it made its grand entrance. As the chariot came to a halt, excitement rippled through the courtyard, with spectators eager to catch a glimpse of its occupants.

Anticipating the fervour of the crowd, organizers had erected temporary metal fencing to maintain order and safety. As the chariot parked in a designated spot within the fenced area, a throng of onlookers gathered, their curiosity piqued yet restrained by the barrier.

With the chariot secured, my security guard assisted me in alighting from the carriage, guiding me toward the wooden platform with gentle care. As I ascended the steps, one of the white-gloved charioteers instructed us to stop, positioning us at the centre of attention.

Confused by the commotion and the significance of our presence, I turned to the guard nearest to me and inquired about the gathering.

"What are all these people doing here? Why have we come to this place?" I questioned, seeking clarity amidst the spectacle unfolding around us.

"These folks thrive on curiosity and gossip. They've gathered here for that very purpose. Even government employees have abandoned their posts to join in the chatter. Business has ground to a halt," the guard explained with a hint of resignation.

Perplexed by his response, I pressed further, seeking to understand the nature of the curiosity and gossip that had captivated the crowd.

"And what, pray tell, is the subject of their curiosity?" I inquired.

"It's not worth discussing," he replied cryptically, his words tinged with a sense of caution.

As the minutes passed, the crowd swelled in size, spilling over into every available space within the courtyard. Even the rooftops of surrounding buildings became perches for eager spectators, their faces alight with anticipation and excitement. The atmosphere buzzed with festivity as people indulged in food, drink, and laughter, spanning generations from the elderly to the youngest children.

Surveying the scene before me, I found myself drawn into the illusion that this gathering awaited the arrival of a renowned singer poised to deliver a captivating performance. The majority of those present were Ethiopian, yet a significant number conversed in various European languages, their diverse backgrounds adding to the tapestry of voices that filled the air.

Parents chatted with their children in foreign tongues, a reminder of the multiculturalism that permeated our society. Memories of conversing with my children in English flooded my mind, a language now distant and faded.

Standing upon the stage, I struggled to maintain my composure, the weight of old age bearing down heavily upon me. My legs trembled with fatigue, threatening to give way beneath me. Sensing my distress, the guard who travelled with me implored the organizers for leniency.

"Oh, please, have mercy. He cannot stand much longer. We must provide him with a seat," the guard pleaded.

"It's the rule; he must remain standing," came the steadfast reply from the organizers, unmoved by the plea.

Before me, a young boy caught my eye, engrossed in conversation in German with his parents as he perched upon a small plastic chair. With determination in his gaze, he rose from his seat and approached the barrier, chair in hand. Gesturing emphatically to one of the men in the bicorne hat, he implored them to grant me the same comfort he enjoyed.

"Give it to him," he urged, his voice cutting through the din of the crowd as he waved his chair up and down the metal fence, a simple yet powerful gesture of compassion. Yet, his plea was met with a stern rebuke from the charioteer, who barked a command for the boy to stand back, his authority brooking no argument.

The child's parents, encouraged by the support of the crowd, confronted the charioteer in German, demanding to know why he had shouted at their son. Their protestations were echoed by others in the audience, each voice raised in their native tongue, creating a cacophony of languages that reverberated throughout the square. The collective outcry was passionate and forceful, urging the charioteer to relent and provide the child's seat to me as a gesture of respect and decency.

Under the mounting pressure of the crowd's demands, the charioteer begrudgingly acquiesced, handing over the chair to me with a grumble of frustration. I sank into the small seat with a sigh of relief, grateful for the respite from standing.

As the clock chimed, signalling the transition from morning to noon, impatience rippled through the crowd, their discontent palpable as they voiced their frustration at the delay.

"Why can't they get on with it so we can finish up and leave?" they grumbled collectively, their words tinged with irritation and impatience.

Lost in my thoughts, I glanced around from my vantage point on the child's seat and noticed a noose dangling ominously from a nearby hanger. A chill ran down my spine as the realisation dawned upon me.

"Who were they planning to hang? Was I brought here to witness an execution thirty years after being kept in prison?" I pondered, my mind racing with apprehension. I couldn't shake the feeling that the intended victim must be someone I knew, for why else would they have brought me here?

Memories of my former comrades flooded my mind, their faces blurred by the passage of time. Some names eluded me, lost to the fog of memory, while others remained vivid in my mind's eye. Yet, in my imagination, they remained frozen in youth, their faces untouched by the ravages of time, a stark contrast to the reality of our aged and weary selves.

As I waited anxiously amidst the murmurs of the crowd, a hushed conversation among the charioteers caught my attention. Their whispers carried through the air, revealing snippets of their discussion as they conferred amongst themselves.

"It's the orders from above. We were just awaiting instructions," one of them murmured into his cell phone, his voice tinged with deference.

"The death sentence was confirmed last week via email. We had prepared for the execution, only to find ourselves in this confusion," another explained to his companions, frustration evident in his tone.

Until that moment, I had not considered the possibility that the noose dangling ominously overhead was meant for me. It had simply blended into the backdrop of my surroundings, overshadowed by the bustle of the crowd and the spectacle unfolding before me. In my complacency, I had forgotten that I was on death row, lulled into a false sense of security by the passage of time.

With a heavy heart, the commander of the chariot turned to the prison guard, acknowledging the mistake that had led us here.

"We have come in error. Let us return," he declared solemnly.

Assisted by my trembling guardian, I rose from the child's seat, my limbs heavy with the weight of realization. Together, we made our way back to the waiting chariot, retracing our steps through the crowd of onlookers.

As we journeyed back to the familiar confines of my prison cell, I couldn't help but feel a sense of relief mingled with sorrow. Before locking the door behind me, the kind, short security guard turned to me with tears in his eyes, a bittersweet smile playing upon his lips.

"Good day," he said softly, his voice choked with emotion.

"Why?" I inquired, puzzled by his sudden display of sentiment.

"Happiness," he replied simply, his tears a testament to the depth of his compassion and the fleeting nature of our shared humanity.

Chapter: XLIV Information and Naughty Crickets

My fellow inmates recounted the evolution of radio usage within the prison walls, tracing its history from a common sight of inmates carrying handheld transistors. Radios were eventually banned following the violent events that followed the national election of 2005. With the prohibition in place, inmates were given a brief window to return their radios to their families. If not they were warned thatthey will be confiscated and repurposed for state revenue—a fate that befell countless devices as families struggled to maintain regular visits, particularly for those serving long-term sentences.

In place of the handheld radios, a centralized prison-wide radio system overseen by the administration emerged. It began to offer controlled access to news and entertainment. Meanwhile, within the confines of Kality prison, satellite TV installations became ubiquitous across all zones and cells, except cells designated for disciplinary purposes. However, the content available was strictly regulated, with approval required for all programming before transmission.

The sourced content for the satellite stations, predominantly emanated from Ethiopian state television, serving as a conduit for government propaganda alongside programming from pro-TPLF domestic broadcasters such as Fana, Walta, EBS, and Kana. Foreign news channels were conspicuously absent from the lineup, reflecting a deliberate censorship of external perspectives.

Interestingly, inmates' content preferences were influenced by gender dynamics, with men gravitating towards English Premier League football broadcasts, while women showed a preference for Kana television soap operas imported from Turkey, meticulously translated and dubbed into the Amharic language.

Within the confines of Kaliti prison. Many mini-media networks thrived under the guidance of handpicked DJs. Mini Media outlets transmit Local radio programs and announcements to all prisoners and sometimes to a particular prisoner.

The prison reverberated with the sounds of music as inmates across all zones tuned in to simultaneous transmissions, creating a cacophony of noise that filled the air. Radio programs, accessible to all inmates, provided a welcome source of entertainment, with the administration imposing minimal restrictions on its usage.

Despite the presence of an old TV connection in our cell, any hope of utilizing it had long been abandoned, and the cables were repurposed for more practical use, serving as makeshift clotheslines for drying laundry. It was evident that the TV and all the connecting equipment were removed specifically on my behalf. The size of the inmates was not the reason, as we knew Andualem and two of his cellmates were provided with a TV.

While there appeared to be no justifiable reason for depriving us of television access, our requests for replacement or repair fell on deaf ears. This left us to rely on tidbits of entertainment gleaned from neighbouring cells, particularly updates on English football matches, much to the delight of an Arsenal fan like myself. Most of these updates came from Andualem's cell, located across the dead-end road leading to the front of our courtyard. Guards stationed on a tower had a clear view of both yards and beyond.

Occasionally, depending on the guard on duty, Andualem and his cellmates would inquire about my well-being. Some guards even took the initiative to relay football results from the other cell to me. However, any attempt to request more substantial information was met with silence. When my cellmates were absent from the courtyard, guards would use sign language to imply that communication between them was risky, suggesting that my cellmates might inform the authorities of any interaction with the guards.

Throughout the day, the sounds of television programs wafted through the thin walls of our courtyard that borders on one side the huge women's cell made from corrugated iron. Their daily transmissions often featured melodramatic domestic dramas filled with mourning and wailing, occasionally interspersed with snippets of news coverage. During such moments, we pressed our ears against the corrugated iron wall, straining to catch every word.

In the evening, we're obligated to tune in to whatever is aired on TV from the confines of our cells. Gripping the metal bars of the corridor windows, we strain to catch the news coming from the women's cell. It's almost a prison mandate that all inmates must listen to the 8:00 PM national television broadcast. We could hear the same eight o'clock news intro melody from far away cells, too.

Occasionally, particularly when something gripping is on the news, we face an unexpected adversary: chirping crickets. Their tiny bodies emit a cacophony that competes with the blaring volume of the television, rendering it nearly impossible to discern the news emanating from the women's cell. It's astounding how such a minuscule creature can disrupt the reception of even the most amplified audio equipment.

In a rare moment of unity during the daytime, my cellmates and I banded together to hunt down and eliminate the pesky crickets whose incessant chirping threatened our precious access to news broadcasts.

Our search and destroy mission took hours, providing us with another way to pass the time. We meticulously inspected every crack and crevice for crickets until we were sure that all had been eradicated. However, no sooner did we eliminate one group than others swiftly took their place.

The captured crickets served as fodder for the lizards that prowled the concrete brick wall bordering one side of the courtyard.

These lizards sought out spots to bask in the sunlight, and our provision of crickets ensured their continued presence, offering a small sense of satisfaction amidst the monotony of prison life.

Despite our attempts to befriend the lizards by offering them crickets as treats, our efforts to domesticate them as potential pets proved futile. While initially approaching us to snatch up the crickets, they quickly retreated to savour their feast at a safe distance from our reach.

One evening, a pivotal moment occurred when the female inmates watched the news with unprecedented silence. Typically, there would be chatter in the background while the news was presented. However, what captured the attention of all the inmates was the nature of the news itself.

The government was visibly upset by a report from foreign media covering the Erecha festival. As the commentator dismissed claims of unrest and highlighted ESAT (Ethiopian Satellite Television) as the source of misinformation, I felt a surge of excitement knowing that ESAT was still operational and continued to broadcast its programs from abroad, challenging the information monopoly of the ruling party in Ethiopia. I understood how the government propaganda machine operated; if there were no issues, it wouldn't have felt the need to deny them.

The events of the following evening hinted at nationwide unrest. Addis TV, a government-owned station, broadcasted news that corroborated the locations identified as hotspots by ESAT, a rival news outlet. This confirmation directly contradicted the previous denials made by the national TV, shedding light on the reality of the situation.

"I find it concerning that the government's dissemination of conflicting information suggests that the situation may be spiralling out of control," I remarked. It was surprising to me that ESAT was viewed as a thorn in the government's side.

Among the select few well-versed in the genesis of ESAT, I stood. One of the primary goals agreed upon by the leadership of the Ginbot 7 movement was to dismantle the TPLF-led regime's stranglehold on media monopolization. Various avenues were explored until the idea of a satellite TV channel based in London emerged. The proposal initially faced significant resistance during discussions within the executive body.

"We can't bear the monthly satellite expenses. How do we fill a 24-hour satellite channel? Developing programs will entail additional costs. Relying solely on free imported content isn't sustainable," voiced many dissenting opinions.

The inception of ESAT stemmed from the minds of three friends residing in London: Girum Yilma, Teddy, and Zelalem. Girum, a member of the Ginbot 7 organisation with whom I shared a close bond, approached me first with the concept of ESAT. While the task ahead seemed daunting, it didn't seem insurmountable to me.

"Provide me with a project proposal that I can present to the Ginbot 7 executive group," I requested.

Girum diligently drafted and submitted the proposal. After extensive deliberation, the Ginbot 7 executive group sanctioned a budget to support the establishment of the television satellite channel.

The executive body wasted no time; on the same day it greenlit the budget, ESAT was established as an editorially independent TV channel committed to steering clear of political propaganda. Abebe Bogale, the Deputy Chairman of Ginbot 7 based in Belgium, was entrusted with legal responsibilities for its inception.

ESAT officially came into being in Amsterdam, with Abebe leading the charge alongside a dedicated team. However, not everyone remained onboard due to instances of management misconduct, leading to early departures.

I couldn't forget the sacrifices made by individuals like Girum, Abiy, and Dereje, who journeyed from London to Amsterdam to contribute. Journalist Fassil Yenealem and ESAT editor Zelalem, hailing from Amsterdam and Belgium, respectively, spent months sleeping on the studio floor in Europe. They subsisted on banana sandwiches as they tirelessly prepared for the launch of ESAT's transmissions.

When Ethiopian TV began citing the same information from ESAT that it had previously condemned, I found solace in knowing that the sacrifices made by Ethiopians worldwide to support and bolster ESAT had not been in vain. Despite the TPLF's ban on television in my cell, our determination to stay abreast of major domestic news from the women's prison wing remained steadfast despite occasional disruptions from the chirping crickets.

Operating during the daytime, our prison's mini media network commenced at 6:00 in the morning and concluded at 5:30 in the late afternoon.

The day would typically start with a headcount for all prisoners, who were instructed to assemble in their respective courtyard areas to be counted. However, our cell was an exception; we didn't participate in the courtyard headcount. With only three inmates in our cell compared to others with over a hundred and with the anticipation that I would refuse to leave my cell for the count, the guards sometimes conducted the count while we were still in our beds.

A police officer from the watchtower, accompanied by a loyal TPLF officer who had access to our cell, would enter and count the three of us before leaving.

Following the headcount, food managers distributed breakfast, and announcements were made regarding inmates scheduled for court appearances or medical visits.

The morning progressed with announcements for family visits, although not all prisoners were eager to receive visitors. When inmates refused visits, the announcer would plead with them over the public address system, often relaying messages from disappointed family members.

Lunch was served after visiting hours, and inmates were summoned back to their cells to eat. Music filled the afternoon air until around four o'clock when the last announcement, including names of inmates scheduled for court or hospital visits the following day, was made.

The variety of music played through the mini media was surprising, ranging from English and Arabic songs to domestic hits like Teddy Afro's "Yastesereyal" (Atonement), which rarely aired on state media. There were no restrictions against Eritrean musician Korchach, whose song "Adey, Adey" (My Country) resonated throughout Kality prison.

Every day, the final announcement from the mini media was associated with a person named Solomon Bayessa. "Solomon Bayessa, you have medicine to take; please come out with water urgently." Though I didn't know Solomon Bayessa or his whereabouts, that closing announcement remains etched in my memory, serving as a poignant reminder of life within Kality prison.

Chapter: XLV: Life in Other Parts of the Prison

I gleaned insights into other prisoners by observing the history and behaviours of my fellow inmates, along with the anecdotes they exchanged about others. Additionally, I occasionally overheard conversations among neighbouring inmates.

I was advised that "prison" was considered an outdated term and that the appropriate designation for the institution was a correctional facility. In Amharic, this translates to "Maremia Bet". The inmates are now referred to as Tarami, which translates to "in need of correction." It sounded like a cruel irony, considering Kality prison offered little in the way of actual correctional measures.

My fellow inmates had been convicted of murder and sentenced to death, yet they exhibited no signs of remorse; instead, they spoke of their crimes with pride, almost as if they were recounting a thrilling adventure. Despite spending over a decade in prison, they had received no psychological support or opportunities for self-development.

Furthermore, the convicts had not received any skills training during their time in the so-called "correctional" facility. This lack of intervention allowed them to believe that after a total of 20 years, they would be pardoned from their life sentences. They hoped to reintegrate into society without remorse or any marketable skills. It was clear that there was no real effort towards correction in this prison, and the inmates themselves seemed resistant to any form of rehabilitation.

I heard disturbing accounts of savage crimes committed by inmates. One particularly chilling tale involved a group of inmates who consumed the liver of the man they had murdered as a macabre display of loyalty to each other. Additionally, there were reports of individuals who, upon completing their entire prison sentence, returned to society only to commit further acts of violence, including murder.

Rather than fostering rehabilitation, the prison environment seemed to cultivate and reinforce behaviours such as cheating, stealing, lying, and instigating conflict. Moreover, both male and female inmates exhibited aggressive and predatory sexual tendencies, and the brutality they displayed towards each other during moments of conflict was deeply disturbing. To me, this was a sign of further brutalization rather than correction.

Furthermore, inmates formed deceitful alliances with law enforcement officers, engaging in the smuggling of contraband such as cigarettes, hashish, and various drugs. This illicit trade resulted in substantial profits, amounting to millions of dollars, for both corrupt police officers and prisoners alike.

Despite a ban on smoking in the prison, cigarettes found their way into the cells, commanding a hefty price of 20 Birr per cigarette.

A pack of cigarettes that can be bought for 20 Birr on the outside fetched 400 Birr on the black market within the prison walls. Many well-regarded prison staff and inmates were involved in the lucrative cigarette trade, with members of the TPLF (Tigray People's Liberation Front) garnering a particularly favourable reputation in this illicit business.

Additionally, contraband items such as alcohol, cell phones, drugs, and various other goods were smuggled into the prison, primarily facilitated by Tigrayan officers loyal to the ruling party. Wealthier inmates, with financial resources and assistance from corrupt police officers, exploited health-related excuses to temporarily leave detention and satisfy their insatiable sexual desires with spouses, partners, lovers or prostitutes outside of the prison confines.

The prison was severely overcrowded, and the quality of food provided was abysmal, with a daily budget per prisoner not exceeding Birr 7.50, equivalent to then 50 US cents. Upon my arrival, I was appalled by the deplorable quality of the bread and injera, which were riddled with grit, and the wot was unidentifiable, tasting only of something salty, not with the consistency of what it should be chickpea, but runny porridge.

Furthermore, the institution's ability to provide meaningful training opportunities for prisoners was severely lacking. With ample time on their hands, inmates often harboured feelings of bitterness and resentment towards both the prison system and the broader community. It was truly disgraceful to label the prison as a correctional institution and its inhabitants as candidates for correction.

Through indirect interactions with women in neighbouring cells and information gleaned from the detention centre housing disruptive prisoners in solitary confinement, I gained further insights into prison life. The women's prison failed to adequately address the needs of those who had a mental illness, leading to distressing scenes of weeping and murmured laments that echoed day and night, painting a poignant picture of their suffering.

The sounds of women groaning in pain throughout the day and night, along with persistent coughing that seemed to strain their chests, created an atmosphere of unbearable suffering within the prison walls. The heart-wrenching cries of those mourning the loss of loved ones - whether it be the death of a mother, father, or child - only added to the overwhelming sense of grief that permeated the air.

The painful experience of receiving news of a loved one's passing while in incarceration is incomprehensible to those who have not endured it. The agony of being unable to attend the funeral, to say a final goodbye, or to witness a loved one's face one last time before they are laid to rest is a grief that knows no bounds.

As I empathized with my fellow inmates and imagined the pain of losing my own family members, I gained a profound appreciation for the depth of their sorrow. Yet, amidst the mourning, the women's prison also witnessed moments of joy and camaraderie, particularly during seasonal festivities. The barn echoed with songs, laughter, and dancing as the women celebrated Christian and Islamic holidays, their prayers and hymns reflecting their unwavering faith.

In contrast, the nearby detention centre reserved for temporary male inmates imposed strict limitations on their movements during the day. Their longing for freedom was palpable as they eagerly awaited any opportunity to catch a glimpse of the outside world, banging on doors in desperate attempts to summon the police and secure their release.

Prisoners in the detention centre would stage scenes of urgency, shouting about a fellow inmate's imminent demise or fabricating quarrels that escalated into what appeared to be violent altercations. They would bang on the doors, feigning distress and calling for help by using the term "Abal," referring to ordinary police officers.

The term "Abal" was introduced during the time of Meles Zenawi, when British influence led to the adoption of English ranks within the Ethiopian police force. However, the use of "Abal" as a slang term for "Constable" in Amharic was not widely accepted or recognized, and other police rankings were similarly unfamiliar and rarely used in everyday language.

Like us, these inmates lacked access to television, and they spent their evenings singing, sometimes resorting to religious songs when needed. Their interactions with female prisoners often involved calling out their names and making silly remarks.

Interestingly, these inmates tended to make the most noise around the time of the evening news, perhaps in an attempt to dissuade others, including women, from listening to the program. However, their noisy behaviour also disrupted our own attempts to listen to the news. These moments served as a test of our shared humanity, seeing both the disruptive inmates and the crickets as part of the same environment.

Chapter XLVI: The Thing About Justice

Gone are the days when a simple declaration like "Freeze in the name of the God of justice" could halt a wrongdoer. The seizure of power by godless rulers ended that era.

Similarly, invoking the symbolism of the flag used to carry significant weight. A call like "Stop, in the name of the flag that many have sacrificed their lives for" commanded respect and compliance. However, over time, the flag lost its symbolic power. It became regarded as nothing more than a piece of cloth. Those who reduced the flag to a meaningless rag and informed the public of their discovery were another set of rulers.

The authority once wielded by invoking the name of Emperor Haile Selassie to maintain law and order also diminished significantly following his brutal regicidal overthrow.

The absence of revered leaders and the declining impact of moral and religious teachings, which underscored principles of justice and fairness under the spectre of divine retribution, further exacerbated a societal erosion of accountability, particularly during the communist regime era.

In this changing landscape, traditional methods of invoking authority and enforcing ethical conduct lost their efficacy, and the mechanisms once relied upon to uphold justice and fairness became increasingly obsolete.

The erosion of the ideal of justice by successive governments has led to a degraded judicial system in Ethiopia.

Throughout Ethiopia's long history, access to justice has never been easy or affordable for many citizens, particularly those who are economically disadvantaged. The system has been marred by wastefulness, corruption fueled by bribery and nepotism, and a lack of empathy. Countless Ethiopians have mourned the decay and loss of justice over the years, but the current state of affairs has left citizens more disillusioned than ever before.

In the past, despite the cumbersome and frustrating process of seeking justice, there was still a sense of faith in the justice system. It was commonly believed that even if it took time or money, one could eventually appeal to higher courts or seek justice from the emperor himself at the court of the crown. However, that sentiment has all but disappeared.

Even during the rules of the military, which was notorious for confiscating private wealth, arbitrary arrests, and killings, the courts were not abused in the same manner as they are in the hands of TPLF. The Derg (a different name for the Junta) never used the courts to legitimize its actions; instead, decisions were often made through political means rather than through the judicial process.

While many members of the Ethiopian People's Revolutionary Party (EPRP) were summarily executed by political decisions, many more survived, for their case was taken to the courts. For example, my brother survived the Red Terror era because his case went to court, resulting in a five-year prison sentence. Some of the Generals accused of plotting a coup d'état at the end of the Derg's rule survived, too, because their cases were seen by the courts without the direct interference of the political leadership.

However, the politicisation of the courts during the reign of the Tigray People's Liberation Front (TPLF) was unprecedented. The TPLF's disregard for the judiciary represents the biggest blow to justice in Ethiopia.

Numerous horror stories circulated within Kality prison, where individuals were arbitrarily thrown behind bars, devoid of trial, often enduring a decade-long confinement. Harsh judgments, fueled by false accusations and testimonies, pervaded the system. Judges openly negotiated bribes in public spaces like cafes and bars, rendering verdicts from these very venues. Justices even abandoned courtrooms to deliberate decisions via cell phone conversations with government officials.

Reflecting on my observations of TPLF leaders in preceding years, it became evident that those culpable for distorting the law included Prime Minister Meles Zenawi and his Henchman Dawit Yohannes.

The justice system devolved into a mockery, with TPLF members initially jesting about it, only to find themselves ensnared within its clutches, becoming subjects of the same ridicule they once entertained. Tamirat Layne, a prime minister of the TPLF era, serves as a prime example, as does Siye Abraha, a former minister of defence and a Tigrayan of Ethnic origin. However, Meles and Dawit, having met premature demises, were spared from the ignominy of being subjected to the justice system they had tarnished.

Under direct government directives, individuals faced false accusations, resulting in severe sentences, including death penalties. Judges affiliated with the ruling party responsible for these cruel judgments exhibited no signs of conscience-induced insomnia. They showed no remorse for the victims of unjust treatment. Each evening, they returned home to serene family dinners with spouses and children, their minds untroubled by the plight of the falsely accused. Among those entangled in the oppressive justice system during my time in Kality prison were Andualem, Eskinder, and Merara Gudina.

Repeatedly, I conveyed to TPLF security personnel that Andualem and Eskinder had no affiliations with the Ginbot 7 movement. This same message was conveyed to British ambassadors and other foreign officials who regularly visited me.

Upon learning of Merara Gudina's (a leader of an opposition party) arrest, I testified, "Merara does not align with violent organizations; he advocates for peaceful struggle. He is cautious and avoids actions that might antagonize the government – he even refrains from accepting interviews with ESAT," I vehemently asserted. "He was falsely accused," I informed visiting foreign government officials. Despite the TPLF security officers being aware of my testimony, it did not deter them from falsely imprisoning political dissenters.

The practices of issuing orders to courts, providing false testimony, fabricating evidence, and exploiting the judiciary and justice system for attacks are not recent innovations by the TPLF. These practices were introduced the day after they assumed power.

The TPLF ruthlessly manipulated the courts, bypassing evidence and political deliberation to detain thousands of former Workers' Party members.

Rather than adhering to the law, the TPLF weaponized the judicial system to criminalize ex-members of the Workers' Party and the former Ethiopian army. Decisions by judges affiliated with the party, not legal statutes, dictated the TPLF's actions. There was no legal basis for the mass arrests orchestrated by the TPLF upon assuming power. Recognizing the dangerous precedent this set, I voiced my opposition to such measures during my brief tenure in the transitional government.

To avoid scrutiny from foreign donors and maintain a façade of democracy for Western allies, the TPLF wielded the courts as instruments of oppression. This tactic was commonly employed to target political and economic adversaries. Before the 2005 election,

Professor Asrat Wodeyes, a medical professional who entered politics to halt the genocidal atrocities against the Amhara people, became a prominent victim of court manipulation. Similarly, after the ill national election of 2005, the courts were utilized to suppress the opposition, mainly CUD (Coalition for Unity and Democracy) supporters, members and leaders, journalists, and human rights activists.

Currently, the incarceration of over one hundred thousand individuals in Kality and other prisons nationwide is widely known. While most inmates were political prisoners, many ordinary criminals languished and perished within the archaic justice system. What is most distressing, however, is the injustice suffered by many who were indicted without due process of law.

I recall a story shared by two fellow inmates about an individual whose name eludes me. Charged with murder, he protested in court, "I did not kill him." Despite his protestations, a false witness fabricated evidence, leading to a guilty verdict and a life sentence. Strangely, no corpse was ever found. Despite his persistent appeals from within the prison, his wrongful arrest was brushed aside, with no one taking his plight seriously. Years passed, and justice remained elusive.

One early morning, the relatives of the prisoner arrived at Kality prison with astonishing news: the man whom he was accused of killing had miraculously returned alive, walking into his own home on his own two legs. They promptly informed the authorities, filled with hope that this revelation would secure his release.

However, freedom from incarceration proved to be a complex process. Despite the presentation of evidence proving his wrongful conviction and the supposed victim's return to life, the path to liberation was not straightforward.

The prisoner was informed that the court could not release someone whose death sentence had been commuted to life imprisonment. The only viable legal recourse was to seek a pardon from the country's President, a daunting prospect for a crime he never committed.

Thus, the man endured additional harsh months behind bars, despite the court's acknowledgement of his innocence, until the President's New Year amnesty provided a glimmer of hope. It was a surreal situation: a victim of false imprisonment and torture, treated as a criminal, forced to seek amnesty instead of receiving compensation from the state. Eventually, his perseverance bore fruit, and he was granted a pardon, finally regaining his freedom.

Nonetheless, my fellow inmates didn't need to labour much to convince me of the existence of a "dead and buried" justice system. Their cases exemplify it vividly. Both admitted to committing murder, but how they were convicted and the events leading to their guilt were shocking.

Assefa, who used a firearm in his crime, managed to conceal the weapon from the police. With no witnesses, law enforcement resorted to introducing a false witness and a pistol to secure a conviction. Assefa argued that even if he hadn't committed the crime, the police and prosecutor possessed the authority to arrest someone under false pretences. Unmoved and unapologetic, he bore the consequences of the charges, which ultimately impacted another individual named Solomon.

Solomon, well into his seventies and hard of hearing, resided in Ambo city and had no prior acquaintance with Assefa. Nonetheless, he was accused in court as Assefa's accomplice, purportedly restraining the victim while Assefa carried out the shooting.

Despite the lack of evidence supporting the accusation, including Solomon's physical absence from the crime scene and genuine alibi witnesses confirming his presence elsewhere, he and Assefa received sentences. Solomon's death sentence was later commuted to life imprisonment. His subsequent shock upon learning of his fate led to his deterioration and eventual demise in prison, a result of calculated revenge by TPLF officials. It was like killing two birds with one stone for the officials, as Solomon was seen as their main economic rival in the area.

Similarly, Dawit confessed to the crime, but the discrepancy in size between the killer and the victim, as well as the small knife used, cast doubt on his ability to commit the murder alone. A partner in crime was found for him to convince the court, despite Dawit's protestations that he acted alone. An innocent man who had no involvement in the crime and suffered from mental incapacity was indicted with the same crime and received a death sentence, later commuted to life imprisonment. This miscarriage of justice is particularly outrageous because it was committed against a person unable to properly defend himself.

The corruption within the legal system isn't solely driven by financial gain or personal favouritism but is rather a systematic encouragement for diligent law enforcement, prosecutors, and judges to manipulate justice guidelines. Performance evaluations prioritise the quantity of criminals apprehended and prosecuted, neglecting the pursuit of true justice.

The reluctance to reverse convictions, even when evidence of innocence emerges, stems from the fear of negative evaluations, resulting in a predisposition to find all accused individuals guilty. It's a disheartening reality.

Chapter XLVII: The Ginbot 7 Special Commando

Something bothered the TPLF, and their actions were difficult to comprehend. Firstly, they restricted my visits peculiarly, allowing only my father to visit, and even then, it was limited to half an hour once a week, specifically on Saturdays.

These restrictions were unprecedented. No other prisoner faced such stringent limitations. The TPLF isolated my father's visits, ensuring that he did not encounter other visitors during his time at the prison. Consequently, I never had the opportunity to meet with my father in the presence of my fellow inmates and their visiting families. As previously mentioned, these visits occurred in the Kality prison administrator's office, and I was transported a short distance, not exceeding 50 meters, to meet with my father there every week.

What baffled me more than the transportation arrangements was the excessive precautions taken. It was customary for an armed soldier to accompany me in the car, as prisoners were not allowed to move without an escort. However, I struggled to understand why they went to great lengths to clear the road of inmates and prison staff during these simple operations.

Saturdays were bustling days at Kality prison, with many prisoners receiving family visits and engaging in financial transactions. I witnessed the chaos firsthand when I was driven around on one Saturday. Male and female prisoners, escorted by soldiers, were busy carrying goods while police officers enjoyed food and coffee at the stalls. This scene was a stark contrast to other days when my passage was meticulously kept clear.

Whenever I moved, I was shielded from the view of other prisoners and police officers until the car made a turn towards the administration office. Berhane, the officer in charge of my transportation, would often have heated exchanges with other police officers who attempted to catch a glimpse of me. Despite Berhane's warnings, some officers persisted in trying to see me, grumbling only after receiving threats.

During our route to the administration office, we passed by a tin shed where female police officers gathered to drink coffee. On one occasion, Berhane remarked on the police officers' behaviour, questioning why they suddenly craved coffee whenever we arrived. The driver, Berhane's fellow countryman, ignorantly responded, citing an incident where a female police officer had greeted me with a salute and how I had reciprocated with a smile. He expressed disbelief that such interactions were allowed in a legal institution.

I shared my observations about the TPLF's precautions during my movements with representatives of the British government. I suggested that they were concerned about the possibility of the Ginbot 7 Special Commando attempting to extract me from Kality prison during these movements. This suggestion elicited anger from the security guard present in our midst.

The precautions extended beyond my movements within the prison. Whenever authorities brought outsiders for repair work in our compound, they instructed us to "go inside," locking us in until the workers completed their job.

Since arriving at Kality, I have faced numerous health problems. Initially, Kaliti Prison doctors were not allowed to see me. A search party was dispatched to find the nurse, Letebrehan, who had looked after me while I was in solitary confinement. Letebrehan was brought to me, and despite being unable to physically examine me in the open, she prescribed medication for my recurring haemorrhoids based on my description of symptoms.

Later, Letebrehan was replaced by a Kality health officer named Asnakech, whose compassion mirrored that of Letebrehan. However, Asnakech was not as assertive and did not insist on privacy when examining me, even in inclement weather.

I suffered from toothaches more than five times during my time at Kality, often resulting in severe facial swelling. Additionally, I experienced pneumonia, cramps, diarrhoea, and recurrent flu-like symptoms. Despite repeatedly requesting to have a bad tooth removed, my pleas went unheard. Medications were not left with me but were kept with the soldiers at the watchtower, who would administer them to me at specific times—morning, lunchtime, and dinner—an unprecedented practice.

Furthermore, when Berhane locked the prison at night, he did so without intending to return until morning, leaving me without access to prescribed painkillers during the night when I needed them most, exacerbating my suffering.

It was inconceivable for TPLF to allow me to have a proper clinic or hospital visit despite my deteriorating health. While my fellow inmates were regularly taken to the prison health clinic, the local health centre outside Kality, and even the Black Lion Hospital in the centre of town for treatment, I was denied this entitlement regardless of the severity of my illness.

Asnakech, my assigned health officer, never suggested I get a check-up elsewhere, despite her authority. Instead, she used a stethoscope and blood pressure gauge for examinations, even outdoors. Despite this odd practice, I couldn't help noticing her beauty each time she tended to my health. Unaware, her beauty unknowingly contributed to my high blood pressure, as the gauge in her hands registered.

Another privilege denied to me by TPLF's strict control was the right to have my hair cut at the prison barber. My shaver had been confiscated upon my detention, and I often wondered if they would have resorted to using a piece of glass to shave my head had I not had my shaver with me.

Initially, I shared my trimmer with Dawit and Assefa, and we took turns giving each other haircuts until conflicts arose between them. Eventually, I encouraged them to request haircuts from Berhane as an excuse to venture outside the confines of our yard. Reluctantly, the prison staff escorted them to other areas within the prison for their haircuts, ensuring they did not divulge any information about me to the barber.

My inmates were always escorted by Captain Berihun or Major Berhane whenever they left the prison grounds for medical treatment or family visits. They never travelled with other inmates in the same vehicle and were often transported to clinics or hospitals in a designated vehicle solely for them.

Even during family visits, Assefa's family had to endure long waits for Berhane to arrive and escort him to them, causing frustration and tears of desperation. Dawit, on the other hand, had very few visitors during the three years he was with me in prison.Yetthe stringent controls were evident even during his limited interactions.

The strict controls imposed by TPLF remain a mystery to me, as they went to great lengths to restrict my interactions and movements, depriving me of basic entitlements and human decency.

Chapter XLVIII: All Forms of Extremism and Reflections on Faith

Kality Prison was a cauldron of religious and tribal extremism. Conversations with fellow inmates revealed that extremism was actively encouraged by the government of TPLF within the prison walls.

At the level of the country, frequent TPLF statements caused friction between the Orthodox Church and other Christian denominations. Sebhat Nega, the chief ideologue of tribalist politics, made toxic media statements suggesting that his party had broken the hold of Amharas and the Orthodox Church on the country.

These type of statements were deliberately crafted to sow division between the people of the north and the south, with the aim of promoting Hailemariam Desalegn, whom the TPLF viewed as a puppet, to the position of prime minister. There was no other purpose than to arouse animosity between Christian denominations.

The TPLF attempted to stir up discord not only between different Christian denominations but also between Christians and Muslims, actively utilizing a policy of division. They interfered in the internal affairs of Muslims, siding with one section against another, causing discord among the faithful.

Similarly to the Crusaders, the TPLF collaborated with Western countries that invaded Muslim countries, as exemplified by the Iraq invasion. The TPLF received orders from the West and became members of the coalition of the willing that invaded Iraq. They were aware that Muslims in our country would be embittered by witnessing the destruction of a Muslim nation and shameful acts inflicted upon Muslims elsewhere.

In Somalia, following Ethiopia's invasion, Colonel Aster (a female code name for male) facilitated Meles' looting by extorting dollars from prosperous Somali merchants and investors. Helicopters were used to transport the money, as one of the pilots informed me, and delivered it to the palace.

Under Meles' oversight, killings of Somalis inside their mosques occurred, with the full knowledge that such actions would enrage Ethiopian Muslims. Meles's actions served no purpose other than to deliberately spread extremism in Ethiopia while garnering support from Western governments under the guise of combating terrorism and prolonging his hold on power.

Despite their efforts, the TPLF did not fully succeed in spreading the level of toxic extremism they had hoped for. Nevertheless, they managed to radicalise individuals from both Christian and Muslim backgrounds, cultivating an audience for extremist ideologies.

In places like Kality, extremism was beginning to take root. The phenomenon of extremist baptisms, seen in prisons worldwide, was also observed in our country. Extremism based on ethnicity and religion was on the rise within prison walls, contributing to the troubling trend.

In the name of religious freedom, the TPLF allowed all religions to do whatever they liked, irrespective of the consequences of their action to the cohesion of the community. Kality Prison was a place where such freedom was allowed. Consequently, the Kaliti mini-media was used to spread religious animosity in the prison. There were three morning broadcasts, conducting services on Thursdays for Orthodox Christians, Fridays for Muslims, and Saturdays for Protestants.

On Thursdays, after the headcount and a call for the catering team to organize the morning meal, the mini-media faith broadcast began with an Orthodox hymn. Fridays started with a Muslim menzuma, and Saturdays featured a Protestant choir. These hymns played in the morning while I exercised. However, I ceased exercising altogether when Muhammad Awel's Menzuma aired on Fridays.

Mohammed Awel's remarkable voice was not the only part of the distraction. His captivating verses differed greatly from those typically praising or beseeching Allah. There was no invocation for divine assistance like "Allah, help me, do this for me."

Instead, his menzuma verses delved into issues that distance a person from Allah and what is considered blessed. They addressed human weakness, malice, and mortality, while his rhythmic voice conveyed a profound message about actions and characteristics that hinder closeness, cooperation, and love. The philosophy of faith conveyed through menzuma was presented in such a profound manner. This musical talent served as a blessing, delivering a beautiful message directly to the soul without the need for instruments.

Muhammad Awel's powerful words resonated deeply:

"When we acknowledge that everything is in the hands of the Creator, What significance does our redemption hold? The remarkable accomplishments of humankind never cease, From the moment of birth to the golden years, driven by worldly passions."

As I listened to his chant, I couldn't help but envision my country's leaders inflicting suffering upon the land and its people for their worldly gains.

"What good can come from harbouring hatred towards a brother? How can one foolishly engage in vanity? Such actions only lead to destruction. In today's world, the true trend is to aid one another, Yet, pride often prevails, accompanied by criticism and gossip. Passing by a brother on the road, with a proud soul, One walks on without uttering a simple greeting."

The verses drew me to the growing selfishness in our country and the evil and deceit that result from it.

These verses echoed in my mind:

"Even brothers turning against one another,

With contempt from the very beginning.

Our actions are so inherently destructive,

The key to this mystery eludes us,

Brothers unable to confide in each other,

The spell that distances us from each other remains elusive."

These words stirred up thoughts of the TPLF's deliberate and unforgettable crime, which tore the country apart along ethnic and religious lines. "Yes, indeed, the spell remains unknown," I muttered to myself.

"Brothers, heed my words of wisdom,

Rebel against the divisive forces,

Embrace love and unity. Do not be swayed by this counsel,

For a nation is strengthened through dialogue."

I couldn't help but ponder whether Muhammad Awel's words were directed at the TPLF, who disregarded such wisdom. "I wish they had the wisdom to heed his message," I quietly reflected.

Nothing in that prison could move me as profoundly as Mohammed Awel's menzuma. Though he never knew of my appreciation, I often whispered to myself, "You've truly served your country well."

Soon enough, I became acutely aware of the religious divisions among the female inmates. Christians of varying denominations engaged in petty arguments, forsaking gratitude and prayer. Fuelled by malice, they competed to sing their hymns the loudest.

The Orthodox adherents resorted to songs of intercession, seemingly aimed at antagonizing their Protestant counterparts who didn't acknowledge the Virgin Mary's intercessory powers.

As for the rest, their hearts' intentions remained known only to the divine. Yet, amidst the discord, many of the male and female inmates persisted in fasting, praying, and engaging with the Bible or the Quran.

Chapter XLIX: Bible Reading and Fasting with Intent

Assefa didn't observe fasting, but he kept a Bible in his possession, diligently reading its contents. On the other hand, Dawit, lacking a Bible, faithfully observed all Christian denomination fasts, including those on Wednesdays and Fridays.

I requested my family to bring me both a Bible and a Quran, but the prison authorities permitted only the Bible due to my Christian affiliation. The Bible I received was my mother's 81-Ahadu large format edition. I delved into its pages, starting from the book of Genesis and proceeding to Revelations, reading it cover to cover three times without skipping a single word. This marked my first encounter with the Bible during my time in prison. Subsequently, I sought out additional books published by the Ethiopian Orthodox Church and immersed myself in their teachings.

I found myself captivated by the 14th-century writings of Abba Giorgis Zegascha, an Ethiopian saint revered and acclaimed by some of the era's foremost philosophers. Through the literature published by the Ethiopian Orthodox Church, I gained a profound appreciation for the antiquity and rich historical legacy of the church, which left a lasting impression on me.

After immersing myself in the Bible, I embarked on participating in the Hudade (Lent) fast, which commemorates Jesus'

40 days of exile. This fasting regime entailed abstaining from both food and water until four o'clock in the afternoon. Additionally, during the holy week of Himamat (Holy Triduum), I extended my fast from Wednesday night until Sunday lunchtime.

To my surprise, I managed to endure the fasting period without succumbing to feelings of fatigue. I undertook fasting as a means to apply some of the lessons gleaned from the teachings of various religions and explore their suggested pathways to both mental and spiritual enlightenment. However, it's possible that I didn't experience the full effects of fasting due to the fast concluding before I could attain such illumination.

Nevertheless, the perspective I cultivated during this time led me to reflect on my generation's shortcomings.

While the Ethiopian people are deeply rooted in religious beliefs, individuals like myself often perceive modernisation as a lifestyle distant from such convictions.

This prompted me to question how we could effectively assist our people when we are so disconnected from their faith. This sentiment echoes the critique made by the Russian literary figure Dostoevsky towards his country's communists, who failed to grasp the religious beliefs of their fellow countrymen. Dostoevsky argued that understanding the beliefs of the Russian people was essential to truly caring about them. This indictment resonates with my generation as well, and it served as the sole revelation I experienced during my fasting period in prison.

The opportunity to delve into spiritual matters presented itself during my time in Kality prison. As I explored these topics, questions arose within me, stirring a sense of alienation.

Among the books I was permitted to bring in was Victor Hugo's Les Miserables, a novel I had previously read at the age of sixteen. Revisiting it once again, I recalled what had resonated with me during my initial reading.

In the book, the devoted Bishop took up residence in a small house to convert the larger building into a treatment centre for the sick. He generously opened his home to the homeless. However, one of the individuals he sheltered repaid his kindness by stealing his silverware and fleeing under the cover of night. The thief was apprehended by the police while attempting to sell the stolen goods and was promptly brought to the Bishop's house.

Upon inspecting the thief's bag, the police revealed the reason for his arrest to the Bishop. In a remarkable display of forgiveness and compassion, the Bishop rose from his seat and handed the thief a seven-branched candlestick, remarking, "Oh, my son, I had also given you this, but you forgot to take it." This act of grace led to the immediate release of the man. This portrayal of a truly 'religious person' left a lasting impression on me, although I had never encountered bishops of such calibre in my country while growing up. Consequently, I maintained a distance from my grandparents' faith and religion.

I found the Bible to be a captivating book replete with profound teachings. Using a pencil, I meticulously underlined every reference to Ethiopia and counted over forty occurrences. Interestingly, it mentioned Syria approximately a thousand times.

What struck me the most was the remarkable overlap between the teachings of the Bible and those of Karl Marx. His principle, as articulated in the Critique of the Gotha Program — "From each according to his ability, to each according to his needs" — bore a striking resemblance to biblical texts.

The apostles established the church by requiring joining members to sell all their possessions and donate the proceeds. I remain uncertain as to when or why this membership requirement was abolished. The sale of possessions enriched the church, enabling it to distribute funds to the needy, as described in Acts 4:32-36.

The apostles established the church based on the principle that individuals would receive only what they needed. For instance, if someone brought in one million dollars but required only 100 dollars for their upkeep, they would receive just that amount. Conversely, if another person brought in ten dollars but needed ten thousand dollars, they would receive the latter amount, as the church had a duty to fulfil its obligation.

This principle aligns with the words of Karl Marx: "From each according to his ability, to each according to his needs." Marx believed that people could achieve this through the development of consciousness obtained from holistic human development. The church asserts that such a level of consciousness is attained only through conscientious submission to Christ.

The Bible explicitly teaches that anyone wishing to join the Christian family must sell all their property and contribute to the church. I emphasise 'strictly' for a significant reason.

In the Bible, Ananias met a tragic end because, after selling his property, he only gave half of the money to the church, concealing the rest under the influence of his wife Sapphira (Acts 5:1-6). Of course, Ananias paid with his life for his folly.

The Bible repeatedly emphasises that the Christian faith regards possessions as akin to sin. "Go sell everything you have and give to the poor, then take up your cross and follow me" (Mark 10:21-22). Furthermore, it states, "It is easier for a camel to go through the eye of a needle than for a rich man to enter the kingdom of God" (Mark 10:25-26).

My grandparents and great-grandparents were Christians. They held a faith that conflicted with the pursuit of personal wealth and possessions. They passed down inheritance not only in the form of houses and land but also in the form of peasants and slaves. While they were followers of the faith, one could argue that they were not leaders in practicing its principles. But the leaders of our church didn't fare better than their laymen.

Anyone can violate the precepts of religion by believing that righteousness is attained not through devotion but solely by the mercy of the Creator. Such a mindset cannot overlook the actions of patriarchs and faith leaders.

As stated in Isaiah No. 3, "The prayer of a vengeful man is like a seed that falls amid thorns. Their spirits remain unbroken, lacking empathy. Sacrificing a lamb in my name is no different from breaking the neck of a dog in my name."

What standard should be used to judge whether a person with a full stomach, adorned in opulent attire, driving a luxury car, and residing in a grand mansion can become a great faith leader? Especially when the country is plagued by hunger, disease, and poverty. It was during my time in Kality that I realized I distanced myself from my grandparents' faith because of this reality. However, simultaneously, I learned to understand and respect the beliefs of my people.

Chapter L: Noise Pollution

Kaliti prison was a raucous place, with noise persisting both day and night. The roar of large jet engines added to the nighttime commotion, competing with inmates' shouts from the urinals and a symphony of snoring and flatulence. The consequences of this din were manifold.

The proximity of Kaliti to Bole Airport suggested that we were directly beneath the flight path, which was especially noticeable as jets began their descent after three in the morning. This contrasted sharply with London's Heathrow Airport, where flights ceased after midnight.

I questioned why our country allowed aircraft to disrupt the night's peace. Was it due to poverty, indifference from our rulers, or factors beyond our control? As prisoners, perhaps it was deemed part of our punishment to be awakened from our sleep. However, the disturbance also affected peaceful citizens, interfering with the sleep patterns and health of children and young people.

Despite my concerns, my fellow inmates seemed untroubled or unaware of the commotion caused by the jets. They were oblivious to the fact that their nocturnal trips to the toilet disrupted others' sleep, leading to heated arguments. While snoring may be natural, I believed the deliberate disruption caused by flatulence was unacceptable, leaving me feeling imprisoned not just among people but among animals.

During the day, the noise continued with amplified calls to prayer from nearby churches and mosques, penetrating the walls of our cells.

Even during my clandestine confinement in solitary, the sounds of nearby faith institutions permeated the city, disrupting its peaceful slumber. I could discern that one of these emanated from St. Michael's Church, where a lengthy and animated service unfolded on the 12th day of each month. This led me to surmise that I was in close proximity to St. Michael's. Yet, uncertainty lingered, prompting me to question whether it was mere proximity or a heightened consecration amplifying the reverberations.

In contemplating the significance of St. Michael's presence, particularly given my great-grandmother's reverence for the archangel, I entertained the notion that perhaps my location near St. Michael's was not happenstance but rather a response to the prayers of my great-grandparents. Such musings spurred vows of offerings, invoking St. Michael's intercession to reunite me with my children and beseeching Archangel Gabriel, revered by my mother, for aid.

When in solitary confinement, I recall that, driven by frustration with the external noise, I resolved to take action. Testing the unsuspecting security guard, I inquired about the proximity of St. Michael's to our location. His inadvertent response confirmed my suspicions – St. Michael's was indeed nearby, fueling my indignation at the cacophony emanating from a mosque nearby.

Regardless of the sanctity of their purpose, I firmly believe that faith institutions should exercise restraint and refrain from polluting the city with excessive noise.

I didn't take issue with the public address system within the confines of the church or mosque. However, allowing the amplifier to echo to the heavens and back felt offensive not only to me but, I'm confident, also to the Creator. Such noise was enough to upset God.

No one should be arbitrarily deprived of peaceful sleep at night. In the civilized world, citizens have the legal right to sleep without disturbance from noise. Laws in Western countries, which often prioritize money and trade, prohibit commercial airlines from flying after midnight. Citizens also have the right to avoid unwanted noise, including amplified messages from religious denominations.

Once the public address systems of faith institutions quieted down, Kaliti prison's internal media would commence operations. Each of the eight zones would transmit announcements in a specific order, covering matters such as headcounts, meals, court and medical visits, hymns, songs, and alerts about health issues like tuberculosis, colds, and various diseases. Other announcements encompassed job assignments, family visits, and radio news, contributing to the cacophony within the prison.

The aforementioned noise primarily pertained to sound. However, the disturbances escalated when accompanied by messages, predominantly through television and radio. Although television wasn't accessible to us, we could overhear transmissions from the women's prison. Our exposure to radio transmissions through the mini-media added to the overwhelming noise.

On one occasion, we discovered it was "Flag Day." I found it puzzling that the same ruling party, which had previously dismissed the flag as a mere rag, now declared a national Flag Day. Despite this contradictory history, the government covered the entire country with flags, as the guards on the tower informed us that day.

I was certain that the commemoration didn't intend to honour the flag but rather served as a business opportunity for the Almeda textile factory in Tigray. Those who facilitated jobs received commissions, while government officials indulged in embezzlement.

In a country where justice was lost, the celebration of justice seemed ironic. Similarly, a nation devoid of peace celebrated peace, while Book Day became a sombre reminder of declining literacy since the Derg regime, with even university students struggling with illiteracy.

Activists abandoned their spouses, and those unable to afford divorce resorted to domestic violence. Government officials shared ill-gotten gains with their mistresses while hypocritically celebrating Women's Day.

The TPLF seized control of the nation, exploiting its resources and governing through intermediaries. The media showcased the "Nations and Nationalities Day" as a display of ethnic costumes and music, masking the suppression of rights.

The incessant recounting of various events provoked impatience, amplified by repetitive news cycles and continuous seminars.

The misuse of English words became prevalent, epitomized by former Prime Minister Hailemariam's erroneous usage of "equivocally" instead of "unequivocally." During interrogations by TPLF security officials, I cited this misuse as a symbol of pedantry threatening national unity.

The trend of inserting English words into conversations worsened under the TPLF rule, a consequence of leaders' limited education. Despite my efforts to address this issue while working with the EPRDF, the practice persisted and spread throughout government briefings.

In France, journalists only used English terms if there was no French equivalent, in adherence to strict regulations. Yet, our government freely adopted English terms like "development" and "transformational," neglecting native alternatives.

The media unabashedly reported ministers receiving honorary doctorates and sergeants promoted to generals without disclosing the dubious nature of these awards. Despite my attempts to expose these lies, my fellow inmates feared repercussions while police officers in the tower silently listened.

I found solace in wax earplugs provided by British Ambassador Suzanne, shielding myself from the incessant noise of the media and my fellow inmates. With the world muted by the wax, I no longer had to endure what I did not wish to hear.

Chapter LI: A Change of Ambassador

Time flies, indeed. I observed its passage across two calendars, spanning from 2014 (2006 Ethiopian calendar) to 2015 (2007 Ethiopian calendar). Winter faded away, summer ensued, and then winter returned. England embraced Christmas, which also concluded. Meanwhile, my children celebrated their seventh and eighth birthdays without me.

In our lives within Kality, days unfold in a monotonous repetition. Confined within a two-foot by six-foot enclosure carved from the vast lands, we are deprived even of glimpses of the sky. As I gazed upwards and then returned my gaze to the earth, I couldn't shake off the awareness of the imposing walls surrounding us. At that moment, my mind drifted to a poem by Kebede Michael, a well-known Ethiopian author. The verses vividly depicted a prison, Asinara, where Ethiopians endured captivity under the Italians in the 1930s.

"Above, they see the sky. Below, they see the earth;

Oh, Asinara, the village of prisoners."

Similarly, in Kality prison, there was no vista to behold. I faced the choice of casting my gaze towards the heavens or downward to the ground. Tall stone and tin fences encircled us from every angle, confining us within their formidable grasp.

Once I resigned myself to the solitude of my fellow inmates, a semblance of routine began to take shape. Each morning, I would rise and embark on a series of relentless exercises, meticulously targeting every limb and muscle group: arms, legs, waist, chest, and extremities. My hair remained the sole organ untouched by this ritual. Push-up after push-up, I would complete up to 640 repetitions daily, commencing at the break of dawn and halting only when Berhane and Berihu unlocked the door for lunch.

In comparison to me, my cellmates are youthful. They engage in physical exercise almost dutifully, perhaps as if to evade some imagined tax fines. Afternoons were dedicated to reading, a habit I nurtured voraciously. I delved into books penned in English, a language that held little relevance for them. Reading wasn't their forte; it seemed to take them an eternity to navigate through Amharic texts.

The TPLF, cognizant of the solace and enrichment I derived from literature and culture, sought to inflict punishment by tethering me to individuals like Assefa and Dawit, who are nearly illiterate.

Under their watchful eye, I was permitted to maintain a modest collection of up to ten books at any given time. These volumes were subject to scrutiny for hidden messages before they were passed to my father at the weekly visit. He would take them home.

After our evening meal, I would immerse myself in reading until the late hours of the night. The books I read were sent to me by kind-hearted souls from various corners of England, a testament to the enduring power of human connection even in the darkest of times.

Security personnel meticulously combed through the books, excising any pages bearing the sender's name before they reached my hands. Yet, certain names managed to evade their scrutiny—Helen, Hobbes, Amanda, and Kate among them. In the desolation of prison, where companionship was scarce, books became my steadfast allies. I delved into hundreds of them, seeking solace and refuge within their pages.

Family visits persisted every week, providing a much-needed lifeline to the outside world. However, the scheduled monthly visits from the British embassy lacked consistency, often disrupted by bureaucratic hurdles. The embassy staff had to secure security clearance before setting foot in the prison, making unannounced visits an impossibility. The authorities took pleasure in mocking the various excuses concocted to thwart these visits.

The change in leadership at the British Embassy saw Greg Dory replaced by Susan Moorehead. Though her interim, Catherine, was delightful, I found myself growing fond of Susan's visits. Accompanying her was her assistant, John, an avid Arsenal fan whose presence never failed to brighten my day.

Susan, a beacon of brightness and emotional intelligence approached her role not merely as a duty but as an opportunity for genuine connection. She possessed a remarkable ability to empathize with my plight as a prisoner, delving deep into the complexities of my sentiments and experiences.

As our visits progressed, Susan astutely navigated the dynamics within the prison, skillfully negotiating with Mr. Gebre Yesus, the prison administrator, to transcend the usual time constraints placed on visits. Thanks to her adept handling, security oversight was no longer an obstacle during her visits, allowing our conversations to flow freely and unhindered.

Our discussions ranged far and wide, traversing topics from family matters to the depths of literature and from literature to the realms of politics and philosophy. Through these exchanges, Susan not only provided a much-needed connection to the outside world but also became a cherished confidante and intellectual sparring partner.

During our discussions, I often seized the opportunity to confide in Susan about the looming political perils gripping our country. I expressed my deep-seated concerns regarding the dangers posed by the TPLF's pursuit of single-ethnic group supremacy, fearing that it would inevitably spiral into an uncontrollable bloodbath. Moreover, I voiced my apprehensions about the potential ripple effects of such a conflict spreading across Africa.

I conveyed to Susan my belief that the British, like many other external observers, seemed more focused on their own shortsighted interests rather than the broader consequences of the crisis unfolding in Ethiopia. Urging her to take action, I implored her to record my concerns and officially relay them to the British Foreign Service. I stressed that such documentation would serve as invaluable insight for future researchers and historians.

"The TPLF's ethnically motivated dominance cannot be allowed to persist unchecked," I emphasized to Susan. "It is a powder keg waiting to ignite, and when it does, the repercussions will be felt far beyond the borders of Ethiopia. British support, if misguided, will ultimately compromise not only its own security and national interests but also exacerbate the crisis in the region. Documenting this belief in the British Foreign Office is imperative for the sake of both Ethiopian and British historians in the years to come."

I urged Susan not to overlook the significance of my point, highlighting the invaluable role that old British Foreign Office documents had played in aiding researchers of Ethiopian history. This was a sentiment I had expressed as far back as 2014 during my initial meeting with British Ambassador Greg. The mere mention of this fact had evidently perturbed TPLF intelligence officers, who had overheard our conversations with the ambassadors.

Chapter LII: Theo Walcott's picture and Neil Wigan's words

Neil Wigan, the UK Foreign Service Director for Africa, joined Susan during one of her visits. I emphasized the rich tradition of British citizens fighting for democracy and freedom throughout history, making it clear that his question, "How do you, as a British citizen, fight to overthrow another government?" failed to resonate with me.

I firmly believed that advocating for change in oppressive regimes was not only a moral imperative but also aligned with the values of democracy and human rights that many British citizens had fought and sacrificed for throughout history.

I reminded Neil of the courageous actions of British citizens in history, such as the British International Brigade's fight against the fascist Spanish government, with notable figures like author George Orwell among them. These individuals stood up against oppressive regimes to safeguard justice and freedom.

I directly challenged Neil, questioning if the British government's seemingly lenient approach to my case was racially motivated. I playfully teased him with a provocative example involving Glenys Kinnock, who became the First Lady of the British Labour Party in 1983.

I pointed out that in the early 1980s, Glenys had illegally crossed into Ethiopia from the Sudan while Eritreans fought for independence. I questioned whether the British government would have reacted in the same manner they had reacted to my plight if she had been apprehended by Ethiopian officials for supporting Eritrean rebels.

Drawing a sharp contrast, I emphasized that while I hadn't physically travelled to Ethiopia, my support for the struggle for freedom in Ethiopia from abroad seemed to elicit disproportionately lenient treatment of the TPLF by the British government in my case. I framed this as potentially indicative of a racist bias in their approach.

Neil responded to my provocations with a straightforward explanation. He clarified that Glenys Kinnock indeed travelled to Eritrea during the war and later wrote a book about her experiences there. He assured me that the British government had made earnest efforts regarding my case and emphasized that there was no element of racism involved in their approach.

Additionally, Neil shared that prominent figures like the British opposition Labour leader Jeremy Corbyn and Lord Dholakia had expressed a desire to visit me in prison, but their visa requests into Ethiopia had been denied.

I was unfamiliar with Lord Dholakia, but Jeremy's stance didn't surprise me. He was my constituency MP, and I had met him several times. He's the kind of person who would travel to great lengths to fight injustice I know Jeremy would do more than visiting me in an Ethiopian jail. While this explanation offered some consolation, it underscored the complexities of international diplomacy.

Despite the seriousness of our conversation, Neil managed to inject a moment of levity with his response to my complaint about the restricted view of the sky within the prison confines.

With dry English humour, Neil remarked, "At least it is not a raining sky." This humorous exchange served as a brief respite from the weightiness of our discussion, highlighting the resilience and camaraderie that can emerge even in the most challenging circumstances.

As Neil departed, I couldn't help but smile at his remark, reminding me of the distinctive traits of both England's weather and its people's humour.

In those moments, as I gazed at the limited expanse of sky granted to me, Neil's lighthearted quip served as a poignant reminder of the small comforts amidst adversity. Despite the hardships and uncertainty that surrounded me, I found a semblance of peace in the thought that, unlike the perpetually weeping English sky, the sky above me remained steadfast and unchanged, offering a glimpse of constancy in an otherwise turbulent existence.

During one of Susan's visits, I recounted Gebreyesus's (the prison chief) surprising statements to her.

"He claimed that it's only thanks to the goodwill of Kality prison that I receive basic provisions like bread rolls, soap, and healthcare. He also mentioned that the committee of inmates has no obligation to provide me with luxuries, like soft drinks during festive holidays, as I am not considered one of them. Furthermore, he asserted that I don't possess a prisoner number, ID, or file," I explained to Susan.

"Why not?" she inquired.

"He simply stated that I am entrusted as a prisoner, but by whom I have no idea," I replied.

"Why don't we ask him?" I suggested, gesturing towards Gebreyesus, who was sitting on a revolving chair behind his desk.

Susan posed the question to Gebreyesus, who responded with a clever smile. Despite his lack of proficiency in English, shared by many of the country's top officials, he used it as a convenient excuse to avoid answering directly. Instead, he brushed off the question with a flirtatious laugh, leaving us both puzzled by his evasive response.

As time passed and Gebreyesus continued to evade Susan's inquiries, I grew increasingly frustrated with the lack of progress in obtaining necessities like pen and paper. Frustrated and determined to bring attention to my situation, I began to strategise ways to sow discord between the trustees and those responsible for my confinement.

During one of Susan's subsequent visits, I confided in her about the denial of pen and paper, hoping she could intervene on my behalf. Susan, ever diligent, managed to secure a promise from Gebreyesus that I would finally receive these essential tools.

Susan also informed me about the Christmas greeting cards prepared by students from Sidcup boarding school in Somerset, England, which she had handed over to Gebreyesus with the request that they be delivered to me. Gebreyesus, with his characteristic smile, assured Susan that he would see to it personally.

Despite Susan's persistent efforts, Gebreyesus' promises remained unfulfilled. While she arrived at each visit with hands full of provisions, including foodstuff that Gebreyesus allowed me to take directly, other items like greeting cards and pens and paper were promised to be delivered to my cell but never reached me. Despite Susan's advocacy on my behalf, the only visitors I received throughout my imprisonment were my father and his wife, Tadelech, leaving me feeling isolated and disheartened.

On another visit, Susan was allowed to give me a picture, and it was an unusual compromise. The photo depicted a young adult alongside my children and Yemi captured on the football turf of at the Arsenal stadium. Without my glasses, I struggled to identify the individual in the picture.

When Susan asked me about the young man's identity, I hazarded a guess, suggesting that it might be Hilawit's boyfriend, my eldest child.

However, upon returning to my cell and putting my glasses, I took a closer look at the photograph. To my astonishment, the young man in the picture was none other than Arsenal's renowned striker, Theo Walcott! That was the only picture I had pinned on my cell wall. Everytime I saw it, I silently thanked Theo for his kind gesture.

The unexpected discovery left me both amused and incredulous as I marvelled at the serendipitous encounter captured in the photograph.

Outside a single photograph and some foodstuff, the only thing I was allowed to take directly from the hands of the members of the British Embassy in Addis was money. The allowance of cash as the sole permissible gift from my British visitors seemed to be a deliberate move by my jailors, possibly intended to underscore the perceived insignificance of the support offered by the British government. This impression was reinforced by the relatively small amount I received each month.

However, unbeknownst to the Ethiopian authorities, the funds I received didn't originate from the British government. The sum of 300 Birr (less than 15 pounds) was sent to me every month from Prisoners Abroad, a British charity established to aid British prisoners held overseas. Both Ambassador Greg and later Susan delivered this amount to me, and while Susan acknowledged its limited value, I remained appreciative of even the smallest gesture of assistance.

"Don't spend it all at once," Susan teased with a playful smile as I signed for the money.

Though her remark was lighthearted, I understood the underlying message: make the most of what little I had. Despite the teasing, I cherished the support, no matter how small, as it provided a semblance of comfort and assistance during my time of need.

Chapter LIII: A Move to Corruption

Corruption is an insidious misuse of authority to gain advantages, regardless of the scale, type of benefit, or the institutions involved. Whether it's government or non-government officials, even the smallest exercise of authority for personal gain, be it monetary, material, sexual, or otherwise intangible, constitutes corruption.

For instance, favouring a female client solely based on the appeal of her smile is a form of corruption, albeit subtle and difficult to quantify. Only the official involved knows the true extent of their corrupt intent. Personally, my disdain for corruption stems from the values instilled in me by my community and family.

Those who actively promote corrupt behaviour are just as morally culpable as those who directly benefit from it. During my time working with the TPLF between 1991 – 1992 in Addis Ababa municipality as the head of the city's economic committee, I consistently emphasized this point to business leaders.

I issued frequent warnings, urging them to conduct their affairs ethically and ensure their staff did the same. I made it clear that municipal services would cease support to any business found involved in bribery or facilitating corrupt practices unless they reported such incidents and refrained from participating in them.

I am fully cognizant of the allure of corruption and its potential for material gain, yet I have steadfastly refused to compromise my integrity. For me, corruption represents a clear boundary that must not be crossed, as it can lead to irresistible temptations.

Regarding moral responsibility, paying money to save human life may not inherently carry moral culpability. However, my personal experience does not involve such scenarios. I have encountered situations where I felt compelled to deliver a bribe, albeit reluctantly and not for personal gain, but rather for the benefit of a just common cause.

Reflecting on such instances, I deeply regret any involvement in bribery, even if it occurred in a context like Eritrea, where corruption is abhorred by people and leaders alike. Maintaining integrity and upholding ethical standards remain paramount to me, regardless of external pressures or circumstances.

Regrettably, you found yourself in such a compromising situation. Paying a bribe to an individual, especially one not directly affiliated with a particular movement or government, can indeed be disheartening and frustrating. Your intention to inform his superiors demonstrates a commitment to transparency and accountability, even in challenging circumstances.

Despite its inherent discomfort, the decision to let the matter go underscores the pragmatic considerations involved in navigating complex political landscapes. While the experience may have been distasteful, it's important to acknowledge the difficult choices one sometimes faces in such environments.

Moving forward, maintaining vigilance against corruption and actively seeking avenues to address such issues within the appropriate channels remains crucial. Your commitment to integrity and ethical conduct, despite the challenges encountered, is commendable.

Two circumstances at Kality prison led to my involvement in corruption. Firstly, I received periodic financial assistance of 300 Birr from the British Ambassador. Secondly, the prison authorities approved funds from my parents for the purchase of bottled water, which Major Berhane and Captain Berihu facilitated by buying and delivering on my behalf, as I was not permitted to access the prison shops.

After informing Berhanu about the 300 Birr I received from the British, the prison authority abruptly halted the allowance provided by my parents. Subsequently, when Susan delivered money to me, I chose to keep it to myself. This enabled me to accumulate a small sum as a contingency fund.

Given my status as a declared diabetic patient, I was provided with plain hot water in a thermos instead of the sugared tea the prison provided. Despite not being allowed to have a kettle within the compound, my parents brought it for me, and it remained with the security police on the tower. They used it to boil water for tea for me and themselves. I ingeniously mixed the hot water with the bottled water to conserve resources. Combining this saving strategy with Susan's funds and the initial 300 Birr resulted in a reasonable sum.

The savings were put to good use to assist Assefa in addressing his challenges, particularly in supporting the return of his children to school. When Dawit confronted me privately, alleging that Assefa was deceiving me and had ample funds from the TPLF for his services, I acknowledged the possibility but affirmed that I had the means to help him regardless of his motives.

Furthermore, we had a collective fund for essential supplies such as washing powder, toiletries, and snacks. However, the idea of engaging in corruption was introduced by Dawit.

"He has agreed, for a bit of money, to transfer messages written by you," Dawit revealed, referring to a security police officer he had befriended at the tower.

This proposition, albeit initiated by Dawit, introduced a moral dilemma and potential involvement in corrupt practices to facilitate communication.

Despite being fully aware that engaging in such practices was corrupt and potentially criminal, the opportunity seemed too valuable to pass up. Acknowledging the deal proposed by Dawit, I agreed to proceed.

To validate the authenticity of the arrangement, I suggested requesting writing paper and pens from the security police officer. Dawit provided the necessary cash for the stationary and a tip for the officer, and to our relief, it worked. I received the supplies as planned.

Dawit cautioned me to keep the supplies hidden from Assefa's view, prompting me to set up a curtain around my bed under the guise of seeking shelter from nighttime lighting. Behind their backs, I seized the opportunity to write a letter to my brother, Bizuneh, residing in the UK.

In my letter to my brother, I expressed concern that my family and friends overseas might hesitate to take action against the TPLF out of fear it could worsen my situation. I emphasized that their actions should not be dictated by the potential consequences for me and urged them to share my written work with the public.

"I'm not imprisoned for petty crimes but for pursuing a noble cause and bearing a responsibility. Sacrifices are necessary for the struggle we've undertaken in the name of freedom and justice for our people and our country," I wrote. "Do not let fear of repercussions deter you from spreading awareness of our cause."

I shared my worries about my children's safety, particularly in London, acknowledging the psychological strain this placed on me. Despite this, I drew strength from the sacrifices made by others in our struggle and entrusted the well-being of my children to my brother.

I addressed the envelope to Miss Lingua Shanka, concealing my brother's identity while inadvertently revealing his address.

Despite Dawit's assurance that he delivered my letter to the cooperating policeman, and the officer confirmed its posting, the anticipated contact with my brother never materialized. The letter contained specific information only decipherable by Bizuneh, including a contact number for him to reach out to. However, no communication ensued.

The dispatch of my letter came at a cost of 1000 Birr, yet it seemed to have disappeared without a trace. This unfortunate outcome underscored the complexities and uncertainties inherent in attempting to communicate from within Kality prison.

Realizing the potential risks associated with communicating through Dawit and the police officer, I attempted to send a second letter. The unpredictability of the TPLF made me wary, and I entertained the possibility that they might have orchestrated the entire situation involving Dawit and the officer.

Subsequently, I received a tip from an external source indicating that both Assefa and Dawit were indeed loyal snitches of the TPLF and were imprisoned with me for that very reason. This revelation came as a shock, especially considering the failed warnings from other inmates who had attempted to caution me about their allegiances.

Any additional savings were allocated towards providing financial support to Dawit and the police officers. On public holidays, I took the opportunity to pass money through the cracked fences that separated us from the policemen, instructing them to enjoy drinks on my behalf.

Before initiating these transactions, I ensured that only one police officer was present, as the officers were divided along ethnic lines and harboured mutual distrust. Despite these divisions, most officers were familiar with me and did not hesitate to accept money. However, they repeatedly emphasized the importance of not involving Assefa or Dawit in our arrangement. This caution stemmed from their concern that Assefa or Dawit might inform the prison administration about the financial exchanges.

Chapter LIV: Hunger Strike

The intimidation tactics employed by the TPLF had a profound impact on my father and his wife, rendering them hesitant to communicate with me while I was incarcerated in Kality prison. Their reluctance to discuss family matters, let alone broader national and international issues, was exacerbated by the abusive treatment they endured.

During their visits to the prison, only the Major and the Captain were permitted to escort my parents onto the grounds. In their absence or when the officers were occupied, my parents were forced to wait on the open on the main highway outside the prison. Additionally, if transportation to move me from my cell was unavailable, the relatively short distance between my cell and the administration office, my parents had to endure lengthy waiting.

Complicating matters further, my father, who was diabetic, occasionally experienced drops in his blood sugar levels while waiting. Despite this, they often encountered friction over the food items they brought for me. These challenges underscored the extent to which the TPLF's intimidation tactics affected not only me but also my family's well-being and peace of mind.

Despite both being members of the TPLF, Berhane and Berihu showed contrasting behaviours during their interactions with me and my family at Kality prison. Despite having moments of evil, Berhane was inherently kind-hearted.

In contrast, Berihu was less tolerant and often made a mess while checking the goods, particularly with grains and biscuit crumbs. He imposed stricter rules, such as requiring my parents to open and taste each tin of sardines and tuna before allowing them to pass. Additionally, he showed disrespect towards the clothes my parents had washed and ironed by handling them carelessly.

Furthermore, Berihu's handling of the list I wrote on scrap paper was dismissive, as he would fling it across the room to my stepmother without regard for its significance. This behaviour underscored the lack of respect and consideration he exhibited towards my family's efforts and presence during their visits.

I noticed administrative and legal issues arising and questioned the authorities: "Why are you harassing my family members?" Their response was a deafening silence, laden with fear, implying that I should keep quiet.

Desiring to take action, I urged my father to sue them, emphasizing that my prison rights were not being respected. Realizing that the courts were not independent, I assured them that I would take full responsibility.

In a bold move, I informed my parents that I preferred they did not visit me the following week and that I would not accept the items they brought. Despite their protests, I stood firm in my decision.

However, when they appeared the next week, I initially refused to present myself. It was Berhane who persuaded me that my refusal was unfair to them, prompting me to relent and meet with them.

Upon entering the office, I was alarmed to find my father absent, but his wife, Tadelech, waiting for me. Worried about his well-being, I immediately inquired about him, addressing him in the affectionate manner my mother used. Tadelech reassured me that he was okay, explaining that he had fallen and broken his arm after their previous visit. Despite my initial scepticism, I closely observed her demeanour and appearance for any signs of deception. Ultimately, I calmed myself, convinced that she was telling the truth.

The absence of my father during visitations always left me with a sense of alarm, not just out of concern for his health but also due to fears of his potential demise. I dreaded the possibility that his sadness and worry could ultimately be his undoing in his old age.

The shock of his broken arm compelled me to retract my request for them to cease their visits initially. However, after witnessing the ongoing mistreatment they endured, I eventually decided to speak out against it. Despite my patient efforts to persuade my parents to stop their visits, they persisted, viewing my request as a mere challenge or dare.

Feeling increasingly embittered, I refused to see them during a particular visit, adhering to my prior directive. Despite their return home with the food and clothes they had brought for me, I remained resolute in my decision, even as my food supply dwindled in the following weeks.

It's unclear exactly what transpired next, but it's possible that my behaviour was brought to the attention of the British Embassy. Subsequently, TPLF officials sent Gebreyesus to persuade me to allow my parents to resume their weekly visits.

In response, I presented Gebreyesus with a list of demands outlining my rights as a prisoner and insisted that my requests be addressed. Despite his attempts to appease me, I remained steadfast in my stance. However, the arrival of Susan later that week brought news of progress – the government had agreed for me to see a lawyer, indicating a potential shift in recognition of my grievances. Consequently, I agreed to accept my family visits once again, feeling a sense of victory.

With this newfound hope and progress, I abandoned my attempt to go on a hunger strike, embracing the possibility of legal recourse to address the injustices I faced.

Chapter LV: Flatulence and a Sleepless Night

Assefa grew increasingly irritated by my empathy towards Dawit. Each time he attempted to portray Dawit as a cog in the system and a malevolent figure, I countered by mentioning that Dawit himself had told me that Assefa was a spy, attributing to him similar malevolence. Despite the prohibition of physical meetings between the two, the exchange of insults and jibes persisted unabated. Their mutual complaints about each other became a relentless barrage.

Gradually, Assefa distanced himself from me, his disapproval of my stance becoming palpably problematic. Meanwhile, I adjusted my eating habits, consuming conservatively as I relied more on weekly deliveries. However, I couldn't guarantee the safety of the stored food. Eventually, I began to experience persistent stomach pains. Subsequent laboratory tests revealed a diagnosis of typhoid, prompting Asnakech, the prison doctor, to prescribe the necessary medication.

That was when Dawit confided in me, suggesting that Assefa was capable of contaminating my food. It was unclear whether his intention was genuine concern for my safety or simply retaliation against Assefa, who had previously informed on him. Assefa had complained to the authorities that Dawit had purposely contaminated his kitchen sponge as he came out of the toilet to wash his hands.

Dawit's revelation started to unsettle me. I began to feel suspicious every time I sat down to eat, though I had little choice in the matter. Seeking some form of control, I asked my parents to find me a canvas bag with a lock and key where I could store all my dry and wet foods securely. My water bottles found refuge in my suitcase. This precautionary measure only served to anger Assefa further.

Assefa seemed determined to find ways to unsettle me. He ceased cleaning the area of the cell where we slept while I persisted in keeping the shower and toilet rooms tidy. In response, I decided to clean only the space around my own bed, leaving Assefa's portion untouched.

Upon realizing that his neglect of duty was not impacting me, Assefa took it a step further by refraining from using the brush and neglecting to flush the toilet. This sparked a new source of contention between us, yet a full-blown dispute did not erupt—at least not yet.

One evening, I was jolted from a deep sleep by an unfamiliar sound emanating from Assefa's bed. Initially, I tried to ignore it and drift back into slumber, but the noise persisted. It became apparent that Assefa was intentionally farting loudly, disrupting my rest. Knowing well my sensitivity to sounds and noise, he seemed to relish in causing me discomfort.

Refusing to engage in a prolonged argument with Assefa, I resolved to exact my revenge. Waiting until he finally succumbed to sleep and began snoring, I seized the opportunity to retaliate. With a swift punch to the plastic chair beside my bed, I startled Assefa awake. Initially disoriented, he returned to sleep. However, as soon as I detected he had entered a deeper slumber, I struck the chair once more, this time with greater force.

Assefa erupted from his bed, alarmed and bewildered by the sudden noise. His shouts pierced the air, rousing Dawit from his sleep in the adjacent cell. Startled, Dawit raised the alarm, summoning the attention of the prison authorities as he complained of a disturbance in our cell.

In the absence of a key, a security policeman leapt over the fence, peering through the bars, demanding to know the cause of the commotion. Assefa wasted no time in reporting that I was disturbing him by repeatedly hitting a chair, preventing him from sleeping.

Assefa's demeanour towards me varied, switching between formal and informal addresses depending on his mood. In contrast, Dawit consistently maintained a formal tone when addressing me.

Assefa's anger erupted into a torrent of insults directed at me, enough to fill both my pockets. In response, I seized the opportunity to share my side of the story.

"He is intentionally disrupting my sleep with his loud farts. I was merely retaliating," I explained.

Despite the security police's attempts to calm the situation, Assefa continued to roar with anger. The policeman instructed his colleagues in the watchtower to summon the keeper of the keys for assistance.

"Try to calm down," the policeman instructed, "Berhane will arrive with the keys and find a solution for you." He maintained watchful vigilance through the window bars.

Aware that Berhane would take some time to arrive from his residence, where he kept the keys, I waited patiently. Finally, around three o'clock in the morning, he emerged from his bed, draped in a voluminous cotton gabi (traditional bedspread), and made his way towards us.

Berhane entered through the front door, his voice tinged with exasperation as he cynically exclaimed, "What is this behaviour? I thought we had adults here."

Accompanied by a night-duty security guard from the watchtower and a high-ranking TPLF officer, Berhane wasted no time in listening to Assefa's account of the situation. Assefa rushed to present his version of events, eager to have his grievances heard. When he finished, I seized the opportunity to share my perspective.

However, Berhane's reaction took an unexpected turn when he heard my side of the story. "Did you interrupt my sleep just to tell me stories about someone farting?" he shouted incredulously.

Berhane's response transformed the tense situation into a moment of absurdity. I couldn't help but burst into uncontrollable laughter, finding the situation utterly ludicrous. Unfortunately, my laughter only served to further incense Assefa, casting him in a different light and igniting his rage. He lashed out with a barrage of insults, and in the heat of the moment, I found myself succumbing to anger as well.

The duty officer observed us with keen interest. "How will they sleep after this type of conflict? Perhaps they should be chained to their beds? We will find a solution in the morning. These deviants have had too much to eat! They are spoiled!" he declared.

Refusing to accept being labelled a deviant brought to a correction centre for reform, I couldn't hold back my frustration. "Listen, I'm not here to be corrected. I ended up in this prison because I dared to challenge your oppressive government. Find someone else to be 'corrected'," I snapped defiantly.

The man erupted into a rage, but Berhane intervened before he could escalate the situation further. Berhane vehemently objected to the idea of us being handcuffed to the bed. It was only the next day, when Susan from the British Embassy paid a visit, that I understood the significance of his objection. It wouldn't have been a favourable report to relay to her had I spent he night handcuffed to my bed.

Chapter LVI: Farts and Punches

It was Assefa's and my turn to get some fresh air following the enforcement of a shift system introduced after Assefa's clash with Dawit. Assefa had risen early and completed his exercise routine while I waited for my turn, making use of the limited space available.

My routine typically took longer than Assefa's, often extending until noon when it was time for meals. As Assefa, already showered and having had breakfast, stood watching me through the bars on the window above the corridor. I completed my exercises and began stretching to wind down, aware of the importance of preventing muscle strain.

As I planted my feet firmly on the ground and pushed my hands against the wall, a noxious smell suddenly assailed my nostrils. Initially, I attributed it to a potential issue with the sewage outside our compound.

Kaliti prison emitted a foul stench every time it rained, as my fellow inmates informed me. They explained that rainwater often overflowed the prison toilets, exacerbating the already unpleasant conditions. However, the odour I encountered that day had nothing to do with rain; the sky was clear, devoid of any clouds. Suspicion lingered in my mind, directed towards Assefa, who watched me from behind the window bars. The nasty smell didn't persist and deciding to dismiss the thought, I continued with my stretching exercises. However, it didn't take long for the foul smell to return.

Suddenly, Assefa burst into laughter, confirming my suspicions. "You're laughing because you know what you did," I accused.

His response was crude, filled with contempt, a testament to his upbringing. "Your mother... I'll do whatever I want, so what are you going to do?" he sneered.

I ceased stretching, stepping into the corridor within the cell and confronting him directly. "What did you say?" I demanded.

Assefa persisted in insulting my mother, prompting me to summon all my strength and deliver a blow to his nose.

What ensued between Assefa and me could only be likened to the legendary 1970s bout between Muhammad Ali and Joe Frazier in the heart of Kinshasa city.

Assefa had little space to manoeuvre, pinned against the narrow corridor's wall, while I had ample room to unleash my punches. I kept him cornered, maintaining my position while remaining cautious of any attempt on his part to grapple and hold onto me. I maintained a safe distance, allowing my punches to fly with precision and speed.

The blows landed swiftly, but Assefa managed to catch the side of my temple, momentarily throwing me off balance. Fortunately, I steadied myself against the corridor walls, realizing the severity of his punches. Without the support of the walls, I would have been at risk of being knocked down onto the floor. Sensing the danger as I staggered under one of his blows, I gritted my teeth and unleashed a flurry of punches with all my might.

The duration of the fight remained uncertain to me. Despite the two-decade age gap between us, Assefa was the first to show signs of fatigue. It seemed that my rigorous four-hour daily exercise regimen had finally paid off, perhaps even saving my life. Dawit's urgent cry to the police on the watchtower echoed through the air:

"They're killing each other!"

The duty officer was Mengesha, whom we referred to as "Mengesha Rayaw" because he was from the place "Raya" in northern Ethiopia. Lacking a key, he resorted to leaping over the barbed wire on the wall to reach us.

Assefa was on the verge of collapse when Rayaw intervened, placing himself between us to halt the fight. In the end, I delivered the final blow, an uppercut that lifted Assefa's chin. Rayaw firmly clasped my hand and urged me to stop, declaring, "That's enough." Assefa remained in shock, subdued and motionless, likely grateful that Rayaw had intervened to separate us.

Although I sustained a few scratches from Assefa's nails on my face, I didn't suffer any serious injuries. Despite my racing heartbeat, the rest of my body remained surprisingly calm. However, the condition of my hands was alarming. The impact of my punches had caused significant damage; my knuckles had lost skin, revealing the whiteness of my bones beneath. Both hands swelled rapidly, with my right hand faring worse than my left. Rayaw stood between Assefa and me, awaiting his superior's response to the situation he had reported.

Mengesha didn't have to wait long before his colleagues arrived, leaping over the wall to enter the yard. He promptly instructed them to locate Berhane and bring him over urgently. Berhane soon appeared, wearing the chain containing the key to our courtyard and cell around his waist. Upon seeing the condition of my hand, he exclaimed in alarm.

"What happened to your hands?" he asked formally, despite my previous requests for informal address. Fueled by rage, I found myself unable to respond.

Assefa wasted no time in speaking up: "I was simply standing here minding my own business. He's the one who instigated the fight," he snitched.

I didn't deny being the instigator, but I explained that Assefa had provoked me by insulting my mother, recounting his insults to Berhane verbatim.

"He's lucky. If we weren't in prison, I would have killed him," I asserted.

Berhane instructed the soldiers to wait and left, leaving the door open behind him, presumably to report to the administrator. Upon his return, he was accompanied by Asnaku, the medical doctor. Asnaku inquired if I experienced pain anywhere else besides my hands, to which I responded negatively. She applied Jibi, an antiseptic fluid resembling running ink, to my hands and wrapped them in bandages. After checking for broken bones and finding none, she wrote a prescription to prevent any infections.

Assefa then requested Asnaku's examination as she prepared to leave. It was the first time since our altercation that I had a chance to examine his face closely. Although his forehead and face were swollen, his nose appeared neither bleeding nor broken, despite my belief that I had targeted it with my punches. Asnaku was prescribed painkillers to alleviate his headache complaints.

"Don't stop moving your fingers even if it hurts," Asnaku instructed before departing.

The next task fell to Berhane. It was evident that Assefa and I could no longer coexist in the same cell. Removing him from the compound was out of the question. The only viable option was to transfer Dawit into my cell and relocate Assefa to Dawit's quarters.

"Pack your things," Assefa was directed.

He complied without hesitation or protest, silently gathering his belongings. With the assistance of the prison wardens, his possessions were piled up outside. Dawit was informed that he would now share a cell with me in place of Assefa. Joy radiated from his face as he swiftly gathered his belongings and entered to take Assefa's place.

Once Berhane and the soldiers had completed their task and departed, the fading echoes of their footsteps were replaced by Dawit's voice, now taking centre stage.

Dawit's voice rang out, taunting Assefa with a mix of sarcasm and mockery. "Hoy, hoy, it's a marvel that a burly young man gets beaten up by a 63-year-old man. Death would be kinder," he began, his words dripping with honeyed sarcasm as he sang at the top of his voice.

"Knock him out, deprive him of a finishing line. They know not their limits, naughty men and dogs. The genuine sniper is known to us. We know the Front Eiserne, who mixed the bandolier with wide open arms. The lion's cave invaded by the baboon, deprived the invader of sleep, and turned into a nightmare," he crooned, his taunts cutting deep.

Despite the psychological and physical pain the fight caused me, I couldn't help but envision it as a professional boxing match. I imagined myself in the ring, hearing the announcer's voice declare our names and stats to the cheering crowd.

"In the red corner, dressed in red shorts and red gloves, the invincible and unrivalled champion, thirty-time winner of thirty though matches, the elderly youth of Abwarey, Andargachew

Tsege; in the blue corner, dressed in blue shorts and blue gloves, desirous of striping off the belt of Abwarey's elderly-youth, winner of twenty mediocre matches, stretching hard to obtain championship, the young dreamer Assefa Kussie," I envisioned, emulating Muhammad Ali's dance moves as part of my daily exercise routine. I thought my fight with Assefa was in the same league as Ali's fight with Joe Frazier's "Rumble in the Jungle" in the Democratic Republic of Congo.

As Dawit continued to tease and taunt, Assefa remained silent, unable to match Dawit's verbal jabs. Time passed with Dawit's taunts and Assefa's sullen silence. Dawit, who had spent over a year in solitary confinement because of Assefa, now found satisfaction in Assefa's daily ritual of emptying his urine-filled plastic bottles into our toilet, mirroring Dawit's past actions. In a way, it seemed that what goes around truly comes around.

Chapter LVII: Sophie's Choice

Things lightened up after Dawit replaced Assefa in my cell. However, it didn't take very long for a mess-up to occur. The biggest problem was the cultural difference between us. I tend to speak openly and frankly, which was primarily the source of all our problems. Dawit and Assefa easily get upset by things that don't bother me. Dawit was more sensitive than Assefa. I quickly reached a point where it became evident that my efforts to get close to Dawit wouldn't work. We soon stopped playing cards and other games.

I focused on my daily exercise routine and reading books, immersing myself in long hours of reading. I challenged myself with the most difficult Sudoku puzzles. Meanwhile, the hostile rapport between Assefa and Dawit had reached alarming heights. They exchanged the most cringe-worthy ethnic slurs, assaulting my ears with their hurtful words. It became evident to me that ethnic extremism was rampant within the walls of Kaliti prison. The environment was characterized by ethnic fights, the exchange of ethnic favours, ethnic games, and ethnic meetings.

Observing the sickness of ethnic extremism and hearing the exchange of ethnic insults between Dawit and Assefa provoked much contemplation. It shed light on the alarming extent to which ethnicism had permeated the country, prompting numerous questions.

Ethnicism in Ethiopia is both disheartening and repulsive. Furthermore, it's challenging to find any ethnic group that hasn't been influenced by mixing, invasions, or being invaded; subjected to war, trade, captivity, slavery, conquest, displacement, and migration due to unemployment and hunger.

Reflecting on the physical features of my own family, I couldn't help but wonder about our ethnic mixtures. Some members bear a resemblance to Portuguese or Turkish ancestry. My great-grandparents would recount tales of Portuguese soldiers who defended Atse Lebne Dengel and Turkish warriors who fought alongside Mohammed Gragn, both showing interest in Habesha women. Even Italian soldiers disregarded Mussolini's warnings when it came to Ethiopian women.

In the Menz area, every farmer owned a slave. Richard Pankhurst wrote, "The number of slaves in Menz transformed its people." There's no need to question whether the mother or father of some of my uncles had Anuak, Mursi, or Hamer ancestry.

Shewa's Amhara and Oromo people mingled and intermarried without restraint. This mingling was necessary for territorial expansion as well as the conservation of expanded boundaries.

The Princes and nobility of Tigray and Gondar, located on the periphery and distant from many centuries of war in Ethiopia, did not label Shewa, the province in the centre, as a land of slaves without reason.

In Shewa, everyone, from peasants to the kings, had mixed blood with slaves. Since the victors of war had the right to treat the victims as slaves, slavery had no racial link in Ethiopia. Many free men and women, Christians and Muslims alike, had suffered the scourge of slavery.

I wanted to share the above with Dawit, who was proud of his pure Amhara heritage, but I thought better of it. I imagined he could twist my words to make it seem like I was insulting him by calling him a slave.

I could have said a lot to Assefa, who also took pride in his pure Oromo lineage. Shewa Oromos have zero chance of claiming a pure lineage. Other Oromos are no different. Sixty-seven per cent of the Oromo people are known to be of mixed race.

Before the expansion of the Oromo, non-Oromo tribes inhabited the lands from the south, where Bale is now located, all the way to Wellega, including Arsi and all of Shewa and the suburbs of Addis Ababa. It's impossible to determine how many of the Shewa Oromos were Amhara or vice versa.

During their second invasion of Ethiopia in the 1930s, the Italians attempted to divide the Oromo from the Amhara in Shewa. An Oromo nobleman by the name of Abba Doyo likened separating the Amhara from the Oromo to the task of separating the white from the red grains of teff (Teffe grain that is too small to pick with fingers). This anecdote is recorded in the book "Summer

Lightning," which delves into the life of an Oromo Ethiopian patriot named Jagama Kello.

What I witnessed of ethnicism from my tiny cell was shocking. I became deeply concerned about the ethnic extremist contagion that the TPLF and its agents were spreading.

It was around that time that I received the book "Sophie's Choice." I had initially read the book before ethnic extremism became such an issue in our country and before the TPLF came to power. Reading it again while experiencing prison and witnessing Ethnic extremism spread across Ethiopia gave me a deeper appreciation and understanding of the book.

"Sophie's Choice" portrays the harrowing tale of Sophie, a Polish woman during the Second World War, amidst the widespread abuse and destruction of millions. Sophie, not Jewish, was arrested alongside her two children by the Germans, accusing her of aiding Jewish people.

The title of the book symbolizes the limited choices presented to Sophie by a German military official. When Sophie and her children were herded with countless others to their potential demise, she was asked to choose which child to save. Refusal to choose meant both children would face death. Faced with an impossible decision, Sophie broke into tears and begged for mercy. The heartless German official, deeming her refusal as an answer, ordered the execution of both children. Sophie agonizingly chose to save her son, condemning her child daughter to death, forced to witness her child's demise while clutching her son.

Reading this story, I couldn't help but think of my own twins and ponder what I would do in such a tragic situation. Yet, I found no answer; the choice seemed unfathomable, destined to lead to a complete breakdown. As tears streamed down my face, I drew the curtains around my bed, seeking solace from the constant glare of the 24-hour lights. While Assefa snored nearby, my mind, consumed by thoughts of ethnic strife, filled me with fear for my country and its people.

Ethnic extremism is a malignant sickness that manifests wherever ethnic clashes occur. Those consumed by ethnic extremism fail to recognize individuals of different ethnic identities as fellow human beings sharing a common destiny. They lack empathy for the vulnerable, deriving pleasure from heinous acts of violence such as grabbing a helpless infant by its feet and smashing its head against a wall like a pumpkin. Tragically, we have witnessed such atrocities not only in Africa but also in our own country. Pregnant women have had their wombs ripped open, and people have been butchered like animals in Ethiopia.

The current trend of ethnic political manoeuvring in our nation has little to do with upholding human rights or respecting ethnic, linguistic, and cultural diversity. Rather, poverty fuels this divisive ethnic politics. Those who have successfully navigated beyond the shackles of ethnic politics and poverty have transcended national borders, forming cross-border international communities.

In Ethiopia, the finite national resources are insufficient to provide the necessary means for all aspiring ethnic elites to lead lives of luxury. Thus, the battle for a larger share of the national wealth is waged along ethnic lines. Political power based on ethnicity is seen as the quickest route to wealth and privilege. Identity politics is employed to mobilize vast segments of the youth and impoverished masses from each ethnic group, leveraging this mobilization as a means to seize power and secure privilege.

Masters of ethnic politics, such as the leaders of the TPLF, exemplify how elites can manipulate ordinary people to seize political power and amass wealth to compete on the global stage. Throughout the federal regions, advocates of ethnic politics may decry the injustices inflicted upon their people, all while keeping their sights set on the power that such politics affords them, often at the expense of pillaging the wealth of their own communities.

Unless individuals choose to be devoured by their own ethnic predators rather than being preyed upon by predators from other ethnic groups, there is nothing to be gained from the peddlers of ethnic political leadership. Any self-respecting community would refuse to be devoured by any type of cannibalistic leadership and would instead bravely rise up against all forms of oppression and exploitation.

It is crucial to understand that those who cannot empathise with people from different ethnic backgrounds lack a sense of humanity, even towards their own. TPLF leaders, who adopted an anti-people, anti-democratic stance against the rest of Ethiopia, are unlikely to become democratic towards the Tigrayan people suddenly. The absence of democracy and freedom and the persistence of poverty in Tigray serve as clear evidence of this reality.

Humanity and democracy are inherently intertwined, rejecting injustice and exploitation in any form. These principles do not tolerate selective application, where democracy is championed in one instance but undermined in another, where honesty is shown in one area but dishonesty prevails elsewhere, or where humanitarian efforts are made here while humanity is disregarded elsewhere.

It is because of what I witnessed and heard in prison that I began to fear for Ethiopia and its people. The unchecked politicisation of ethnicity and the subsequent use of this brand of politics to further the material enrichment of the ethnic elite is a cocktail for serious disaster. My observation led me to question the future of Ethiopia and its citizens.

Chapter LVIII: Face to Face With a Lawyer

My hunger strike won me legal representation, albeit with a catch. I selected Temam Ababulgu to advocate on my behalf. He had previously defended a group of Muslim individuals wrongly accused of terrorism for speaking out against bad government policies affecting Muslims.

Prior to my abduction, I had heard Temam's interviews on Voice of America and German radio stations, where he discussed his pro bono work for the accused individuals, earning him recognition as a hero. I believed Temam wouldn't falter under pressure from the TPLF. Confident in his abilities, I informed my father and British Ambassador Susan that Temam was my choice.

However, in Ethiopia, prisoners lack the right to select their own legal representation. One day, Ambassador Susan presented me with a list of five lawyers, none of whom included Temam. When I inquired about his absence, she explained that the list contained reputable lawyers from whom I had to choose. It became clear that I could only select a lawyer from the provided list, handpicked by the government, presumably the TPLF.

Despite my suspicions being confirmed later, I felt powerless, knowing that my options were predetermined by those who held me captive. Tragically, the British foreign office had agreed to this travesty of justice by telling me that I had no option.

Susan obtained permission from Gebreyesus and had me examine the background, experience, and qualifications of each lawyer listed at the back of the document.

"Study the documents carefully and select one," Susan instructed.

I returned to my cell with the file and scrutinized it closely. After deliberation, I chose Berhane, whom I suspected may have been born in Tigray. As it turned out, my suspicion was correct. I presumed he might have affiliations with prison authorities and intelligence officers without much ado.

I didn't harbour high hopes of winning my case when I requested a lawyer. I was well aware that the justice system was structured to validate any accusations made by the TPLF. Innocent individuals like me lacked support when falsely convicted. However, my curiosity drove me to seek legal representation. I wanted to understand the TPLF's motives. Would they allow me to exercise the rights they had denied me? Would they grant me an appeal if requested? How would they respond to the evidence I had against them for my self-defence? These questions motivated me to request a lawyer. In essence, I sought amusement while under the watchful eye of the TPLF.

When Susan visited next, I informed her of my choice of Berhane as my lawyer. My father relayed that Ato Berhane had been notified and agreed to visit me. However, he delayed his visit due to a severe leg injury sustained at the airport terminal. Weeks passed before he finally arrived by car, still in pain and with his foot bandaged. He expressed his willingness to represent me, exuding an old-school, knowledgeable, and empathetic demeanour. We immediately connected, and I found myself liking him.

Our meeting took place in the administrator's office, arranged with the usual meticulous care. For the first time, I conversed with someone without Major Berhane or security agents looming over me. I couldn't comprehend why the TPLF suddenly respected the privacy between a lawyer and his client.

Despite leaving the door ajar and Berihu stationed outside within view, we lowered our voices, assuming he wouldn't overhear us. It was evident that he was instructed to keep an eye on us, with inanimate objects likely serving as surrogates if needed. I harboured no doubt that our conversation was being intercepted by TPLF agents elsewhere. I always cautioned my visitors about this.

I disclosed everything to Ato Berhane, outlining my requests for action. He meticulously jotted down my instructions in his notebook. Our discussion lasted over an hour, during which he posed pertinent questions and promised to return promptly with answers. Returning to my cell, I felt a sense of triumph at manoeuvring beyond its confines and gaining some physical movement.

Ato Berhane's visits were infrequent compared to other lawyers due to security office authorization akin to those granted to the British Ambassador. These visits were subject to revocation if the authorization ceased. He endured lengthy waits before gaining permission to see me.

During our subsequent meeting, Ato Berhane's foot had yet to heal. He regretfully informed me that he hadn't obtained answers to the questions he had diligently noted. Queries regarding prisoner rights yielded no responses from the Kaliti Correctional Facility, which asserted its role as a host rather than a custodian. Security agents claimed innocence, citing adherence to their duties without involvement in correctional matters. Both entities disavowed responsibility for my inquiries.

I had held onto a glimmer of hope that the TPLF might feign adherence to the law for propaganda purposes. However, I soon realized that allowing me legal representation was merely a mockery on their part. Ato Berhane soberly conveyed the complexity of my case.

Yet, there remained one avenue unexplored. I proposed suing the government for violating my rights as a client. Ato Berhane explained that such a move required consultation with my father. It dawned on me then that he was my father's representative, not mine. Only my next of kin possessed the authority to retain legal counsel on my behalf, a right denied to me as a prisoner. Ato Berhane was advocating for my father, not me.

The prospect of my father's involvement only added layers of complication. Would he dare confront the threats he undoubtedly faced to pursue a case against the government? I doubted it. It felt like a cold awakening, dousing all the dreams and aspirations I had harboured, including the impassioned speeches I had envisioned, inspired by figures like Mengistu Neway, a failed coup plotter against Emperor Hailselassie and Fidel Castro at his trial defending the July 26th movement. Ato Berhane offered his assurance to do his utmost, but I returned to my cell with a heavy heart, my hopes dashed.

Chapter LIX: Assefa is Madder, and We Are Not That Far Behind.

We found ourselves confined in the smallest cells within the vast expanse of Kaliti prison, an unforgiving circumstance. Unlike other prisoners, we couldn't opt to avoid each other if conflicts arose, nor could we maintain distance during the day; we were constantly in close quarters, day and night.

The TPLF deliberately selected unlikely cellmates and crammed us together in the tightest of spaces, a situation tailored to torment me. I was the focal point of this prison's cruelty, evident in the frequent clashes between Assefa, Dawit, and myself, orchestrated by this oppressive design. My relationship with Dawit wasn't marked by physical violence, but it was far from healthy.

Each of us spent solitary moments lost in thought or simmering with resentment. Forced into incessant self-reflection and internal debate, there was little opportunity for meaningful conversation or emotional release; the intimacy we craved remained elusive.

During my time in solitary confinement, the saying "People heal people" resonated with me. I repeatedly implored British Embassy staff to advocate for my transfer to a regular prison, where interaction with other inmates was possible.

Upon being transferred to Kaliti, I initially rejoiced. Yet, my elation quickly turned to despair as I discovered that not everyone possessed the capacity to heal. Disillusioned by my fellow inmates, I found myself longing for the isolation of solitary confinement, devoid of human contact and the stark reminder of the outside world. I confided in Susan, expressing my belief that I was better off alone. Moved by my distress, she appealed to Gebreyesus for a change in my cellmates.

Life continued amidst the disagreeable company of my fellow inmates. My intense longing for conversation drove me to engage somewhat assertively with the soldiers on the tower. We discussed a myriad of topics, both trivial and profound, whenever Major Berhane arrived to deliver our meals or escort Assefa to the bathroom.

Assefa's movements were restricted; he couldn't even access basic necessities like water or the toilet without an escort. In the absence of external interaction, my fellow inmates conversed with each other in their dreams and during waking hours, and I'm sure they observed me engaging in self-talk as well.

Assefa was the first to begin conversing with himself. His mental state had been in question ever since he was transferred to solitary confinement. Isolated from us, he resorted to talking to himself, a behaviour that escalated as he began experiencing hallucinations and contemplating unthinkable thoughts. Then, one day, the unthinkable became reality.

It was New Year's Day, and I was up early, engaging in my usual exercise routine. Assefa watched from between the bars of his cell window, a position he often assumed in recent months when he felt inclined to taunt or insult me in a muffled voice. However, over time, his teasing had ceased. I played a part in that; my boasting about the old man from Abwarey, the undefeated champion, had faded, and I refrained from backing Dawit when he occasionally joined in with provocative remarks. Despite this, Dawit continued to provoke Assefa, and the latter reciprocated. Their conflict stemmed from years of animosity, not just the tensions within our prison cells. Given the opportunity, they would have gladly done each other harm.

The peace that had settled between Assefa and me afforded me the freedom to utilize the full six meters of our prison grounds, which meant I had to pass by Assefa's window. As I approached, Assefa surprised me with his unexpected greeting.

"Happy New Year! Forgive me," he said, acknowledging the Ethiopian New Year on September 11, 2017.

Though I had only known Assefa for a short time, I believed I understood him well. I didn't consider him the type to seek forgiveness, so his request caught me off guard. I felt a sense of pity for him, suspecting that his mental and physical health had deteriorated during his extended solitary confinement. It had been months since our altercation, and my bitterness toward him was diminishing. Despite my reservations, witnessing the toll of his isolation became increasingly unbearable, even for me. Startled by his request, I didn't hesitate to offer my response.

"Happy New Year to you as well, don't worry," I replied, clarifying that forgiveness wasn't necessary. I found it difficult to believe his request was genuine, especially considering his deteriorating relationships with others. Assefa had previously been close with Major Berhane, and I had witnessed their amicable interactions. He had also been on good terms with Lieutenant Berihu. However, now he was embroiled in conflicts with both.

The altercation between Assefa and Berhane began when Assefa accused them of "adding poison to the food they were fetching from the prison caterers." Assefa scrutinized every meal closely, convinced that it had been tampered with. He adamantly refused to eat, surviving solely on barley meal (Besso, roasted barley flour, that can be turned into smoothy with water) or the occasional hot meal delivered by his wife. Despite efforts by the two TPLF prison wardens to persuade him otherwise, Assefa remained steadfast in his belief. Even my offer to exchange bread with him was rejected. Concerns about Assefa's health weighed heavily on my mind, as did my own uncertainty about my well-being.

As I pondered what the TPLF would unveil next, the realization that my hopes of expressing my frustrations through the lawyer had been dashed hit me hard. Left with no other outlet, I resorted to talking to myself aloud. I sang songs, concocted riddles, and even communicated with the neighbouring women's prison by knocking on the wall and inquiring about their well-being. I even asked if Emawayesh, a middle-aged lady accused of involvement with Ginbot 7 and implicated in the failed coup attempts linked to me and my associates, was among them.

I sang out EPRP (Ethiopian People's Revolutionary Party) revolutionary songs, long past and forgotten, emphasizing verses that resonated with current times. The prelude to the communist International Anthem felt particularly fitting. I adapted the verse about the international struggle to focus on the national struggle:

"Our national struggle is upon us,

Let us fight for all of Ethiopia's children,

A brighter tomorrow is in sight.

This is the ultimate battle,

Let each one stand guard in their rightful place."

I sang.

While singing these verses, I had no inkling that the struggle of the Ethiopian people was engulfing the country like a prairie fire. During moments of cheer:

"For the unity they've shattered,

For the land they've desecrated,

For the freedom they've stolen,

For the yoke they've burdened us with,

Our response is to rise and say no."

Those verses were from "It's for You, Ethiopia," the song of the Ginbot 7 popular force that I composed before my abduction. I found myself singing the song on various occasions, especially after hearing the distressing news from Kaliti Mini Media or the television blaring from the women's cell. The abuse our sisters had to endure in Arab countries deeply affected me.

"Filthy paws defile your honor,

Slavery bows your shoulders low,

Skies pierced by the grief you mourn,

Eyes robbed by tears stained with blood,

It's for you, we gather, Ethiopia."

I repeatedly sang the verse containing these words as the thought of fellow women facing abuse and daily suffering in the cell adjacent to our cell tortured me endlessly.

When I heard the news on the radio broadcast from the mini media about the landslide at Koshay, the city's rubbish dumping ground, and the death of scores of children, I turned to a verse from the same song.

"For the children who snatch food from stray dogs' mouths,

For the fetus sold in the global marketplace,

This is why we find ourselves behind bars."

With an unruly voice, I sang for the deceased children of Koshay, aware that our country's children were being sold under the guise of adoption, and our virgin land was being handed over to Indians and Arabs not for free, as we were told for attracting investment, but for huge sums paid into Ethiopian officials' personal accounts overseas. Embittered by the fabricated charge of terrorism against me, I made a mockery of it by introducing myself to new security guards as the country's leading terrorist, Bin Laden's little brother, the Secretary-General of the Ginbot 7 movement, Andargachew Tsege.

When I felt sorrow:

"If it were up to me, according to my wish,

My insides pierced by bullets,

I would prefer to see myself

Dead on the cliffs of Mount Semien." (A mountain in Northern Ethiopia)

I echoed the embittered verses above by wasting precious years in the hands of TPLF. Describing to the soldiers on the tower the nature of my imprisonment in riddles, I was referred to as an entrusted prisoner, unsure whether my captor was the devil or a mere human being.

"My captor differs from the one watching over me,

One is unseen; the other has a face I see." I said.

The security guards listened and laughed. I crafted prose and poetry, critical of the television commentary that filtered through to me from the neighbouring women's cell, offering some free entertainment to the security guards. When television portrays the lack of effective administration as the root of all problems:

"Lack of good administration is a convenient excuse,

A cloak for theft, a hoarder of shame,

Unless cast into the sea like the cursed pigs,

Development and growth are false promises,

No hope of healing for Mother Ethiopia's woes." I sang.

If television speaks about eradicating poverty:

"Ethnic apartheid, theft, looting,

Spreading its wings, covering the country,

Bugles may sound with declarations of development,

But alas, wishful thinking, poverty will not end." I mocked.

For the endemic corruption within the system:

"For the conscientious leader to stop corruption,

Would require the ability to create humans like the Lord above."

I continued to ridicule the mocking words aired by the state broadcast authorities.

Assefa used to occasionally sing a sorrowful Oromo tune. It had a haunting quality, like a deep lamentation. He had translated some of the verses for me, but I struggle to recall them now. Perhaps one of the blows he landed on my head had hindered my memory for creativity.

Dawit had a melodious voice and would often sing. However, he didn't have much recollection of poetry and lyrics. He was fond of the musician Neway Debebe. His favourite morning exercise music was Neway's "I owe you a favour." Although he didn't know all the lyrics, he would repeat the ones he remembered in a deep voice:

"Not just any favour,

You're my right hand when troubles confront me,

But with a humble title,

you're the Queen of Kindness,

Firmly rooted, you're the statue in my heart.

Where are you, my friend, my support, my beauty? How are you?"Thank you,' he ended.

Dawit never disclosed why he held that song dear or who the lady was that he felt owed him favours. However, I never doubted that the women in the large cell next door empathized with him every time he sang that song. I'm certain he used his best voice, knowing they could hear him.

Chapter LX: Clemency Revisited

I met Ambassador Gregg a month after I was kidnapped at Sana'a International Airport and brought to Ethiopia. He inquired about my well-being and health before raising some issues. I told him that my urgent need was for TPLF to expedite the execution of the death sentence passed by its Kangaroo Court in my absence. I have already detailed some aspects of his response in previous chapters. Another point he raised was suggesting that I should ask for clemency and seek my release. Uncertain if his suggestion was his own initiative or influenced by his Foreign Affairs Ministry, my response was unequivocal.

"It is the TPLF who should be seeking forgiveness for the injustice and abuse it inflicted on the Ethiopian people," I asserted.

This idea of requesting clemency was raised multiple times by British officials. What I hadn't fully grasped or investigated was whether TPLF had promised to release me if I sought clemency or if the idea originated from the officials themselves. "Would requesting a pardon aid their efforts to secure my release?" I pondered. However, I didn't ascertain the genuine motivation behind this initiative.

The suggestion that I should seek clemency came from the British a few months after my lawyer, Ato Berhane, informed me that he couldn't achieve what I had entrusted him to do, that is, to get me a chance to appear in front of a court.

Ambassador Susan conveyed, "I met your partner, Yemiserach, and your brother, Bezuneh, in London. They urge you to request clemency. They see no reason why you can't seek pardon and get out of prison."

Yemserach, not involved in politics and managing two young children alone, didn't surprise me with her message urging me to request a pardon. However, I was perplexed by Bezuneh's concurrence.

I questioned Susan intently; "does Bezuneh support the idea of me seeking clemency? Did you hear it directly from him?"

"Yes," came her firm and affirmative response.

I pondered why Bezuneh would endorse such a notion. "Bezuneh is an executive member of Ginbot 7. He wouldn't take that stance without consulting other executives. They must have deliberated and reached a consensus. It was difficult for me to discern their decision, but I knew they were aware of my steadfast stance against seeking a pardon, making it illogical for them to convey conflicting messages. I reached this conclusion, bearing in mind a similar experience from before.

In 2005, executives and senior officials of the party of the Coalition for Unity and Democracy (CUD) held divergent views on seeking pardon. They were put in prison for refusing to take up their seats in parliament on the grounds that the national election was rigged by the ruling party. One faction believed it was appropriate to seek release after requesting clemency, reasoning that there was no fair court or law under TPLF's rule. Seeking pardon wouldn't compromise our innocence known to the public, nor would it reflect negatively on us. Conversely, another faction questioned the propriety of requesting a pardon from TPLF, the perpetrators of the crimes they accused us of. They viewed such actions as shameful for both themselves and the electorate who supported them.

The division among CUD executives was deemed perilous by Dr Moges Gebremariam, deputy chair of the CUD international committee, who received this information from his friend Professor Ephriem Yishaq. At that time, Dr Moges and I had travelled to Australia to establish and bolster CUD support organizations.

We were both concerned that the debate over seeking a pardon could potentially lead to a political catastrophe. To bridge the gap between the factions, Dr. Moges suggested that I write to those who were debating against seeking pardon. We already understood the reasoning behind the faction in support of seeking pardon.

During our flight from Sydney to Perth, based on discussions with Dr. Moges, I penned a five-page letter. The document was divided into various subheadings and aimed to assure CUD members that they would not face any repercussions if they decided to seek pardon and regain their freedom. It delved into the question of pardon from legal, public relations, moral, and political perspectives. The conclusion asserted: "The public knows that

TPLF is deceitful, criminal, and incapable of tarnishing your reputation for seeking pardon. The worst-case scenario would be to witness division among yourselves on this issue and create a rift. Avoid division, stay united, sign off on your pardon, and depart. We know the sentiment of the public outside, which will not deny you the heroic honour because you sought pardon for your release. Do not fear."

This document was sent to Professor Ephrem Yishaq, who had access to the prisoners in Kality. As a result of this letter, CUD executives and others were able to leave prison together and without any division among them. This experience prompted me to carefully consider the idea of seeking pardon, which Bezuneh and many other friends were urging me to accept. I reasoned that they must know better than I that such a move would not entail any risk of political disaster.

I informed Susan that I would contemplate her suggestion, and we parted ways. It was agreed, according to the law, that seeking a pardon would be facilitated with the assistance of a lawyer. I informed my family that, for better or worse, I wished to consult with my lawyer. Ato Berhane promptly arrived at Kality upon receiving security clearance. His stance mirrored that of the embassy staff.

"There is no alternative. As you know, I am not allowed to take your case to court. It has been unceremoniously closed. Going through the courts is shut. The only way out is to seek pardon and depart. There is no need to wait any longer. People know who you are. Don't worry," Ato Berhane advised.

After that, I had to make a decision. I was reluctant to draft a pardon letter that could potentially be used as propaganda material by the TPLF. I found the lawyer's suggestion of submitting a half-page pardon letter to be unacceptable.

I informed Ato Berhane that I wished to write the letter myself and requested him to arrange permission for my access to writing stationery. Ato Berhane spoke to the Kality Administrator, Commander Gebreyesus, and secured permission for me to get pen and paper.

"How many sheets of paper do you need?" Gebreyesus inquired through Major Berhane.

"Twenty," I replied.

Gebreyesus meticulously numbered every single page with a pen to ensure that not a single sheet would be taken without authorization. I utilised 15 pages to draft my request for pardon.

Fourteen of the pages detailed my rights and duties to combat TPLF's corrupt and abusive governance. In that context, I stated, "In this just struggle, the actions that were deemed unlawful are those that challenged the peaceful and legal processes of the constitution in pursuit of freedom and justice. If these actions were against the law, I still had valid reasons to argue that the peaceful struggle, closed off by the EPRDF itself, warranted a new form of resistance. I wasn't seeking pardon for resisting the EPRDF government but rather to highlight that while it may have appeared as defiance, it was in response to the violation of the procedures of a legal and peaceful struggle. I acknowledged that my resistance was intertwined with a degree of rebellion fueled by numerous grievances, which I requested be considered in the assessment of granting me pardon."

I mentioned in the letter that I would consult with my lawyer and send the letter through him. Ato Berhane was summoned to Kality, where he sat next to me while reviewing the text. After reading through it, he remarked:

"This letter does not explicitly request a pardon. It reads more like a historical account. I wouldn't have been able to write it myself. There's nothing I could possibly add or remove. I will submit it as it is. What they require is a sentence clearly stating that you are seeking pardon, which is already included. I don't anticipate any further discussion from them. I've heard this from intelligence sources. They are not expecting anything more from you."

Ato Berhane departed with the document, and I returned the remaining stationery. I imagined that Ato Berhane might keep a copy of the file. However, I am uncertain about what the Intelligence Bureau did with the document once they received it from Ato Berhane. Ultimately, I was released based on a general pardon declaration to all political prisoners, not as a result of my request for pardon.

Chapter LXI: Wind of Change in Ethiopia

Assefa's wife's visits had unexpectedly increased in frequency. The woman who used to take weeks to come and see him was suddenly visiting him every week. When Ever Berhane came to take Assefa out for a visit, he looked unhappy, as if he didn't want Assefa to meet with his family.

The wardens who normally announced Assefa's wife's arrival seemed to vanish when it was time for family visits. I first noticed their absence during a dispute with Assefa. His wife had to wait hours before they let her see Assefa. The delay was caused because the coordinators of the visit were no where to be found. Later, I learned from the information his wife passed on that something was brewing in Ethiopia.

Assefa's wife is from Ambo, some 100 KMs from the capital Addis Ababa. Each time she visited him, Assefa returned with news of rebellion not only in Ambo but throughout the Oromia and Amhara regions. Gripping the bars of his cell, he told me:

"They're nearing their end." They meant the government.

"What's happening now?" I asked.

"Young people all over Oromia are rebelling. Nothing is entering or leaving Addis Ababa. The government has killed many in the Amhara region," he replied. Such news became routine.

We learned of worsening situations from the information flowing through the women's cells. The women had forsaken their beloved TV soap operas, now tuning into the news instead. They cranked up the volume, knowing it was our only source of information.

We somehow adapted to terms like "emergency declaration" and "command post." The usual TV commentary on the 'command postu' made me ponder the term's exact meaning. Was it Amharic or English?

I'm aware that such casual usage of English was encouraged under the TPLF to mask their limited education levels when they seized power. Their belief that sprinkling English words and expressions into speeches signalled sophistication is a testament to the TPLF's inferiority complex. I feel a twinge of embarrassment every time the TV reports on the command postu.

Nevertheless, reports about the command post indicated that Ethiopia was far from peaceful. Incidents of burning and property destruction were regularly reported. Clues about the specific locations of these problems began to emerge as some reports discreetly revealed more unstable areas. We managed to sift some truth from the misinformation disseminated about the command post activities.

Once, a security guard from Southern Ethiopia surprised me by gesturing wildly and then boldly writing on a piece of cardboard the name: "Arba Minch." He pointed at me and mimicked, firing a rifle. Confused, I watched as he inscribed "Ginbot7" on the cardboard. It dawned on me that Ginbot7 had some form of armed resistance in Arba Minch. This revelation was startling since Arba Minch was in the south, while the main forces of Ginbot 7 were situated in the north of Ethiopia. It took the warden considerable effort and bravery to relay that message. I was impressed by his determination.

Other security guards also seemed emboldened. They discreetly passed me information. Once, a young Oromo warden informed me about some online activity concerning me on Facebook. He added, "They will release you not because they want to but because they'll be forced to."

"What makes you think that?" I inquired.

"They are under pressure from all sides; they have no other option," he replied.

Desperate to cling to hope, I wanted to believe the security guard. Yet, my conscience cautioned against raising my hopes too high.

However, emboldened by the words of the security guard that afternoon, I found myself singing loudly the lyrics of a song by Ethiopia's most famous musician, Teddy Afro, which had become a recurring feature in the recent mini media broadcasts.

"Gondar, Gondar, land of valour, The pillar and bond of unified Ethiopia"

At the time, I was unaware that a Colonel named Demeke Zewdu, a native of Gondar had defied TPLF orders to surrender to the soldiers dispatched and had bravely fought and defeated them. Nor did I know that the entire population of Gondar had risen in rebellion against the state, which had sent additional soldiers to either capture or kill Colonel Demeke, leaving the situation in Gondar spiralling out of control.

Despite my lack of detailed knowledge, I accepted the information provided by the wardens at face value and proceeded to compose verses appropriate for the news of the rebellion.

"Wails from Gera Meder to reach Gondar,

No response echoes from Quara, what transpired?"

That verse is inspired by Donald Levine, an American historian whose book titled "Wax and Gold" examines the relations between Menz and Gondar power centres in earlier centuries. The author portrayed Gondar as a province of intellectuals, rich in knowledge, where individuals from the Shoa Province, particularly Menz, sought education. Simultaneously, he noted that Menz provided the military strength for Gondar to thrive as a centre of learning. The author metaphorically likened Gondar to the head and Menz to the foot.

The verses urged Gondar to repay its debt to Shoa by becoming the "footsoldier" to save it. They expressed hope for relief for those of us languishing in prison in Shoa. At the time of writing, there was no awareness that Gondar had already risen.

Events began changing rapidly. Television commentary from the neighbouring women's cell indicated chaos within the EPRDF, the ruling party. One announcement concerned EPRDF's self-assessment, admitting to decay, a surprising revelation. EPRDF shifted from denying the existence of political prisoners to announcing their release, particularly those with international renown.

The release of a prisoner, especially Colonel Demeke, received enthusiastic support from the women. Consequently, you started inquiring about Demeke, learning more about him and understanding Ethiopian women's love for heroes.

Women prisoners also began following Amhara regional and Addis Ababa media, which provided more information than Ethiopian Television.

During a discussion among media professionals, Zeray, a powerful media official, complained about inappropriate news distribution. Bold responses from media officials representing Amhara and Oromo regions hinted at the weakening of the TPLF.

Around the same time, there were reports that EPRDF member organizations would release a joint statement with representatives from various regions. While Hailemariam, the PM and Demeke's speeches lacked directness, Lemma Megersa's, president of the Oromia region, bold message caught our attention, signalling potential change.

Although Debretsion's presentation failed to impress, Obbo Lemma Megersa's bold message, "We cannot continue business as usual. We need change and, if necessary, sacrifice," resonated with me, leading me to mutter, "Last days," to myself.

The government began releasing prisoners one after another. Andualem Arage, Eskinder Nega, General Tefera Mamo, Merara Gudina, Bekele Gerba, Olbana Leylisay, and many others regained their freedom. Before my abduction by the TPLF, I had authored numerous press releases advocating for the release of Andualem, Eskinder, and Bekele in my capacity as secretary and on behalf of Ginbot 7. Their release gave me hope that I, too, would soon be free, but reality did not align with my expectations.

Days stretched into weeks and weeks into months. The news of prisoners being released nationwide became commonplace, but there was no mention of my release. My family had no updates on my case when they delivered my weekly food ration. I began to believe that the EPRDF had not considered my release. Recalling the wisdom of my grandmother, I muttered, "Archangel Michael knows," and resigned myself to the situation.

Chapter LXII: Abiy is Elected. A New PM

Towards the end of February, news broke that Prime Minister Hailemariam Desalegn had resigned from his position. I had never taken him seriously, so the news of his resignation left me unimpressed, almost as if he were resigning from a non-existent Prime Ministerial role.

This reminded me of an interview I had given to Sisay Ageyna on ESAT television. During the interview, Sisay asked, "What is your impression of Ato Hailemariam?" I responded, "A piece of woodwork dancing to TPLF's tune every time they pulled the strings." (In English, my words would translate to calling him a 'pantomime character'). Interestingly, Hailemariam himself did not refute my impression.

"I didn't have any independence. I worked under the influence of others," he claimed afterwards. While I didn't doubt that he was under undue influence, I couldn't help but question why a person in his position couldn't find the courage to say "no." My objection towards him stems from wondering why he was unable to do so. TPLF entangled him in numerous compromising situations simply because he lacked the ability to refuse. If they could, they would have likely involved him in the execution of my death sentence as well.

ESAT radio and television extensively reported on how TPLF's spies failed in their attempt to assassinate me in Eritrea. We obtained, and ESAT possesses, a recording of a last-minute telephone conversation between the security advisor of the Prime Minister and the individual authorized to carry out the killing.

I couldn't help but wonder how many decisions like mine Ato Hailemariam executed before declaring his resignation. While I escaped death, I witnessed the dismantling of Hailemariam's government, the very administration that sanctioned my death sentence. I pondered over the fate of those who were less fortunate than me.

Nonetheless, Ato Hailemariam became the first Ethiopian to resign from such a high position. Ethiopian Television hailed this event as a historic achievement, a first-time occurrence on the African continent. Despite the constant blaring of the television on the resignation and its historical significance from the adjacent women's cell, it provided no clues about Hailemariam's potential replacement.

February yielded to March, reaching mid-month. The sole source of news for us remained the women's cell, making it impossible to gather information about the direction the Prime Minister's position was heading. I had a hunch, akin to peering into a crystal ball, that the next Prime Minister would likely be an Oromo.

I understood that Tamirat Layne and Hailemariam Desalegn couldn't truly represent the Amhara and Southern regions, respectively, as they were perceived as puppets of the TPLF. It seemed plausible that EPRDF could strategically argue that both Amhara and the Southern regions had been given a chance at the Prime Ministership. However, what wouldn't be debated by EPRDF was the timing for an Oromo Prime Minister. Given the intense protests in Oromia, I believed the next Prime Minister would need to hail from that region to bring stability to the country.

In such a state of limited enlightenment, I once asked one of the security guards about the speculation regarding the next Prime Minister. The guard on duty happened to be Oromo.

"There are rumours it may be Dr. Abiy Ahmed," he responded.

The name was unfamiliar to me, so I sought clarification.

"Who?" I asked.

He repeated the same name.

Assefa, who was nearby, noticed my confusion briefly explained Abiy and his work. This conversation occurred just weeks before Abiy was elected.

One day, we learned that EPRDF was in session for the election of the Prime Minister. Anticipating an announcement on the evening news, we relied on the women prisoners to keep the television volume high, no matter how late, so we could receive the news. We waited anxiously for a long time, but no announcement came. Disheartened, we eventually retired to bed.

The next day brought surprising news: Ethiopia had elected a new Prime Minister whose name matched the one the young security guard had mentioned just one week prior. Many months later, I discovered that Abiy's election involved a tense, strategic, and complex process. It left me puzzled as to how the security guard had so confidently disclosed Abiy's future role as Prime Minister.

Television reports claimed that the election was conducted fairly and democratically at the EPRDF Council. However, I couldn't shake the suspicion that the election result was a foregone conclusion by the OPDO. It seemed unlikely for an ordinary policeman to confidently predict Abiy's election.

It appeared to me that the OPDO was steadfast in installing Abiy as Prime Minister, regardless of any objection. Both non-Oromo and Oromo wardens, as well as Assefa, an Oromo inmate, reiterated that OPDO had resolved not to accept the election of a Prime Minister from outside the Oromo ethnic group. Assefa's wife had also informed him of Abiy's imminent elevation to Prime Minister. Later, I learned that the country was labouring to install him as Prime Minister. Despite this, I remained convinced that OPDO had orchestrated Abiy's ascent well in advance before the actual event.

When the Prime Minister's name was announced, we could hear his voice emanating from the women's cell. All prisoners at Kality, and indeed the rest of the country, were familiar with his face and appearance. My two cellmates and I were the only ones unaware of his identity.

We strained to listen to Dr Abiy Ahmed's speech when Parliament endorsed his election as Prime Minister. Pressing our ears against the corrugated iron sheet walls of the women's prison, we absorbed his words. His repeated invocation of the name Ethiopia caught my attention. He spoke not of hatred but of love, emphasizing unity over division, peace over conflict, and kindness over cruelty—a stark departure from past rhetoric that the parliament used to hear.

Suddenly, we had a leader invoking the Creator and praying for the blessing of our people. He concluded his speech with the rallying cry, "Long Live Ethiopia!" That evening, I, too, congratulated Ethiopia and its people before drifting off to sleep.

Chapter LXIII: The Caprice of Television

One month had passed since Abiy's election, yet there was no noticeable change in our lives. The prison food had improved, with rumours circulating that the food budget had doubled. However, Assefa remained fixated on his fear of bread and sauce being laced with poison. His meagre rations from home were dwindling, and he was rapidly losing weight.

One morning, our sombre mood was interrupted by a surprise visit from the prison administrator, Commander Gebreyesus. It was unusual for him to visit unless there was a problem, and I had been on my best behaviour. Assefa was scheduled for his outdoor time that day, leaving Dawit and me locked in our cell when the commander arrived. Major Berhane called to us through the barred windows, informing us that someone was there to see us.

Gebreyesus greeted me and then asked a peculiar question: "What problems are you experiencing?" I replied that I didn't have any problems. He then shared the purpose of his visit: "It has been decided that you can have a television."

I didn't inquire about who made the decision. The prospect of a television didn't excite me; my mind was preoccupied with thoughts of why I hadn't been released with other political prisoners. Gebreyesus seemed to sense my thoughts. "Courage, don't worry," he reassured me before leaving.

That afternoon, a television was installed in our cell—a small flat screen just the right size for our confined space. We watched as cables were installed and the antenna fixed, with the wardens unable to conceal us from the installers due to the installation process about to take place inside our cell. As the workers completed the installation, we exchanged glances with them.

However, our TV lacked the satellite service other prisoners had in their cells. We could only access transmissions available through the analogue aerial: ETV, ETV Entertainment, ETV Languages, Addis TV, and EBS. When we inquired about the exclusion from satellite signals, Major Berhane relayed Gebreyesus's response: "It's only a temporary arrangement which will change soon."

Despite its limitations, I found some solace in finally having access to television. I reasoned that having something, even if imperfect, was better than nothing at all, particularly regarding the lack of satellite connection. Greeting the TV screen that had been inaccessible for four years, I eagerly delved into its offerings.

Initially, the novelty of television consumed our time as we absorbed news and entertainment. Witnessing the new Prime Minister for the first time was a highlight. However, my enthusiasm waned quickly. The programming lacked quality and was rife with government propaganda.

The capacity of journalists was noticeably low, with poorly researched and prepared programs. All of this contributed to my loss of appetite for television, and soon, all I could stomach was limited to the news.

In contrast, Dawit loved the TV. He switched it on first thing in the morning, and asking him to lower the volume proved futile. While I wouldn't have minded if he indulged in television programs when I was out or during our outdoor time, the incessant noise disrupted my peace of mind when we were locked in together. Despite my attempts to explain my concerns to Dawit, he was unwilling to listen.

In the meantime, the prison authorities decided to transfer Assefa from his cell to a different zone. Berhane came over to break the news after the gates had been locked for the night. I peered out from behind the barred windows to see who had opened the gate after dark.

Berhane opened Assefa's cell and instructed him to gather his belongings. Assefa tied up his bundles and lined them up outside his cell. He approached the window and let me know he was being transferred to Zone 1. He reached out his hand and asked for my forgiveness. I reached out my hand to him and wished him good luck. He didn't want to say a word to Dawit. He looked at him with an indifferent gaze and went away.

After Assefa's departure, my relationship with Dawit deteriorated due to our conflicting habits of television usage. The cell was polluted with noise round the clock. I attempted to mediate the problem.

I suggested that he only switch the TV on from midday meal times up to 10 o'clock at night. Dawit replied, "I can do as I want." I told him that I, too, could do as I wanted. "We can't arrive at a solution if we both start focusing on our individual rights," I told him. I tried to explain the difficulty of the situation we were confronted with.

"There is nobody to give judgment between us. If we were numerous we could have had a vote. The only choice we have is to come to a common agreement," I pleaded. He saw my attempt at civil dialogue as a sign of weakness and didn't want to reply. He switched the TV on and off as he pleased and let it blare loudly.

I was compelled to take decisive action. One afternoon, Dawit walked out of the cell, leaving the remote controller behind. I seized the opportunity to change and lock the television passcode.

Upon Dawit's return, he attempted to switch on the TV but couldn't access any other program except for the news. "You did this. Give me the code," he demanded, his contempt only serving to embitter me further.

"You said it was a matter of individual rights. So, I can also do whatever I want," I replied, standing my ground.

Dawit erupted in rage. He flung the remote control onto the ground and crushed it under his feet. "You can smash the TV set for all I care," I retorted.

My response further angered him, and he raised his voice, hurling insults. The security guards on the tower heard our commotion and realized something was amiss. They urgently summoned Major Berhane.

Berhane arrived swiftly, overhearing Dawit's tirade. He could foresee the situation escalating into a physical altercation, and Dawit showed no signs of being calmed down.

"Gather your belongings then," said Berhane.

Dawit understood where this was heading. He knew he would end up in Assefa's tiny cell. He tried to save himself and said:

"I fought with him because he was trying to influence me to hate Tigrayans as he does," Dawit said this, knowing that Berhane was of Tigray origin.

Berhane, however, was not easily swayed by Dawit's malice.

"Stop your idle talk, grab your belongings and get out," he said and locked him up in the tiny cell.

I had dreamed of having my own cell for the past three years and finally had my way. I vowed I would never carelessly repeat the old Ethiopian adage "Humans heal Humans."

Chapter LXIV: News of My Release

It felt as though all prisoners except for me were set free. Months had passed since the most renowned politicians were released. Of course, I questioned why not me? I tormented myself, wondering if I was kept under detention because the TPLF refused my release. I had good reason for that, given the bold statements I made on many occasions in many public media against the ethnic apartheid they set up and the plundering of the wealth of impoverished Ethiopia. I know my statements have tormented TPLF officials. Anyway, everything I said was backed up by evidence.

The TPLF believed that I, Andargachew, had organized a diaspora protest against them following the rigged Election of 2005. Their repeated statements during interrogations made that clear. "We know that you execute all of the organized work for Ginbot 7. What will the movement do without you now?" they had asked.

In previous years, I noticed the TPLF had an exaggerated perception of my role. We once recorded one of their security officers telling the assassin they sent to Eritrea to kill me that "killing me would amount to a major event in the history of Ethiopian intelligence."

All these thoughts led me to the conclusion that "the TPLF would not agree to my release that easily." As days passed and I began to lose hope, I resorted to believing that life would continue in prison. I exercised, read, and watched television news.

Dawit did not waste his time displaying his true worth as a bad boy. He sent me insulting comments and gestures from the confines of his tiny cell.

Those were the circumstances of my hopeless life. One midday mealtime, my ears perked up to the sound of the unexpected. It was a Saturday. I was prepared for my father's visit and had organized items that needed to be returned and clothes for the laundry.

Saturday was the one day I could have a hot meal. I had taken a small snack just before, washed up, and was drying the plate with a ragged tea towel when I heard my name being announced on television. At first, I thought the devil was calling.

My eyes were planted on the TV screen. Two journalists sitting next to each other were engrossed in a program called 'Browsing the Internet'. They were discussing topics that were given prominence on social media.

One of the journalists said, "There was a substantial campaign requesting the release of Andargachew Tsege," and the other one continued, "The government has responded to that public request today."

"Ato Andargachew and another 547 prisoners have been granted pardon," said his colleague.

I stood watching with my mouth wide open. I couldn't believe my ears, and the truth sank in as I read the captions repeating that same announcement at the bottom of the screen. Seeing is believing; hence, I believed in my release.

The news sent me into a turmoil of confused emotions and thoughts. I felt both happy and sad. I was delighted at the thought of seeing my children and ending my father's distress. I was devastated by the thought of the years I had spent in suffering.

Of course, I was used to life in prison, and now I would have to get used to the free world. The anxiety that sparked was tremendous. I wondered if I would find things as I had left them or if everything had changed. I wondered what kind of imprint four years of life in prison had left on me and what challenges I would face as a result.

I entered a turmoil in a matter of minutes, which was triggered by the thought of breaking this news to my father. I expected he wouldn't have heard the news as he was on his way to see me at the time the announcement was made. I thought about how I would greet him and how calmly break the news of imminent freedom. I was still thinking when Berhane unlocked the external gate.

There was nothing untoward about Berhane's expression, just the usual.

"Family, family," he repeated, but nothing more. I thought perhaps he hadn't heard the news, and I couldn't help telling him what I'd heard on television. He looked genuine when he replied:

"Congratulations," he said.

The announcement did not change my compulsory drive to the office next door, where I would meet my father. I hopped into the car and turned up at Gebreyesus's office where I expected to see my father.

My father surprisingly sprang up to greet me without any support. After I greeted him:

"You're full of energy! You sprang up like a lively young man today," I said.

"I'm full of happiness," he replied and urgently recounted how he heard about my release on Sheger radio. My effort to break the news was wasted, and yet it was a relief. His wife, Tadelech, beamed at me with joy flooding her face.

Half an hour passed quickly as we talked about meaningless things. Even though the media reported my release, both my father and I had no idea when that would happen. My head was full of such thoughts as I returned to my cell. My father left, probably thinking the same thing.

Chapter LXV: Goodbye Kaliti

The news of my release was officially announced by the media on a Saturday. However, the Kality prison administration said nothing, and the day passed by. Sunday and Monday went by as well. I wasn't surprised that nobody came to see me on Monday, May 28th (Ginbot 20), as it was TPLF's day of victory against the military regime it removed from power, hence a national holiday.

However, I had expected a visit on Tuesday. The morning passed with no visits. In the afternoon, Commander Gebreyesus himself turned up.

"We've only heard about your release on the media. No instructions had arrived until just 15 minutes ago. Could you please sign here? This copy is yours. The rest belongs to the correctional institution," he said.

I didn't even try to read what he was asking me to sign. I didn't have my glasses on and had to ask him to point out where exactly my signature should appear. He checked to make sure I had signed all three pages.

"You will need this; it proves you have been released. Now, please organize your belongings. I have a couple of things to prepare and will be back shortly. You won't be sleeping here tonight," he said and left.

I was amazed by the belongings that I had accumulated while in prison. The washing basin, jug, bucket, plastic food container basket, thermos, plastic mug, an assortment of plates, and many other knick-knacks, including clothing.

I didn't want to keep most of the items. I decided to take some of my clothes and all of my books.

In the afternoon, around half past four, I heard the engine of a car coming toward my cell. I understood they were coming for me.

The duty officer was Berhane. He opened the gate:

"Are you ready?" he asked.

"Yes," I replied.

"Is that all you are taking?"

"That's right." "Could I ask you to give the remaining items to the women's cell?" I asked. "I'll do as you ask," he replied.

Berhane instructed one of the security guards on the tower to descend and help load the car. I didn't need any help. The tall young one who drove the others mad by constantly winning games of draughts skipped up to us. He picked up my belongings swiftly and loaded them into the back of the car. I held on to two plastic bags of books and followed him.

Dawit was watching through the window of his tiny cell. I couldn't work myself up to say goodbye to him. Not that I hated or felt contempt for him but only because I felt he wouldn't appreciate the meaning.

The car parked outside was an ambulance. I bumped shoulders with Berhane, the traditional way of saying hello and good buy. He was a good man. He insisted on addressing me formally throughout the three years we knew each other; a kind, empathic person. His own story would tell a sad and dramatic tale.

I bid goodbye to the security guards on the ground and up on the tower. They all placed their hands on their hearts and flashed warm smiles as they wished me good luck. These guards were brothers and a source of courage during my three years in prison. I won't ever forget them.

I sat on the ambulance stretcher next to two intelligence officers in plain clothesmen. All of my belongings found a place on the floor and in the corners. Our journey started.

During my three years in Kality prison, I had travelled by car countless times to Commander Gebreyesus's office but never went past it as we did then for the first time. Instead of taking the usual right turn to the office, the car whizzed past and headed for the prison exit. From a distance, I could see the decorative arrow protruding from the top of the gates, which swung open to let us out. The avenue that passed in front of the prison led away and to Addis Ababa. That depended on which way the driver decided to turn. Reassuringly, the car turned to the right. I felt a bit of relief.

I saw an unexpected crowd at the prison gates, and I wondered what they were waiting for at that time of late afternoon. The ambulance stayed on the right lane and sped off towards Addis. The windows were glazed, so people couldn't see what was inside, but we could see the outside.

It didn't take long before we reached the ring road. Nobody had mentioned where exactly we were going. I expected to be taken to the British embassy because I am a British national.

We travelled a short distance before the person sitting next to the driver in the front passenger seat took out his cell phone. He was discussing my father's address, so I understood that was where I was heading. Something clicked.

My father had heard I would be released but had no idea when and wouldn't have known where I would be taken to. I wondered how he would feel when the ambulance arrived at his house without any warning. I started imagining him fainting or having a heart attack.

The vehicle made its exit from the ring road and headed towards Bole Road. The city had changed so much that I couldn't help which direction my father's house was located. Eventually, we found the right junction.

I was alarmed by the crowds just before the junction. When we eventually took the right turn, it was obvious the crowd was getting hopelessly bigger.

I thought the city must be in some kind of turmoil, for it was too late for so many people to be taking to the streets. It looked like a population explosion had just happened. How could feeding, employing, sheltering, and providing health and educational services equitably and sustainably happen? I asked myself.

I found an answer that relieved me from anxiety. A young man following the ambulance cried out: "He must be in here!" All those people that I had just been worrying about heard the young man and ran after the ambulance. The people who had been standing on the edge of the street leading to my father's house started milling onto the street in front of the ambulance and behind it. It was with effort that the vehicle managed to push through the crowd up to a left-hand turn then came to a stop.

The driveway that led to the family compound was jammed with people who did not respond to the driver's persistent horn. I saw my younger sister standing outside the ambulance. Her name is Ayne. I couldn't hear what she was saying but she was shouting out like a madwoman. Her son Suleiman was standing next to her. He was holding his mobile phone over his head. I didn't recognize the faces that surrounded the ambulance. There were all kinds of people.

The security staff inside the ambulance looked anxious. They didn't dare to get out and manage the crowd. The ambulance was surrounded in every direction. From behind, people pulled until the door handle and forced it to swing open. "Stop, you can't do that," said the security staff, but nobody listened to them.

Suddenly, the sky opened, and a downpour began. A couple of youths pulled at my arms. I arose. Others joined the young people and groped me all over until they had me suspended above the crowd. I was carried up into the air.

The rain was pouring, but it was the sound of people that filled the air. I could hear women ululating. I thought I heard gunshots, but it was only fireworks. I looked down at the heads beneath me as the rainwater flushed down my face. I'm not sure how long it went on. It felt like a long time. At last, they put me down on the veranda of my father's house. My father stood before me, dressed in a cape.

Chapter LXVI: At My Father's Place

I embraced my father, his wife, my aunt and her husband Ato Merid, my sister, her son, my cousin Tiruneh, and numerous other relatives with kisses. A young man whom I did not recognize halted me. "That's enough," he declared.

"You must acknowledge the crowd outside and reassure them. Once done, we'll proceed with our program calmly," he directed.

Unfamiliar with him, I complied without question. The young man draped a ceremonial cape over my damp shirt before ushering me outside.

Perched on a chair in the courtyard, I surveyed my father's expansive compound, now densely packed with people. They lined the surrounding walls, spilling onto the street beyond the wide-open gates, which resembled a bustling venue hall.

As I ascended the chair, applause erupted around me. I delivered a brief speech, though the words were a blur in my mind. I likely echoed the sentiments conveyed to me by the young man, promising a swift return. With that, I descended from the chair.

Guided by the same young man, I was led to a nearby bedroom. "You're soaked through. Change into these," he instructed, gesturing towards a neatly laid-out traditional white cotton ensemble on the bed. Once he left, I swiftly changed into the clothes.

Upon his return, he fastened a slim, tri-coloured band - echoing the Ethiopian flag - around my waist with a safety pin, then draped the ceremonial cape over me. Once again, we emerged into the crowd, making our way towards my house within the complex.

As we traversed the throngs of people, I marvelled at the sight. Never could I have imagined my father's courtyard teeming with so many individuals. What I once feared might overwhelm him now revealed itself as a display of solidarity and celebration, a testament to the bonds he shared with his community.

I was initially struck by the sheer number of people below, their mobile phones twinkling like stars in the night sky. Such widespread use of technology was a stark contrast to just four years prior, highlighting the rapid pace of change.

Once settled on the balcony, I was taken aback by the amplified sound of the Ginbot Popular Force anthem, "For You, Ethiopia!" - a composition I had authored. The voice of Meron Semeneh, sister of the renowned artist Alemtsehaye Wedajo, resonated deeply within me as she chanted the prelude with remarkable power.

The crowd joined the singing. It was unbelievable to hear thousands in Addis sing the words;

"For the unity shattered, for our country debased,

For the freedom stolen, replaced with chains,

My bare chest meets the flames, defiance unchained."

In that moment, I was overcome by an overwhelming disbelief and near-hysteria. It was as if my senses were momentarily blinded and deafened by the magnitude of the occasion. The fact that "For You, Ethiopia!" was being amplified in the heart of Addis Ababa signalled a profound shift in Ethiopia's political landscape, one that I had not fully comprehended until that moment.

Meron sang those lyrics, accompanied by the voice of her back singer, Abiy Kassa - my friend from London. Despite my lack of detailed information about the Ginbot 7 movement, I couldn't help but wonder how many of those familiar faces had risked everything to bring me to this moment.

While I may not have known all the details, I was aware that our struggle had played a significant role in the declaration of a national emergency and the establishment of command posts by the regime. I couldn't help but feel gratitude towards the women prisoners who had access to television and bravely used it to inform me by putting up the volume despite the penalty they would face for doing so.

Thoughts raced through my mind at lightning speed as I observed the crowd singing the anthem with such fervour. It was astonishing to see how deeply they knew the lyrics by heart. Inspired by the moment, I felt compelled to share the story behind the anthem.

After the song ended and the crowd fell silent, I recounted the experiences that had inspired me to write it. I spoke of a documentary I had seen in the Eritrean wilderness, depicting the hardships faced by a young woman from Menz who had ventured to the Arab lands in search of a better life. I expressed my gratitude for their love and support. On their part and in a touching gesture, they presented me with a golden necklace bearing the words "For You, Ethiopia!"

After the welcome ceremony concluded, I stepped down from the balcony and retreated into my house. Despite the joyous occasion, I had yet to speak to my children or Yemi. Moments later, my nephew Suleiman facilitated a call to London, allowing me to hear my family's voices after four long years. The emotions that flooded me during that conversation reminded me of the moments when I had lost hope of ever hearing from them again. Though our conversation was brief, it filled me with immense comfort and joy. After the call ended:

As the excitement of the ceremony gradually subsided, I found myself appreciating the meticulous planning that had gone into organizing the event. Details that had initially escaped my notice now stood out: the careful arrangement of tents, chairs, and posters, the coordinated attire of the hosts, and even the printed t-shirts bearing matching text and images. The ceremonial garments provided for my father and me added to the occasion's significance.

Despite the dispersal of the crowd, many lingered late into the night, a testament to the hospitality and efficiency of the organizers.

Their foresight extended to practical matters, such as managing the crowd's desire to take photographs with me in a careful and orderly manner. With their approval, I graciously acknowledged each person before retreating to my room for some much-needed rest.

Alone in the quiet of my room, I reflected on the extraordinary events of the day and night. The profound impact they had left on me was undeniable, and I marvelled at the depth of emotion and gratitude that filled my heart.

Chapter LXVII: Face-to-Face with PM Abiy Ahmed[1]

Old habits die hard. I awoke early, at the same hour when the counting of prisoners would begin in Kality prison. For a few moments, I couldn't remember where I was. It seemed almost surreal to think that I had been released. Lying on my back, I stared up at the high ceiling. The walls, painted blue, surrounded me. The soft woollen blanket draped over me served as a reminder of my new reality. In front of me stood a wardrobe, a fixture of my newfound freedom. With a sudden jolt, I realized, "Yesterday was not a hallucination."

It was still very early, the sunrise yet to grace the sky. Everyone else was still fast asleep. Quietly, I dressed in my exercise attire and slipped out of the room. The compound was now as empty as it had once been full. Silence enveloped the surroundings like a heavy cloak. I walked past the posters that still adorned the walls, each one holding a story of its own. With each step, I absorbed the newfound sense of freedom that surrounded me.

---

[1] Words of Caution for readers; Subsequent developments revealed that much of what PM Abiy Ahmed told me in our first meeting were elaborate lies, carefully crafted to win me over. I have left the words on these pages unaltered to remain faithful to the original Amharic version of this book, published five years ago. However, I no longer share the enthusiastic opinions I once expressed about the person.

I was particularly struck by a poster featuring an image of me chopping firewood in Eritrea, accompanied by the text: "A freedom fighter that knows freedom." These words were drawn from my book "Freedom Fighters that Know No Freedom," published in 2005. As I gazed at the poster, memories flooded back of the controversy surrounding the book's difficult-to-understand writing style, which had irked many affluent readers.

I couldn't help but wonder if my imprisonment had inadvertently popularized this controversial book. How many more people had read it now? I recalled asking the intelligence officer who brought me books during my extrajudicial imprisonment to find me a copy, only to be told, "We looked everywhere and couldn't even find a second-hand copy."

It was ironic that the TPLF government, which had branded me a terrorist, was now crumbling. I had satirically labelled TPLF types as "freedom fighters" without any understanding of true freedom. And now, people were hailing me as a "freedom fighter who knows what freedom is." The historical irony was not lost on me.

After reading the posters, I resumed my physical exercise routine, completing it before anyone else woke up. Following a refreshing shower and dressing, I prepared to embark on my new life. However, decisions about my daily routine were still being made by others, including the organizers of my welcome party and my family, who were offering advice on how to proceed. In accordance with our agreement, I readied myself to greet the large number of visitors expected to arrive.

Since I had no immediate plans, I didn't mind the lack of an itinerary. After all, I couldn't plan a trip to England without travel documents. Therefore, I quickly noticed the presence of British embassy staff among the crowd. They informed me that I needed to submit a photograph for my passport.

Katie, the embassy consular, took several photographs with her cell phone, assuring that one of them would suffice. However, she also mentioned that we needed documents confirming my release from prison, which are typically given to prisoners upon their departure. I initially struggled to locate them but eventually found the papers I had signed for Commander Gebreyesus.

My sister, who was the only one aware of the day's schedule, shared it with me, emphasizing that the PM, Dr Abiy, wants to see me before I leave for the UK. She revealed that she had been in regular contact with him regarding my release and that he had taken significant action when I remained in detention on Monday.

I expressed my willingness to meet with Dr. Abiy if he desired. However, we were uncertain about the timing of the meeting, expecting his call while entertaining our guests.

As more people arrived, some mentioning they had travelled from Gondar, nearly a thousand kilometres from Addis, I found myself constantly rising to greet them, engage in hugs and kisses, and ensure their comfort. It wasn't until lunchtime that I could finally take a break.

The welcome party worked tirelessly, receiving guests and announcing lunch. A generous buffet of injera, bread, and four different sauces awaited everyone, inviting them to indulge to their heart's content.

I named the lunch party "The First Meal Consumed in Freedom." The buffet was thoughtfully prepared, taking into account the dietary needs of various religious and fasting communities. The food was not only delicious and varied but also entirely vegan-friendly.

Around half past two in the afternoon, my sister received a phone call from the Prime Minister's office, instructing us to accompany me to his office at three o'clock sharp. We arrived punctually at the Prime Minister's Office, housed in the same building that the former Workers Party of Ethiopia had occupied. As we entered, a person named Tawfik, known to my sister, greeted us, and we were ushered into the waiting room.

Shortly afterwards, the Prime Minister's Chief of Staff, Fitsum Arega, arrived and personally escorted me to the Prime Minister's office. Dr Abiy greeted us warmly at the door, shaking my hand before pulling me into a hug—a traditional gesture inherited from the TPLF era.

Dr Abiy expressed his desire to speak with me privately, asking Fitsum to arrange some coffee. It struck me that the Prime Minister rarely met visitors unaccompanied. Observing him up close, I noticed his youthful appearance and approachable demeanour.

As we settled in for our conversation, Dr. Abiy remarked, "I know Andargachew. He is not a political merchant," initiating our discussion. His words left me wondering about his intentions, but he quickly shifted the focus to my health, expressing concern over my weight loss and pallid complexion. I reassured him that I had been exercising and felt healthier than ever in terms of appetite and well-being.

Then, Dr Abiy made a surprising revelation: "You spent four years in prison, and because of you, I have been locked up for six years. You still owe me two years." His statement left me perplexed yet intrigued as I realized he was sharing insights into events I knew were unfolding but remained unclear about the orchestrators behind them. He was not actually locked up but had to endure six years of stress in isolation, having sent his family to the US, fearing detection of being the source of information that was delivered to me and which I inadvertently shared with others.

It became evident to me that Dr Abiy had been working against the TPLF even when it was risky to do so. Despite being a party member, he had actively worked to undermine its influence, a stance that few dared to take openly during that time of political repression.

I felt a pang of sadness hearing about the sacrifices Dr. Abiy and his family endured because of me. Learning that he had sent his family into exile in the US while he remained behind to face the consequences of his actions weighed heavily on me. Our discussion continued, delving into the reasons for my prolonged detention while other prominent politicians were released.

Dr Abiy revealed that he had intervened on my behalf, issuing an ultimatum to his colleagues in power: either release Andargachew or accept my resignation. It appeared to me a bold move that highlighted his commitment to justice and human rights. As we conversed, our dialogue touched on various issues plaguing the country, from political and economic challenges to social unrest.

I didn't hesitate to express my concerns about Ethiopia's future, particularly regarding its youth unemployment crisis. I emphasized the urgency of addressing this issue to prevent widespread unrest, highlighting the need for leaders to empathize with the struggles of the youth and demonstrate tangible efforts to create opportunities for them.

Dr Abiy displayed a deep understanding of the complexities facing Ethiopia yet remained optimistic about the future, often repeating the phrase "we shall overcome." While I couldn't fully share his optimism, his determination was evident.

Our conversation also touched on the prospects for peace between Ethiopia and Eritrea. Dr Abiy expressed his belief in my potential role in facilitating this peace process. This discussion ultimately led to the resolution of the decades-long stalemate between the two nations, bringing an end to a chapter of conflict and paving the way for renewed cooperation and stability in the region.

An hour and a half flew by in our discussion, covering an astonishing array of topics that extended far beyond the issue of Eritrea. Despite the breadth of subjects we tackled, I found myself in rare agreement with Dr. Abiy on every point. It was a testament to the depth and complexity of our conversation that could easily fill the pages of a monumental historical volume.

As our discussion concluded, Dr Abiy walked me out of his office to the waiting area where my sister awaited, surrounded by empty coffee cups that hinted at a lengthy wait. Their warm exchange of greetings suggested a familiarity that predated our meeting that afternoon.

The visitor's reception area resembled a spacious corridor adorned with a full-length portrait of the late Meles Zenawi, his finger pointing towards a distant horizon. While Dr Abiy and my sister conversed, I found myself momentarily captivated by the portrait, my hand clasped in Dr Abiy's as Fitsum snapped photographs on his mobile phone.

Before the photography session ended, Dr Abiy instructed Fitsum to immediately share the images. It was clear they would be released on the Prime Minister's Twitter feed. Later, I discovered an error in the accompanying wording, which falsely implied that I had visited the Prime Minister's office to convey my thanks. In truth, I had agreed to the meeting at Dr Abiy's request, confident that I could offer valuable insights amidst the ongoing changes.

Silently, I addressed the portrait of Meles, a surge of mixed emotions prompting an expression reminiscent of the British and American phrase: "You f...er! Are you watching?" It was a moment of raw emotion, a silent acknowledgement of the tumultuous journey that had led me to that point.

Chapter LXVIII: 31 May 2018

The house and compound buzzed with activity upon our return from meeting with Dr. Abiy. Hospitality and private visits stretched late into the night, finally bringing an end to the eventful day.

The next morning, I rose early, no longer disoriented by my surroundings but rather settling into my new reality. With plans in mind for a night flight to England, the decision weighed not only on an urgent visit to my family but also on concerns voiced by many regarding my safety. Given the lingering presence of the notorious intelligence service established by the TPLF, dismantling it remained a priority amid fears of potential risks.

A small group comprising members of a welcoming committee convened for an introductory meeting. Though unfamiliar with the committee members, we gathered in a room within the house, a property I had believed to be mine but had been auctioned by the government during my time in prison. Fortunately, my nephew had secured its purchase, allowing us to convene without interruption.

Though not all committee members were present, I was briefed on their identities: Berhanu T/Yared, Shewakegn Abatnew, Eyerusalem Tesfaw, Meskerem Aberra, Ephraim Solomon, Natnael Yalemzewd, Daniel Shibeshi, Sentayehu Chekol, Temesgen Adane, Yidnekachew Kebede, Habtamu Menale, Merkebu Haile, Abel Wabela, Solomon Decheisa, Fassika Adugna, Woineshet Sileshi, and Emebet Girma.

Gathered with welcoming organizers and family members, we shared our impressions and laid out our collective guidance. Expressing gratitude, I took the opportunity to thank each committee member for their sacrifices and efforts in organizing my reception.

My sister, growing impatient with the duration of our meeting with the reception committee, interjected, "Let's go and finish our tasks and return home before people start to arrive."

Curiously, I inquired, "Where are we going?"

"We will first go to Bole St Michael church to light a candle at our mother's grave, and you will greet the head of the church (Debru's Aleka,)" she explained.

"Okay," I replied, accepting her plan.

She then added, "We will then go to Entoto Kidane Mihret, the famous St. Mary's church."

Perplexed, I questioned, "Why?"

"We have a matter to conduct there," she cryptically replied.

Satisfied with her response, we set off for Bole Michael.

Understanding my sister's intent, I realized she wanted me to visit our mother's grave, knowing the significance of my mother's presence in my life. Additionally, she intended to convey a message to our late mother, expressing the efficacy of a supplication my mother made on my behalf to St. Gabriel during the Red Terror era.

As we stood at her grave, my sister addressed our mother, affirming that "St Gabriel is still looking after your beloved son." My mother, in the 1970s at the height of the red terror, had made the ultimate self-humiliating vows to the saint to protect me from the butchers of Addis.

After paying respects at our mother's grave, we also visited the burial ground of my grandmother, Emahoy Getenesh, who was laid to rest in the same church.

Reflecting on the changes since my return from England nineteen years ago, I noted the alteration in burial practices. Originally interred in a proper grave, my mother's remains had since been relocated to a shelf within a concrete wall, a stark contrast to the English tradition of burial.

Comparing Ethiopian customs to those in England, I found the difference unsettling. In England, despite its smaller size and large population, Ethiopians living there are afforded the freedom to choose the disposition of their remains upon death. Even in a foreign land, they are not deprived of the dignity of a proper burial, contrasting sharply with the Ethiopian practice of stacking remains on communal shelves.

In Ethiopia's capital city, Addis Ababa, however, corpses are dug out and stacked away like books. That practice began during the TPLF era, a period marked by immorality and depravity that also infiltrated the church.

My heart swelled with anger as I thought about how patriots and their descendants were denied the simple dignity of six feet of burial land by the descendants of traitors who had invaded Addis Ababa.

Taking the candle my sister handed to me, I lit it bitterly and placed it in the designated opening. I couldn't help but feel a deep sadness, knowing that my mother's remains lay within that concrete block, far removed from the natural ground she deserved.

Muttering to myself, I whispered, "She would have been better off without a marker, exposed to the rain and wind amidst the fields where birds sing in the sunshine. It would have been a more peaceful rest, even if her body had to be buried alongside others."

The catacomb had been specially opened for our visit, and after we concluded our time there, we proceeded to the office of the head of St. Michael. He awaited us in a large, modern office, his eyes brimming with tears as he greeted me with profound emotion and affection.

After exchanging greetings, the ecclesiastical chief shared, "The entire nation was worried about you. We did what we could to show our support. Your sister kindly provided us with your baptismal name, Haile Selassie, and we conducted a nationwide prayer using that name. I am the only one who knows the actual identity of Haile Selassie."

I was astonished by the revelation. The words of the Aleka and the church's execution of the prayers were truly remarkable. It

366

reminded me of the conviction I held during my time in prison, believing that my great-grandmother's St Michael was watching over me.

Concluding our business with St Michael church, we proceeded to Kidanemihret (St Mary's church) to fulfil my sister's vows. She had promised to bring me to the church, among other things, if her prayer for my release was granted. It hadn't occurred to me that similar requests from countless other mothers and sisters, made in devotion to St. Mary in different corners of the world, would find their way to me while I obediently followed my sister from one venue to another.

Upon our return from Kidanemihret, I insisted that we pay a visit to Ato Aberra, my Godfather, who was around 90 years old. My father had informed me that this elderly gentleman would make the arduous journey from Piassa to our house in Bole every week to inquire about the outcome of his regular visits to the prison. My Godfather, whom I had known since childhood, undoubtedly shared my father's deep concern for my well-being.

Before heading to see Ato Aberra, we made a stop at the British Embassy to collect my travel documents. Unfortunately, Ambassador Susan was not present during my visit. However, I later learned from Yemi that Ambassador Susan, along with my partner and my brother Bizuneh, had been closely monitoring news of my release online. Yemi recounted how Ambassador Susan was moved to tears upon seeing images of me being carried into my father's compound by a jubilant crowd.

At the embassy, the staff inquired about my preferred mode of return to England. They suggested arranging a private exit from the airport to a meeting venue where I could reunite with Yemi and the children discreetly. However, I declined this option firmly. I was confident that my friends in London were aware of my arrival date and were already planning a welcome celebration. It didn't sit right with me to sneak away through a private exit after all the effort they had put in. We parted ways, agreeing to proceed according to my choice.

Back at the house, which had been empty when we departed but was now filled with people, I learned that some visitors had left in disappointment during our brief absence. This saddened me. Throughout the afternoon, visitors continued to come and go, and I diligently followed the welcoming organizers' instructions. I granted short interviews to television and radio channels, which seemingly raised concerns among security overseers, as visitors were subsequently subjected to thorough searches before entering the compound.

As sunset approached, a dilemma arose within my family. They were concerned that announcing my departure to England and bidding definitive goodbyes could stir up a commotion. It was decided that I would leave the house discreetly.

Staying at my sister's house near the international airport seemed like a practical choice. This would have been inconceivable in the past, as the thought of interacting with my sister's husband, Teferra Walewa, a well-known TPLF loyalist and minister, made me queasy. Fortunately, Teferra Walewa was travelling outside the country, sparing me from the awkward encounter.

We made a brief stop at my sister's house, just enough time to organize my personal belongings and take a shower. As I stood in front of the full-length mirror, examining my reflection for the first time in years, I was taken aback. I had known I had lost weight, but seeing my scrawny appearance was startling. My reflection seemed unfamiliar, like that of a different person. I couldn't help but trace the outlines of my collar and chest bones, questioning their prominence.

During my time at Kality prison, I had only been allowed a small mirror for shaving, which barely reflected my face, let alone my entire body. I had dismissed the comments about my weight loss as an exaggeration, but now, faced with my reflection, I understood why my well-being and health had been a topic of concern.

After dressing in the clothes provided for me in Addis Ababa, I realized that these, along with the shoes I was wearing, comprised all the clothing I would be taking to England. My sister and I were travelling business class, which afforded us a substantial luggage allowance. It felt wasteful not to utilize it, so I decided to pack some of the books I had marked with notes during my time in Kality prison.

In total, I had read and sent back to my father's house 306 books over three years. I packed them into five suitcases, reminiscent of the choices I made forty years ago when leaving Sudan for England, travelling with only the clothes on my back.

As I sat beside my sister in the business class section of the Ethiopian Airlines Airbus A350, I reflected on the overwhelming show of affection, courtesy, and respect from my country folks, including the airline staff—a stark contrast to the clandestine manner in which I had been abducted and brought into the country.

Chapter LIXX: Bon Voyage; Back to London

The decision to opt for a cheaper flight through Yemen rather than Eritrean Airlines business class ultimately led to my abduction, underscoring the consequences of that choice. While I understood that Eritrean Airlines business class didn't offer significant advantages over economy class, the experience with Ethiopian Airlines business class was truly impressive.

The hospitality began even before takeoff, with a glass of champagne and delicacies. The luxurious armchairs, TV screens, audio system, and comfortable pull-out bed all contributed to a sense of novelty and comfort, particularly after my years in prison.

Curious about the cost, I inquired with my sister, learning that the business class ticket cost around ninety-something thousand Birr, significantly more than the twenty thousand for economy class. The substantial price difference gave rise to thoughts about the treatment of officials in Ethiopia, many of whom likely travelled in business class or even higher.

Reflecting on this, I couldn't help but wonder if I truly deserved such treatment. The disparity in travel accommodations highlighted broader issues of inequality and privilege within the country's leadership.

Despite my internal musings, I hadn't discussed the cost of the ticket with anyone, leaving me to ponder over who had footed the bill for this unexpected luxury.

As the aeroplane prepared for takeoff, my mind raced with a flurry of thoughts, attempting to organize them into coherent patterns. The familiar announcement wishing passengers a pleasant flight, spoken in Amharic as "melkam berera," resonated through the cabin, signalling the beginning of our journey.

The announcement filled my mind with a whirlwind of emotions. After four years, I was on the brink of reuniting with my children, Yemi, my brothers, my sisters, my relatives, my friends, and acquaintances, as well as my beloved London community. My heart raced with anticipation even before the plane touched down, and butterflies fluttered in my stomach.

Upon landing in London at seven o'clock in the morning, we swiftly gathered our personal belongings and made our way to the exit. Despite the bustling airport atmosphere, I felt a profound sense of inner turmoil. In silence, I pushed my trolley beyond the usual greeting area for passengers. Suddenly, the air was filled with the familiar sound of my country people singing "Ya Ho" in the distance.

As I approached the crowd, I noticed numerous green, yellow, and red-striped Ethiopian flags waving among them. The singing seemed to cease as they caught sight of me, replaced by shouts, whistles, and ululations that filled the airport with joyous chaos. The sheer number of people overwhelmed me, making it impossible to distinguish individuals.

Efforts by the group tasked with controlling the welcoming party struggled to maintain order as I drew nearer to the crowd. It became clear why the British Embassy staff had suggested a private exit – everyone seemed eager to greet me with kisses and hugs. Despite pleas to prioritize my family, the organizers had to assert themselves physically to clear a path for them to reach me.

The first person to catch my eye was my son, Yilak, holding a poster with "Welcome back Dad" written in English. It seemed someone had given it to him to hold above his head, but he looked bewildered amidst the commotion. His older sister, Hilawit, stood just behind him.

As I approached, I noticed they were both in tears. I felt a surge of emotion welling up inside me, threatening to spill over. My throat and chest burned with intensity as if pierced by shards of glass. I knew that if I let myself cry, it would be uncontrollable, and I feared the impact it might have on us all. So, despite the overwhelming emotions, I fought to hold back the tears, clinging to a fragile sense of composure.

I couldn't spot Yemi and my younger daughter, Menabe, Yilak's twin.

"Where are they?" I called out, trying to locate them amidst the crowd.

The organizers hurriedly made their way through the crowd and eventually found them. As soon as Menabe caught sight of me, she burst into tears and retreated. I wouldn't see her again until much later when we were on our way home in the car.

Curious about Menabe's reaction, I turned to Yemi and asked, "What's going on with Menabe?"

"She says you're not her father," Yemi replied.

The news wasn't entirely unexpected. I understood how shocking and confusing it must have been for Menabe to process.

I also noticed Bezuneh's children, my brother's, among the crowd. They were younger than my own children. Along with them was his wife, Selam. The familiar song, "For You, Ethiopia," which had echoed through my father's compound, was now being played again at Heathrow Airport. People were singing and dancing, creating a spectacle that had never before been seen at Heathrow Airport. Passersby stopped to watch the joyous celebration.

British television channels such as Sky News and BBC News, along with journalists, were actively reporting the news of my arrival. They politely requested comments from me, and I obliged. ESAT television colleagues were also present, recording the historic event. Abbay Media was broadcasting the event live, and I heard that the welcoming event in Addis Ababa had been shown to international Ethiopian audiences as well.

Individuals were taking photos on their mobile phones and sharing them with friends and family. The technology for direct mobile transmissions was something I hadn't experienced before my time in prison, and I was amazed to see how individuals could essentially become their own TV stations.

I marvelled at how five years in jail in these times would equate to the equivalent of 25 years in the past. Judiciaries need to reconsider their penalties to ensure they are appropriate for the times. A person leaving prison after five years may find the world to be a completely changed place, especially with rapidly evolving technology.

Many representatives of NGOs who fought for my freedom came to the airport. Organizations like Reprieve and Redress were among those that applied pressure on the government, and their representatives were present at the airport.

We slowly made our way through the crowd with the help of the welcome party organizers and finally reached the car park. My Ginbot 7 friends, including Major Mamo, Yifru, and Ephraim, were among the lead coordinators. Zelalem used a loudspeaker to control the crowd.

A limousine had been arranged to transport my family and me, and we were escorted right up to the vehicle. The driver was

Turkish. Everyone appeared to have a copy of the address to which I was to be driven. While people rushed off to fetch their cars, I sat in the limousine with my children, Yemi, Bizuneh's children, and the journalist from Abbay Media, Tigist.

The children, who were alarmed by the crowd in the hotel, had now calmed down. They found soft drinks in the back of the limousine and sat admiring the vehicle between gulps of their sweet drinks. Other family members had started the day early to welcome me back home. The narrow street where the limousine was waiting suddenly filled up with cars and blocked the passage as they all assembled around the vehicle.

"That's enough, let's start our journey," the limousine driver was instructed. Yifru drove ahead with an Ethiopian flag hoisted on his car. Behind us, more Ethiopians followed, waving the same flag on their vehicles all the way to my residence.

We were driving towards North London, and the route options were plentiful. The chosen route went straight through Central London, passing by the Ethiopian Embassy. Protestors had spent the last 27 years outside those gates and wanted to make their voices heard once again. All of the cars escorting us drove by, pressing hard on their horns.

That's how I was finally escorted back to my home in North London with my children and Yemi. I was freed after just short of a few days from four years in prison. The London crowd granted me some privacy with my family but promised to come back and fetch me for the celebration the welcoming party had organised. That brought the end to my experience as an abductee.

www.ingramcontent.com/pod-product-compliance
Lightning Source LLC
Chambersburg PA
CBHW051455030726
47592CB00006B/1940